Chicken Soup for the Soul®

Thanks Dad

101 Stories of Gratitude, Love, and Good Times

Jack Canfield
Mark Victor Hansen
Wendy Walker
Foreword by Scott Hamilton

CSS

Chicken Soup for the Soul Publishing, LLC
Cos Cob, CT

Chicken Soup *for the* Soul

www.chickensoup.com

Contents

Foreword, *Scott Hamilton* xi

❶
~How Dads Say "I Love You"~

1. My Father's Approval, *Bryan Gill* 1
2. From the Only, *Heidi Durig Heiby* 5
3. Very Important Papers, *Sallie A. Rodman* 8
4. I Knew, *Adrian R. Soriano* 11
5. The Silver Flute, *Sharon Beth Brani* 14
6. Tools for Life, *Caitlin Q. Bailey* 17
7. The $20,000 Haircut, *Jess Knox* 19
8. One Father's Sacrifice, *Abby McNutt* 22
9. Morey, *Heather Simms Schichtel* 25
10. It Was My Dad, *Joel Schwartzberg* 28
11. Silence Is Golden, *Kathleen Shoop* 30
12. Knight in Shining Armor, *Natalie June Reilly* 33

❷
~Lessons for Life~

13. This Is How We Practice Not Quitting, *Karyn Williams* 39
14. Okay, Fine, My Father Was Right, *John Lavitt* 42
15. Living in My Heart, *Teresa Armas* 46
16. His Final Lesson, *Megan Tucker-Hall* 50
17. The Car, *Cathy C. Hall* 53

18. Getting Back to Abnormal, *Mark Damon Puckett* 56
19. Blind Determination, *Janet Perez Eckles* 59
20. Life Coach, *Curtis Silver* 62
21. The Power of Encouragement, *D.R. Ransdell* 65
22. How to Build a Sailboat, *Gail Wilkinson* 69
23. Thanks for Letting Me Fail, *Tim Brewster* 71
24. The Preacher's Kid, *Patti Callahan Henry* 73

❸

~Dad to the Rescue~

25. A Father's Persistence, *Michael Jordan Segal* 79
26. Always at My Back, *Wendy Walker* 82
27. Words of Wisdom, *Tracy Cavlovic* 86
28. Just Wait, *Charles E. Harrel* 89
29. Daddy's Little Girl, *Christine Trollinger* 92
30. The Cape of Good Hope, *Jennifer Quasha* 95
31. A Shorts Story, *Amanda Green* 97
32. The Hero Who Broke the Rules, *Brenda Nixon* 99
33. Saying No to No, *Jenna Glatzer* 101
34. Mooning Misfortune, *Ashlan Gorse* 104
35. Watching Over Me, *Terrilynne Walker* 107
36. Daddy to the Rescue, *Marla H. Thurman* 109

❹

~Making Gray Hairs—Fathering Teenagers~

37. Wrong Way Reuscher, *Eric T. Reuscher* 117
38. Johnny, *Robin Pepper Biasotti* 121
39. Dud and the Catcher's Mitt, *Cindy Beck* 124
40. Showing Up, *Rachel Furey* 127
41. Cool Dad, *Heidi L.R. Zúñiga* 129
42. Driven, *Robyn Kurth* 133
43. Melody of the Heart, *Tina Haapala* 136

44. My Unfair Father, *Melissa Face*................................140
45. Valentine's Day Ambush, *Kathleene S. Baker* 143
46. Runaway Letter, *Debra D. Peppers*.............................146

❺

~Through Thick and Thin~

47. Crazy Curtains, *Michelle Sedas* 153
48. The Track Meet, *Fracia Heter* 155
49. Pops, *Lizy Herrera* 158
50. Flowers that Never Die, *Kathy Irey*........................160
51. Dad's Secret Ritual, *Victoria LaFave* 163
52. Coach Dad, *Ronda Armstrong*.............................166
53. The Constant, *Kimberlee Murray*..........................170
54. An Orphan's Daughter, *Karen Gray Childress*................173
55. Always a Winner, *Al Serradell* 177
56. The Final Gift, *Marsha D. Teeling* 180
57. Handstands, *Amy Lyons* 184
58. Manhood 101: Having Your Masculinity and
    Your Marriage Too, *Sheila Curran*..........................186

❻

~Stepping Up to the Plate~

59. Finding a Friend, *Kirsten Ogden* 193
60. A Real Dad, *J. Aday Kennedy* 197
61. The Christmas Present, *June Harman Betts* 200
62. My First Bike, *Ray M. Wong* 204
63. Finding Home, *Diane Stark*................................208
64. First Place, *Linda Apple* 211
65. A Real Father, *Barbara Edwards*...........................213
66. The Stepfather, *Sally Schwartz Friedman*...................215
67. As Time Goes By, *Cynthia Blatchford*.......................218

❼
~Making the Ties that Bind~

68. The Cheslatta River Race, *James S. Fell* 225
69. The Man Who Learned to Unravel, *Kerrie R. Barney* 229
70. Love in a T-Square, *Sheila M. Myers* 232
71. The Best Gift of All, *Mary Jo Marcellus Wyse* 235
72. Breakfast, *Donna Buie Beall* 238
73. Coach, *Stefanie Wass* 241
74. The Garage, *Christine A. Brooks* 245
75. Dad's Tomatoes, *Tina Bausinger* 247
76. Alaskan Adventure, *Elaine L. Bridge* 250
77. Dodging Failure, *Paul Winick* 253
78. Building 101, *Barbara Canale* 257
79. Waterskiing with Dad Is Okay, *Jill Barville* 261
80. The Saturday Treat, *Sara F. Shacter* 264

❽
~Everyday Heroes~

81. Hero to Many, Father to Me, *Danielle* 271
82. A Quiet Hero, *Timothy Martin* 273
83. My Dad Is as Nice as a Fish, *Stephen Rusiniak* 276
84. The Shopping Trip, *Jane Choate* 279
85. Laughter, *Elissa Stein* 281
86. Rules of Engagement, *Jill Olson* 285
87. Living My Father's Dream, *Lola Di Giulio De Maci* 289
88. The Greatest Lesson Never Spoken, *Dave Ursillo, Jr.* 292
89. Not Afraid Anymore, *Sydney Wain* 295
90. A Faithful Father, *Bonita Y. McCoy* 296

9

~Moments that Last Forever~

91. The Cradle, *Shawnelle Eliasen* 303
92. Fathers, Sons and the Angel in the Stadium,
    Marni Chris Tice 307
93. Seven Minutes, *Lura J. Taylor* 311
94. Caught on Tape, *Nick Walker* 315
95. When Daddy Held My Hand, *Annmarie B. Tait* 318
96. Tuesdays with Daddy, *Sharon Dunski Vermont* 321
97. One Last Reminder, *Jan Hamlett* 324
98. Heart Strings, *Cynthia M. Hamond* 328
99. Just a Little Phone Call, *Kierstan Gilmore* 331
100. The Shrubbery Massacre, *Ron Kaiser, Jr.* 334
101. Is Mom There?, *Andrea Atkins* 336

Bonus Chapter
Truly Grand Dads

102. The Pinch Hitter, *Dawn Lilly* 343
103. Everlasting Lessons, *Kevin Price* 347
104. Doting Dad, *D. B. Zane* 350
105. Running the Gauntlet, *W.S. Gager* 353
106. I Call Him Papa Jim, *Donna Reames Rich* 356
107. My Father—My Son, *Gary B. Xavier* 359

Meet Our Contributors..362
Meet Our Authors 380
About Scott Hamilton..382
Thank You!...384

Foreword

I have a theory. It goes like this.

The second you hear your first child cry for the first time, a chemical is released in your brain that makes you mildly psychotic for the rest of your life. The world is now forever different. You have been transformed. Changed. And you are probably better than you have ever been.

I am pretty sure that it is more than a theory. Whenever I am around other dads at different events with my sons, I can see the loving glow that can only come from absolute, unconditional love. It is not the love you have for your wife, siblings, or parents. It is a love that you can only have for your children. It makes you stronger, weaker, braver and filled with more fear than you ever thought possible.

If you have a son, you have probably lost count of how many times you have saved his life in the first few years. If you have a daughter, your instincts create a radar that is always on to protect her from everything. You would do anything for your children and it is something that is unique and hard to articulate. Right now, if you are reading this and don't have children, you probably don't get it.

No one can prepare you. No one can accurately describe what it is all about. And the funny thing is, when you make the decision to start the process of fathering a child, no one can talk you out of it. It is nature working its best, most amazing, beautiful, complicated magic.

I was adopted. I was told what that meant as soon as I was old enough to understand. My sister was my mother's only pregnancy that didn't end in heartbreak. She simply couldn't go through another failed attempt and decided adoption was the best option. My parents wanted me. They chose me. I loved and respected them. They are both gone now and I miss them terribly.

Their sacrifices were beyond reason or logic. I was sick as a child and they did everything they could to find the answers to bring me back to health. When we found skating, I miraculously started to recover. But as I got to the higher levels of competition, the expense became unbearable.

My father was a professor at Bowling Green State University and did everything he could to support the family even as he was losing the love of his life to cancer. We all knew he was suffering, emotionally and financially. My father and mother had to make incredible personal sacrifices to keep the family from going bankrupt. My brother and sister felt it too. I carried a lot of guilt about the sacrifices my parents made for me until I had children of my own. It was then that I understood there is no sacrifice too great for your children.

When Tracie and I got engaged, our friends Sterling and Stacy Ball threw us a party. I mention Sterling and Stacy by name because when their son Casey was five years old, his kidneys stopped functioning. Sterling, without hesitation, gave one of his kidneys to his son. Casey is alive and thriving due to the sacrifice that his father gave without a second thought.

Toward the end of Sterling's party, I lined up some friends who had children and I asked them what made them decide to start a family. Tracie and I knew that we wanted children, so my question was about gaining perspective. Each one of them gave a different answer.

One said, "Because we have a responsibility to continue our family." Another said, "That's why we are here. To be parents." Then there was, "We all emotionally need to have that responsibility." Or, "I wanted the unconditional love that you can only get from a child." And yet another said, "I knew it was going to be a lot of fun to experience another childhood."

You get the idea.

But knowing I was a testicular cancer survivor, I thought it might be unlikely that I could become a father. A miracle might be necessary. We got one a little over nine months after we got married. When my son Aidan was born, it was the first time I had seen the flesh of my own flesh.

Being adopted, that was one thing I could never share with my parents. Physical characteristics. Eyes, nose, body type, etc. I never craved those things. I didn't really think they were important until I looked in Aidan's eyes. They were MINE! Identical! And I'll never forget the moment I realized that. After struggling with health issues on and off throughout my life, and wondering if I would be able to have my own children, I suddenly realized my own reason for becoming a parent. No one will ever look at me the way my children can — with complete love, need, fear of the unknown, and trust. *With my own eyes.*

My second son Maxx was another miracle. He was very unlikely to happen after I suffered a pituitary brain tumor in 2004 that changed my body chemistry in a way that inhibited fertility. I gave myself six injections a week for two years. Three in the leg and three in the belly. It was at the end of the second year that I gave up. Tracie understood and we accepted the fact that one miracle was more than enough. It was the very next month we found out we were expecting another child. Another boy, Miracle Maxx.

I have the magnificent duty and honor of being the most important man in my sons' lives. And they are the most important men in mine. I will never be the same.

I'm now better than I have ever been because I have to be. They deserve it, and it is my life's mission to fulfill this tremendous responsibility.

This is the magnificent duty and honor all dads share.

To love, and be loved, unconditionally.

To be looked up to.

And for me, with those identical eyes.

~Scott Hamilton

Chapter 1

Thanks Dad

How Dads Say "I Love You"

My Father's Approval

You don't raise heroes, you raise sons. And if you treat them like sons, they'll turn out to be heroes, even if it's just in your own eyes.
~Walter M. Schirra, Sr.

It was a cold night in late November. A perfect night for high school football. The harvest moon drowned out the stars as it hung high above the stadium lights. I was a senior and team captain as a middle linebacker. We were a good football team with a 12-1 record so far in the season. This particular game was the semi-final round of the Alabama 5-A State Championship Playoffs.

We trekked from Eufaula to Mobile via Greyhound to meet our cross-state nemesis. If we won this game we would play Etowah High School in the State Championship game in December.

JaMarcus Russell, a mere freshman at the time, played quarterback for our opponent. Russell later played college football for LSU and then became the first pick in the NFL draft in 2007, going to the Oakland Raiders. Another kid by the name of Carnell Williams, also known as "Cadillac" Williams, played running back for Etowah. He later played for Auburn University, and then the Tampa Bay Buccaneers. This was a tough team.

That November night the chilling air stung our noses and burned our lungs as we ran during pre-game warm-ups. The stadium engulfed the one hundred or so faithful fans that followed us to our battle. The opposing legion roared with ten thousand strong. My parents sat dead center on the fifty-yard line about halfway up in the section closest to the field.

Our team was the closest any Eufaula team had come to winning the State Championships in nearly twenty years. But first we had to cross this Goliath-sized hurdle in Mobile to move on to the finals in Birmingham. Playing in the championship game in Birmingham was something my dad did as a senior in high school. Hoping to make it that far was a dream of mine. I wanted to do something my dad had done, but better.

The game commenced and we burst out of the gates fighting. It was a fight to the finish with both teams leaving everything they had on the field. We scored first. 7-0. Then they reciprocated. 7-7. Then we pulled ahead with another touchdown. 14-7. They scored again but we blocked the extra point. 14-13. They took their first lead of the night with a little over seven minutes left in the fourth quarter. A failed two-point conversion made the score 14-19. With under a minute left in the game we fumbled. They ran the clock down and then took a safety with nineteen seconds left on the clock. 16-19. With three seconds left to score, we fought, bit, scratched, tore, grabbed, and ripped to break through the end zone one last time but time ran out.

I tackled a lot of guys but I also missed a lot of tackles. I made some good calls and made some bad ones. One play that haunts me was my chance to sack JaMarcus Russell. I closed in on him as we both neared the sideline. He cut left and I cut left. He shook right and I shook right. I was about to sack a future NFL quarterback but just before I placed my helmet on his shoulder pads I tripped. I fell and lunged for his legs and we both rolled out of bounds, however, not before the ball spiraled out of his hand and into the receiver's for the first down.

I was humiliated. I had my chance and blew it. I completely screwed up. The embarrassing part was that we rolled out of bounds into my team's sideline. I knew where my parents sat and hid my face from their seats. I could hear the disappointment in the sighs of the crowd. I couldn't bear the thought of what my dad was thinking.

The clock struck zero signaling that our chances of making it to the finals were over. We were numb. No tears, just disappointment.

Not enough energy to cry. Time slowed to a crawl and the cheers of our opponent echoed in our helmets. I remained silent. My head throbbed. I didn't want to speak to anyone. No cheerleaders, no coaches, not my fellow linebacker whom I had played next to for six years, and especially not my dad. I feared how the conversation would go. I didn't want to hear, "Good game" because I knew it wasn't true. I didn't want to hear, "You'll get 'em next time" because there was not going to be a "next time." I didn't want to stomach, "You should've made this tackle or that tackle." I wasn't ready to face the reality of falling short in my father's footsteps.

With my helmet in one hand and my shoulder pads in the other, I walked alone across the field to the clubhouse. I looked up into the stands where my parents once sat. Empty. Every seat was empty. I guessed they'd decided to leave early. Could it have been my missed tackles? Was it the score that drove them away? Was it something worse, something as bad as shame? I didn't blame them; I was disappointed too.

It is funny how the air can be cold, your body hot and your emotions frozen as a familiar sound falls on your ringing ears. It was a whistle. A familiar whistle. Amidst thousands of cheers, a marching band, air horns, fireworks and sirens, I recognized that whistle. It came from the sideline. My head jerked and zeroed in on the source.

There he stood dressed in his game attire: red hat, red shirt with my number embroidered on his left breast pocket, khakis and a red tiger-pawed stadium cushion. It was my dad's whistle. Why did he come to the sideline? What would he say? What could be so important to call my attention away from my self-pity? What news couldn't wait until I got home? Why was it so important to remind me of the disappointment I had become?

Our eyes met; both red from heartache. I stared at him awaiting the verdict. He didn't say, "Good game," or "You should have done better." No expression fell on his face. Then he said something I'll never forget for the rest of my life. He extended his muscular arm, raised his thumb in a thumbs-up gesture, and said, "I love you, son."

He loves me? Even though I screwed up? Even though I blew

it? Even though the weight of the game rested on my shoulders and I messed up? He loves me? That's exactly right. He loves me! All of those negative scenarios left my head. I didn't have a father whose love was contingent on my successes or failures. I had a father who loved me because I am his child and he is my dad. My dad approved of me because I am his son, not because I do or do not adorn a State Championship ring. So, thank you Dad. Thank you for showing me the perfect picture of my heavenly father's love.

~Bryan Gill

From the Only

Dad, your guiding hand on my shoulder will remain with me forever.
~Author Unknown

I thought I might die. It was the first semester of my second year in college, and my freshman-year boyfriend had just broken up with me. I didn't know what to do. I had not been without a steady boyfriend since my sophomore year in high school, and this one was special. I had seen it as my first legitimate adult relationship, being that I was almost twenty. I was miserable, unable to eat or sleep. My roommates were worried, but had given up after trying to cheer me a thousand different ways. I had even written my estranged sweetheart a poem about an old doll that had been left on the shelf. Me. I was so hurt and so young.

I began to call home almost every day after the break-up to muster sympathy from my mom. My dad and I, however, continued to have those bare bones dad-and-daughter phone conversations during our official Sunday phone call, the ones where I reassured him each time that I was studying and had enough money. My mom and I, on the other hand, really talked. She wanted to know everything that was happening around campus, what I was learning in my classes, and what was good in the cafeteria. These were the days before cell phone "anytime minutes" and unlimited long distance, so we began racking up some bills. I waited for the "other fish in the sea" speech that, thankfully, never came. My mother was supportive and patient through my tears, but after weeks had gone by, she finally told me that I was being silly continuing to pine. I knew she was right, so I tried to mend my broken heart by burying myself in my studies even more than before, and joining a few more college organizations. Dad stayed away from the topic altogether. I knew that he felt bad that I felt bad, but he generally left emotional rescue to my mother.

One day when I returned to my dorm room from an afternoon class, I found my roommate sitting at her desk, grinning up at me. An arrangement of pretty, pale flowers sat on the table in the middle of the room.

"For you," she said. My heart stopped. This was it. My ex had finally realized the error of his ways and wanted me back. He hadn't actually fallen for that Barbie doll freshman in his RA orientation group after all. I approached slowly and lifted the fragrant basket, opening the little card with shaky hands. Written there was simply: *From the only man who has loved you for twenty years.* My eyes filled with tears. My roommate looked at me with confusion.

"These are from my dad," I choked, sitting down to cradle the bouquet in my hands and gaze at the delicate blooms.

"Your dad? What for?" My roommate crossed the room and sat down next to me, arm around my shoulders. I handed her the card. She smiled again.

"Your dad's so sweet."

"I know," I sniffed. Right there something shifted in me. I gained perspective. My mom's steady counsel had aided in my slow recovery, but this was the shot that I needed to heal completely.

Many years have passed since then and I am happily married with a daughter of my own. My father has had his own battles to face in recent years, with failing health and forced retirement, but the grand image of Dad as protector never really goes away. As it turns out, a father's physical strength is just a metaphor for what he really gives his children. I don't think I realized the absolute fortress of my dad's character, the strength of his morals and convictions, until he began to fail physically. Mom had been telling me over and over again how my father never complained about the deterioration of his quality of life, no matter how bad he felt, but that he often lamented no longer being able to do things with and for us. I wanted a way to reassure him that not being as active anymore had nothing to do with his ability to be a great father. We had traveled together all our lives, Dad and I, and I did miss that aspect of our relationship. But the foundation and support that he had given me had never weakened. In fact, it had strengthened.

I had all but forgotten about the boyfriend, my desperation, and Dad's flowers, until I saw a picture in an old album that jogged my memory. My eyes filled with tears again at my father's sweet gesture. It was just a week before Father's Day and I had an idea.

My dad opened his simple card with a weak smile, as smiles come harder with Parkinson's. The flowers had surprised him, although he had always been the rare man who appreciated flowers as a gift. The card read: *From the only woman who has loved you since the day she was born.*

Then I hugged him, asking him in a whisper, "Do you remember?"

"I remember," he assured me softly. We nodded at each other. As always, there was no need for words.

~Heidi Durig Heiby

Very Important Papers

Education is simply the soul of a society
as it passes from one generation to another.
~G.K. Chesterton

"Impressive résumé," Mr. Green said, perusing the paper in his hand.

Oh good, I thought. Maybe I've cinched the position.

"Just one last thing. We'll have you take a little aptitude test and then we'll chat once more," he said.

"Well, I'm certainly ready," I replied with more enthusiasm than I felt. Must keep that smile on my face and look calm, I thought. I could hear my dad saying, "Never let them see you sweat."

I took the test and was pretty sure I'd flubbed it terribly. My nerves were frayed and I was overwhelmed. This interview had started at breakfast and it was now past one o'clock. Mentally drained, I summoned the Human Resources Manager, Cleo, and told her that I was done. Then I waited. Finally, the results were in.

"Well, Ms. Rodman, I see you're certainly well equipped for this position. I'll have Cleo take you over to her office and we'll get the paperwork started. Can you start on Monday?" Mr. Green stated.

"Uh, certainly," I said rather stunned. Then I asked what I really wanted to know. "Can you tell me how I scored on the tests?"

"I'm not allowed to give out that information, but let's just say you did very well."

"Thank you," I replied meekly.

And with that I had my dream job. I mused about it in the car on the way home and wondered how I had done so well.

My dad's words rang in my ears, "Education, my dear, education. That's what it takes to get ahead in this world."

My dad valued education tremendously. He had been forced to forego college since his father died when he was a senior in high school. As the oldest male, he was expected to go to work and support his mom, two brothers and two sisters. Many years later, he married and supported my sister and mother working as an electrician. When he came to California the year before I was born, the World War II boom was on, and one of the aircraft companies saw promise in him and sent him to USC to get his degree as an engineer.

He made sure I was sent to the best schools his money could buy. I went to a private grammar school, and then a girls' Catholic high school. I eloped at nineteen and my father was very disappointed that I didn't attend college. I had been accepted at USC and I think he wanted his offspring to follow in his footsteps.

While my children were in high school I went back to college and finished my degree at age thirty-seven. Dad came to my graduation and there wasn't a prouder parent in the crowd.

After that all-day interview, I realized I had never thanked my father for the sacrifices that enabled me to obtain a quality education. That night I sat down and wrote him a letter. I wanted to be able to say these things without him becoming emotional. Dad would get misty-eyed when they sang "The Star Spangled Banner" at baseball games. Sometimes I had a hard time handling his emotions. So I chose my best floral stationery and put my pen to work expressing my gratitude. It went something like this:

Dear Dad,

Every time I know the right word to use in a business report or how to calculate the rate of return in a marketing analysis sheet or successfully proof a report for a shareholders' meeting, I think of you.

Thank you, Dad, for all the times you made me do my

homework or quizzed me on my times tables or spelling words. I realize now how much you sacrificed to make sure I got the best education possible.

I love you, Daddy, and am so thankful you are my dad. I hope I always make you proud and just know I will always be your little girl.

Love,

Sallie

I waited with anticipation for him to receive the note I sent. Days, weeks and then a month passed. Nothing. I finally called my mom.

"Mom, has Dad mentioned any mail he got lately?"

"No, Sallie. Is he expecting something?"

"Nothing special, Mom, I was just curious. I mean… I mailed him a short note but it wasn't that important," I replied. I was too chicken to tip my hand.

And so time passed and nothing was ever said. I didn't know if he had received it and ignored it, or if he even got it at all. Meanwhile the years flew by and I moved ahead in my career. Dad was always there to call and congratulate me.

After my father died, we were searching his apartment. He had told me that there was money stashed all around the house — in the sofa, ottoman and his recliner. Being a product of the Depression, he didn't entirely trust banks. I needed to be sure we didn't miss anything so I searched everywhere.

When we cleaned out the bedroom, there in his dresser drawer we found documents wrapped in a rubber band and marked "Very Important Papers." Among the title to his car, his life insurance policy and savings account book was a ragged, yellowed piece of floral note-paper. Knowing he had received my note made my heart leap for joy. He had known how grateful I was to him. And even though he had not been able to tell me back then, I knew the extent of his love when I found my letter.

~Sallie A. Rodman

I Knew

The most important things are the hardest to say,
because words diminish them.
~Stephen King

A couple of years ago on a warm summer day, my family gathered at my parents' home to celebrate my oldest brother's birthday. This was sort of a regular occurrence for our family, since there were five siblings and fifteen grandchildren, all of whom, at some time in their lives, had celebrated a special occasion there. Close friends of the family, including a priest known as Father Mike, were also present.

As my wife, kids and I walked up the driveway, we noticed a few adults sitting under the carport, a few adults standing by the barbecue pit, and most of the children running loose in the backyard. As my children ran quickly past me to be with their cousins, my wife and I began our rounds of greetings with everyone.

I walked up to my father, who was sitting next to Father Mike. His eyes were red and watery from standing over the barbecue pit preparing my brother's birthday meal. We made eye contact, and my father greeted me with the universal acknowledgement that all male Hispanics give one another—a quick nod of the head in an upward motion, basically translating into "what's going on" or "how's it going." I responded with the same head nod, and the gesture completed our greeting. Father Mike, obviously bothered by this, said to my father, "That's no way to say hello to your son. Stand up and give your son a hug so he knows how much you love him." Without hesitation, I spoke to Father Mike. "He doesn't have to. I already know." My father looked at the priest with the biggest grin and gave a small chuckle.

I am the youngest of three sons and my older brothers often comment on how easy I had it growing up. They were the guinea pigs for my father's disciplining techniques. By the time it was my turn, my father had mastered the art of disciplining with a single stare—a stare that could stop me in my tracks and make me adjust my attitude.

That, of course, is not the only thing my father is about. He is a good man, with integrity and a strong work ethic. Throughout my childhood, and even into my adult years, my father's actions demonstrated his love for me. For that reason, telling Father Mike "I knew" was something that I said with conviction.

I knew my father loved me when, as a young boy, he took the time to show me how to tie a fishing hook on my fishing line. I knew he loved me when, even when he didn't want to, we came home early from our fishing trip because I was tired. I knew he loved me when he came home from work with a pack of basketball trading cards for my collection. He would watch me open the packages with excitement, then ask me if I got anything "good." I knew he loved me when he took me to school on rainy days, never once complaining about being late for work. I knew he loved me when, during my high school basketball days, he yelled, "Use the backboard!" every chance he got. I knew he loved me when, during one of those basketball games, I fell to the floor with a twisted ankle and he ran from the bleachers to be at my side. I knew he loved me when he told me stories of how he grew up, and how I should do my best in school so I wouldn't have to work so hard. I knew he loved me because, during my high school graduation, as soon as my named was called, he yelled, "Alright Adrian!" in front of hundreds of people.

I knew he loved me when he showed me how to change the brakes on my car for the first time. He said to me, "I'm only going to show you once, so you can learn." Once was all it took. I knew he loved me when, right before I got married, he pulled me aside and told me, "You know you're going to work for the rest of your life.

Always take care of your family first." I knew he loved me when he came as fast as he could any time I needed help within my own home. I knew he loved me when, on my birthday, he and my mother called me first thing in the morning and sang to me. I knew he loved me because he was always present when my children were born.

I am a blessed man to have a father like mine. There are others in this world who will never know these kinds of experiences. They will never know a man as good as my father, a man willing to give of himself, without complaint, and never expect anything in return. He is a good father, a good husband, but most of all, a good man. He has taught me to value what I have, to be good to people, to work hard, to love my wife and to be strong in whatever I do. Thank you, Dad, for being there for me. I am forever in your debt. I wish I knew how to repay you for all the things you have done for me. If you ever wonder whether or not I know how much you love me, don't worry… I know.

~Adrian R. Soriano

The Silver Flute

There is no greater loan than a sympathetic ear.
~Frank Tyger

"**M**ommy, what's this?" my youngest daughter called from the living room.

I turned my head to see what she was referring to. My eyes fell on the black-and-white rectangular instrument case in her hand. Memories flowed over me as I stepped towards her.

"Oh, my," I said choking back my rising feelings. "It's my flute."

I took the case from her and gently laid it on the dining room table. Clicking the snaps on each side I slowly opened the lid. There lying on a red velvet lining was my old silver flute that I had played more than forty years ago.

"Play it, Mommy," she squealed with excitement.

"Oh, I don't know," I hesitated. For a few minutes, I was carried back in time to another world. In the background I could hear the beat of the drums and the sound of the instruments.

I was playing in the marching band again. Wearing my heavy navy uniform and hat, I walked with all the others back and forth in formation. My fingers played the Sousa march and my heart beat with pleasure. Another football game. Another half-time.

It had been difficult for me growing up in a family of six. I was the shy and quiet one, always willing to stay in the background. My parents did the best they could to provide for the needs of my two brothers, younger sister and me. Even so, something was missing from my life, and I didn't know what it was. I was always a good student and played the piano for the choir. But, at fifteen, I was insecure and longed to feel a part of something.

One day, I was wandering around in my unsettled life feeling burdened and out of sorts. I tried playing the piano, which I often did to quiet my soul and refresh my spirit. But this time it just didn't seem to help. As I rose from the piano I saw my dad walk into the room. He went over and sat down on the sofa and began to open the newspaper.

"Hi, hon," he said keeping his eyes on the newspaper.

"Hi, Dad," I answered softly. At that moment I felt like the weight of the world was on my shoulders and I really wanted to be alone.

"What's the matter?" my father questioned, putting down the paper.

"I don't know," I answered, feeling embarrassed by the question.

"Come over here." He motioned for me to sit down beside him.

He looked at me as I sat down. The more he probed, the more I began to spill out my feelings of being alone and not accepted at school.

My father seemed to take it all in stride and tried to solve the problem.

"Well, what can we do?" he asked.

"It might help if I could play in the band like David," I responded. My older brother always seemed to blaze the way. "He gets to go to all the football games for free and ride the bus. A pianist doesn't get to do anything but play the piano."

"Well, okay. We will get you an instrument. Which one would you like to play?"

"The flute," I answered, hardly believing my own ears. "That way I can have lessons with the others and play in the band."

Before I knew it my father had dropped the paper, stood up and moved into action. Grabbing the telephone book, he located the closest music store. Next thing I knew, he and I were off to buy a flute.

When I got to the store, I was mesmerized by all the shiny instruments. The manager led us to the flutes. Carefully, he opened a few different ones, but I already knew which one I wanted.

"Well, what do you think?" my dad asked.

"I like that one," I said quietly. There it lay so new, so shiny, so absolutely perfect.

"That's a very good flute," the manager explained. "You will get a beautiful sound from it." Within minutes we paid for the flute and walked out of the store with me carrying the treasured instrument.

My heart was spilling over with joy, not only about the new flute but because I knew that my father loved me. The worth of that love meant more to me that day than all the instruments in the store put together.

True to my word, I took lessons and began playing in the high school band. In a matter of months I started playing at football games and marching in parades. For the first time in years, my heart felt settled and at peace.

"Please play it, Mommy." My own child's words jarred me back to the moment.

"I don't know if I can," I said as I put the pieces together.

I ran my hands over the silver flute while listening to the trilling of flutes and piccolos in my memory.

Placing the flute to my lips, I slowly began to play, first one song and then another. Amazed that I still remembered the fingerings, I grabbed an old book and for the next few minutes was lost in the music.

Thank you, Dad, I thought, for knowing my heart and for being so willing to do what you could to help me that day.

There was more to be treasured in that flute than met the eye. And I will always cherish the love that it represents.

~Sharon Beth Brani

Tools for Life

A child enters your home and for the next twenty years makes so much noise you can hardly stand it. The child departs, leaving the house so silent you think you are going mad.
~John Andrew Holmes

It was December when my father had to live the moment every dad dreads — times two. I, with my bachelor's degree in hand, was officially and permanently leaving the nest for Connecticut. My sister, clutching her master's degree, was heading off to New Jersey to start her new life.

And to make matters even worse, there was a long-time boyfriend waiting for each of us. Not only was my father losing both of his girls at once, he was losing them to other men. He had us hostage for the holidays, but after that, all bets were off. The clock was ticking.

So that's the year he gave my sister and me the best presents we ever received.

A pony? No, I'd given up on that dream years ago when he bought me a stuffed horse instead. A car? Nope, my father insisted the old Buick he'd procured from our elderly neighbor was "a great car!"

Sitting underneath the tree on Christmas morning were two identical gifts my brother, muscles straining, pushed in front of his sisters. Large, slightly lumpy, and heavy enough to make me question what I'd do with a box of rocks.

"This is from your father," my mother said, eager to re-distribute the credit. With slightly nervous glances cast each other's way (my father does not do his own shopping), my sister and I tore open the paper to reveal... toolboxes.

Just what every little-girl-at-heart wants for Christmas.

"Open it, open it!" our very own Santa announced gleefully, clapping his hands.

So we did.

Hammers. Wrenches. Nails. Duct tape. Tire gauge. Tape measure. Screws.

The fun just kept coming, and he couldn't have looked prouder.

We couldn't have been more confused.

Like your average girls, we dutifully ooh-ed and ah-ed over our loot and kept our eyes glued to the clearly denoted GAP box under the tree.

"He did that all by himself, you know," Mom confided to us later when all of the crumpled wrapping paper had found a home on the floor and presents lay scattered about. "It took him hours to pick all of that out."

Suddenly, it was clear—tightly packed into those cumbersome, clunky toolboxes were all of a father's lessons and love. He may have been passing us on to other men, but his girls were going to be able to take care of themselves—and always remember who it was in their lives that first built a foundation and always picked up the pieces and hammered them back together.

Yes, my father gave me a tire gauge for Christmas, along with the forethought to avoid problems before they happen.

A spare key holder—and the knowledge that everybody's human and forgets their keys sometimes.

A hammer—and the strength to know that girls can swing them, too.

Nails—and countless memories to hang on the walls.

A toolbox—and all of the love and support to get through the good and the bad in life. No matter what's bent out of shape or broken.

Thanks, Dad. For all of the tools you've given me.

~Caitlin Q. Bailey

The $20,000 Haircut

It is not what we take up, but what we give up, that makes us rich.
~Henry Ward Beecher

My dad is a non-traditional dude. He let me call him by his first name when I was a kid. He got a tattoo and was so excited about it he offered to get me one. (I was sixteen.) He owns exactly one tie and it has pool balls on it. And for as long as I can remember, he proudly wore his hair in a ponytail.

As easygoing as my dad was, though, some aspects of growing up with a freethinker weren't so easy. Paying for college was one of them.

"Why don't they have a box on those financial aid forms that you can check that just says 'my parents aren't paying for this'?"

"Because most parents do," I said.

"Mine didn't."

"You didn't go to college."

"College isn't for everyone," he said in a spiel I'd heard many times before. "You could get a job. Or go to school part-time. Or join the Army and have them pay for college. Just the Reserves. It's like two weekends a month and you won't actually go to war."

He wasn't kidding, even though I weighed ninety pounds and HATED the outdoors.

Needless to say, it became pretty apparent that I would be financing my college education myself. Even if he wanted to, my dad wasn't in much of a position to help. We simply didn't have an extra $100,000 lying around.

The scholarship prospects looked grim. There were plenty of $500 scholarships for being of Native American descent, $800 scholarships for playing the bagpipes, and $100 scholarships for essays that weren't worth writing. But I didn't even qualify for those and anything better than that was few and far between or came from the school directly.

Finally, after weeks of scouring every resource available to me, I stumbled on a scholarship I actually qualified for—and this one was a doozey.

"$20,000?!"

My dad was stunned. His eyes literally bugged out of his head.

"Get it," he said. "Get that one. Make sure you get that one." He was dead serious.

For the next few weeks, I devoted myself to the application process. I polished essays. I prodded teachers for glowing letters of recommendation. I made a list of everything that could possibly be considered community service.

After about a month of selling myself on paper, and another month of waiting impatiently, my work paid off.

"They want to interview me!" I told my dad. "They want to interview me with you and Mom! I'm a finalist!"

For the first time, it sunk in for my dad that I might actually get this thing. He'd wanted me to win the scholarship from the start, but until I landed the interview, I don't think he actually believed it could happen. That day, the money felt within reach.

The morning of the interview, I spent way too much time picking my outfit. I wanted to look professional, but not like I was trying too hard. I settled on jeans and a turtleneck. That would work, right?

"Ready to go?" my mom called from the living room.

"Just a second," I said as I threw on one last splash of body spray. I had a really good feeling about this. I was confident that my smarts would impress the interviewers and that my personality would win them over. I had faith my mom would make them smile and that my dad would crack them up. We were a good team. A genuine family. I liked us.

As I bounded out of my room, fully ready to tackle what would likely be one of the most important interviews of my life, I stopped dead in my tracks, speechless.

There in the living room was my dad. Without his ponytail.

"Your ponytail," I said, pointing to the empty spot on the back of his head.

"I cut it off. I don't want you losing a $20,000 scholarship because they don't take your dad seriously."

It was bittersweet. I was touched that he would take this meeting so seriously—especially after all the times he teased me about paying for college. But I felt bad that he literally cut off something that had defined him for years.

"People have lost jobs over stupider things," he said when I tried to tell him it wasn't necessary. "I didn't even want the possibility of it keeping you from this money."

The interview went well, and a few days later we found out I got the scholarship. I was one of five recipients, and the $20,000 I got literally changed my life. It gave me the guts to apply to the University of Southern California when I found out they had a screenwriting program, and it gave me the means to enroll when I got in. USC led me to my job in Hollywood, and to friends I never would have met.

I don't know if cutting off his hair really changed anything. I suspect that, really, it didn't. But like my dad said, it didn't hurt. And if it did sway the judges, I am even more grateful for the gesture.

Thanks, Dad, for cutting off your ponytail. You really did do everything in your power to help me.

~Jess Knox

One Father's Sacrifice

Any man can be a father. It takes someone special to be a dad.
~Author Unknown

I f you asked anyone about my relationship with my dad, they would tell you that I am Daddy's little girl. He rarely said "I love you" or "I'm proud of you," but I always knew that he believed in me. Even though he wasn't a very affectionate man, I never questioned his love for me. His primary role was as the provider for our family. It meant Dad worked many hours at a local tire plant and wasn't home much. That didn't change how I felt about him. I idolized him, like most girls do when it comes to their fathers. We had a special bond that even my mom didn't understand, a bond that I cannot describe to this day.

But things in our family would change. In the fall of my senior year in high school, my mom decided to leave our family for a man she had met on the Internet many months before. This turned my world upside down and devastated my dad. I lost my mom that night, and I needed Dad more than ever. Fortunately, our relationship as a family bloomed. We began eating dinner together, going to church together, and spending time together. The special bond between us grew even stronger that year and would continue to do so throughout my four years in college.

When I began choosing a college that January, Dad told me that I could attend any school I wanted. To his surprise, I chose a very expensive private university about an hour and a half from our home. I was awarded enough scholarships to cover half of my tuition and fees, but Dad would still have to pay the rest. When I told him this, all he said was, "Okay." He had made a promise, and he was going to keep it.

I started school that fall, and I loved it! I excelled in my classes and joined activities that forced me out of my comfort zone. I participated in student government, campus ministries, and other things that not only strengthened my organizational and people skills, but also required me to conquer my fear of public speaking. Through it all, Dad was always there. When I needed money, Dad would send it in an envelope marked "Daddy Moneybags." It made me laugh every time. He even drove to school to take me shopping for a new homecoming dress.

There were times when Dad's sacrifices made me feel guilty. But one Sunday, I came to understand why he did the things he did for me. I sat in church that morning listening to the pastor speak about the meaning of a shepherd warrior, when one of the points on the outline grabbed me. It said, "A shepherd loves sacrificially." The pastor described a sacrifice as "giving up something you love for something you love even more." At that moment, I finally understood. Dad loved me so much that he was giving me what I wanted no matter what it cost him. He sacrificed so I could attend a school I loved, and he did so without question or complaint. To him, allowing me to go to this school was more than keeping a promise; it was his way of showing his love for me. His love, along with the love of those around me, helped me complete this chapter in my life.

A few short weeks later, Dad watched me accept my two Bachelor's Degrees, one in Biology and one in Psychology. Like always, he didn't say much. He just let me relish my accomplishment. With a hug following the ceremony, Dad told me what I needed to know: he was proud of me and would always be regardless of what I did in my life.

I thank God for my dad every day. I thank God for the countless hours Dad and I spent in the car driving to and from school on the weekends and holidays as we talked and listened to our favorite radio program. I thank God for the notes, my favorite fruit, and the chocolate rose Dad hid in my laundry or grocery bags to remind me that he loved me. I thank Him for the hugs I got just before Dad would leave when he took me back to school, and I thank Him for Dad coming to see me for no other reason than because he missed me. I thank Him for the large basket of goodies Dad brought me during finals week because he forgot to purchase a ready-made "survival kit" from the school. He overflowed the basket with chocolate candy bars, crackers, and chips. He even glued fabric to the basket to make it more special!

It is said that your earthly father is a reflection of the Heavenly Father here on earth. He protects you from those who might hurt you. He corrects you when you are wrong. He guides you as you become the person you are supposed to be. He loves you even when it seems that no one else does. I see the Father in my father's sacrifice. I see God's love through my dad's love, and I thank God for blessing me with such a wonderful man—a man I call Dad.

~Abby McNutt

Morey

*He who would learn to fly one day must first learn to stand and walk
and run and climb and dance; one cannot fly into flying.*
~Friedrich Nietzsche

Change had blown in on the winds of spring air and catapulted my family into a new era. My brother had graduated from high school in May and would be leaving for college. I had finished my studies and was leaving for a new job in Europe. We only had a few precious months left as a family living under the same roof. Everything would change in the fall.

Dad had quite the reputation for being the gushy, sentimental type. Surprisingly, he was doing okay as an impending empty nester. A few tears were shed when "Pomp and Circumstance" was played at the graduation ceremony, but for the most part he was holding it all together. We were very proud of his composure.

May also brought a family of magpies that would take up residence in our maple tree. This family returned year after year to bicker, squawk, build nests and raise baby magpies.

This particular generation of magpies seemed to be extraordinarily noisy. The tree shook with their daily skirmishes, leaves dropping and horrible sounds coming from the inside of the branches. One early morning, the ruckus was so bad that my dad ventured out to see what the birds were doing. He found a lone, fledgling magpie hopping around the yard, flapping his little wings and yelling his little birdie head off.

Dad bent down to talk to the bird. "Hey there little guy. What's going on? Did you fall out of your nest? Poor birdie. Where's your family?"

He looked up in the tree to find Mommy and Daddy Magpie sitting on a branch and glaring ominously at him. "Oh, there you are. You should keep a closer eye on your baby. We have nasty cats."

Dad went inside to take a shower. As he was leaving for work, the poor magpie was still hopping about, flapping his wings and trying to fly. He had to do something for the poor little thing.

Dad called the zoo. "Yes, well I have this baby magpie in my yard. He's trying to learn how to fly but he can't yet and I just don't know what to do to help him. Should I catch him and put him in a box? Should I put him back in his nest? Should I bring him to the zoo? I think I should probably just leave him alone but I'm so afraid something is going to happen to him."

"Sir?" replied the zookeeper, "You do realize that this is a wild animal."

"Well, yes."

"And that learning how to fly is a natural process?"

"Sure."

"Then you should probably just leave him alone. He'll learn. No offense, but your presence in the yard might be frightening him."

Dad no longer followed the magpie around the yard. He did, however, watch him vigilantly from the living room window, just to make sure a rogue cat didn't turn him into lunch.

The next day I got a call at my summer job. It was my father. He never called me at work. "Dad? Is everything okay?"

"Heather, have you seen Morey?"

"Morey?"

"Yes, Morey… Morey the Magpie."

"You named the bird?"

"I saw him this morning but now I can't find him. I've walked the yard three times. I even looked in the tree but he's not around. I'm worried."

"You named the bird?"

"I'm very worried about him."

"Maybe he finally learned how to fly."

There was a long pause. "I hope so."

"Dad, it's lunch rush. I have eight tables. Gotta go."

Driving home from work, my Psychology 101 class finally paid off. It wasn't about the magpie. It was about his own little fledglings who were leaving the nest. It was about my brother and me.

Dad felt as helpless as the mommy and daddy bird watching in the tree. He couldn't make us fly once we left the nest. He couldn't will us to be successful and happy. He couldn't ward off the tabby cats. In fact, once we left his nest, he could only watch from his own branch, provide love and support and hope for the best.

No wonder he named the bird.

I got home and found him looking out the kitchen window.

"Did you find Morey?"

"No, but I also didn't find any feathers or signs of a fight. So I think he's okay. I think he might have learned how to fly."

"Of course he did. He had very good parents who raised him well, loved him and taught him how to catch worms. They made a nice cozy, warm nest. When it came time to fly, he already knew how to soar."

My dad had big tears in his eyes. "Well, I'm still going to miss him."

I snickered. "You're a funny dad."

The summer was spent playing, laughing and enjoying time as a family. Dad never did find Morey. I would point out a magpie and ask, "Is that him?"

"No, that's not Morey."

"Dad, it's a magpie. You really can't tell the difference, can you?"

"Of course I can. We bonded."

Soon it was the end of August. Bags were packed and it was time for my brother and me to leave the nest. In the end, Dad had nothing to worry about. He raised his little fledglings well….

And we flew.

~Heather Simms Schichtel

It Was My Dad

Silence is the mother of truth.
~Benjamin Disraeli

Back when I competed in middle school debate, my dad—a lifelong teacher—would wake up early to rouse me on Saturday tournament mornings. With night still engulfing the morning sky, he'd help me into my suit and suggest tactics as we drove to the waiting school bus. If there was time, we'd get a box of doughnuts for the team.

Roughly twelve hours later, the bus would pull back into the dark school parking lot as if the day had never touched it. I'd see my dad's car, its dome light illuminated so he could grade papers while he waited. He got a lot of work done on those nights.

"So… what's new?" he'd ask sarcastically while I climbed inside, as if the plastic-and-marble trophies entering with me didn't already answer the question. As I shared the day's details, he'd consume each word thoughtfully.

"So what's new?" is the closest my father ever comes to saying "I love you," as if the word "love" might burn his lips on the way out.

But looking back, I realize my father expresses love, as dads are so prone to do, in deeds more than declarations. My father's love is cloaked in attention, sacrifice, and selfless generosity. Love is the quiet battery that powers those human qualities.

It was my dad who told me not to worry about the cost of college—that he and my mom would somehow "make it work." It was my dad who drove to where I worked to hand-deliver my SAT scores, hot off the mailman's truck.

It was my dad who called with weekly encouragement when I was unemployed in Los Angeles and sleeping in a friend's living room. It was my dad who supported me as I started law school, and just as much when I quit six months later. And it was my dad who visited me at the mall where I competed with a teenager to be the assistant manager of a tiny video store.

It was my dad who opened his home and every possession to me when I moved into my parents' condominium following my divorce. He treated it like a routine event, even though it was the first divorce in the history of our family.

I remember how my dad insisted I try on his work shirts and pants, as if sensing the holes the separation had left in me, and desperately trying to fill them in with pieces of himself.

It was my dad who steadfastly held the ladder as I climbed back up to resume my life.

"Love" or no "love," he comes in loud and clear.

Sometimes on Friday nights, while I wait in my ex-wife's driveway for the children to emerge, I play with the dome light and wonder about the kind of father I am.

The kids knock the thought out of my head as they enthusiastically pile in.

"So… what's new?" I ask, instinctively.

They smile broadly, and start telling their tales.

~Joel Schwartzberg

Silence Is Golden

The older I grow the more I listen to people who don't talk much.
~Germain G. Glien

My dad sat in his rocking chair. The chair bucked, agitated just like he was as he plucked peanuts from their shells and popped them into his mouth. He glanced at me every so often, grimacing. It seemed from his furrowed brow that he was the one who was slogging hour upon hour in a swimming pool, counting tiles and laps, with arms like lead, heaving for breath and somehow, getting slower!

"Just a plateau, Kath," my dad said. Plateau my you-know-what. I was actually getting worse.

"How am I supposed to keep this up?" I sat on the couch across from my father, my arms hugging my legs to my chest. Each breath tripped over the sob before it. "I'm not getting any faster!"

My dad rose from his chair. My heart seized a little bit. He'd had enough of my weeping and was making an exit. But then I felt his strong hand grab the back of my neck and squeeze, giving me a little shake on the scruff. He'd done this a million times throughout my life. It was his answer to other dads' bear hugs.

"Are you working as hard as you can?" he said.

"Yes!"

He stopped squeezing. No more words. That couldn't be it. I looked up at him from my curled position on the couch, waiting for magic words, the sentiments or advice that would immediately reveal my next steps toward becoming a faster swimmer. He was my father after all, and pep talks were his specialty. It had always seemed as though he'd had a crystal ball that doled out advice that actually worked. But this time, silence.

"Well," he started squeezing again. "You wake up tomorrow and you go back and work even harder. Oh, and trust God. A little faith helps."

I shrugged out of his grip and gaped at him. "That's it? I'm working as hard as I can. So that's it? This is the best I'll ever be?"

A tiny hint of a smile did not cancel out the warmth in his eyes. He had told me my entire life I could be anything I wanted if I set my mind to it and there I was doing just that and still somehow drowning in my own mediocrity. Could he have been completely wrong?

"Dad, I mean it. Is this the best I'll ever be?"

"I don't know," he said. "Is this as good as you can be?" And then he was gone, to help my mother with a clogged toilet.

I woke up the next morning and was back in the pool working as though I had a spot on the U.S. Olympic team. Working hard had already been forged into the creases of my brain. Even if I wanted to quit, I couldn't. And there in the pool surrendering to the very thing that frustrated me so much, I found my answer.

• • •

Seventeen years, a Ph.D., husband, two children, and a multiple sclerosis diagnosis later…

I was back on my parent's couch for a visit. This time my two toddlers crawled over me, around me, on me, squalling for attention. I wrapped them in my numb arms and felt grateful they were too young to notice my silent tears or realize that I couldn't feel their soft skin with my prickly fingertips. As long as my warm body was near, all was right for them. They had no idea what multiple sclerosis was or what it meant to me.

My dad sat across the room in his rocking chair, narrating the TV news as though I couldn't hear it myself. "Damn politicians!" the rocking chair moved with his mood.

My dad glimpsed me every so often and caught my gaze with a forced smile. I waited for his encouraging words, his worldview that's tethered to his heart by the belief that anything is possible with a little faith and hard work.

Sitting there, I floundered in my self-pity, wondering where those sentiments were. He'd offered them through my swimming life, as I scratched through full-time work and Ph.D. studies, premature births of two children, and while I waited to see my writing published. But this time, with my immune system attacking the coating on the nerves of my brain, he had nothing to offer?

I closed my eyes and laid my cheek on the top of my daughter's head, sniffed the baby shampoo and listened to her coo and sigh at the pleasure of merely being alive.

Then I felt it. My dad's hand on the back of my neck, squeezing. And I waited for the words. But none came. A few more squeezes and he was gone to the kitchen, foraging for his favorite shelled nuts. I remembered all the times he'd offered his advice.

And I realized that as I got older he said less and less about how to handle things. He passed me on the way back to his chair, and there it was, the squeeze on the back of the neck. The one that said everything he couldn't.

~Kathleen Shoop

Knight in Shining Armor

*Certain is it that there is no kind of affection so purely angelic
as of a father to a daughter. In love to our wives there is desire;
to our sons, ambition; but to our daughters there is something
which there are no words to express.*

~Joseph Addison

One of the sweetest things in life is stumbling upon precious moments in the everyday lives of everyday people and discovering everyday truths. A few years ago, I was dropping my boys off at the school bus stop on a cold winter morning. I noticed a lumberjack-looking man standing quietly with his hands dug deep into his pockets amongst a herd of wiry elementary-aged kids. These kids had this man completely surrounded. However, this burly-looking man had eyes for only one little girl — his daughter, a petite little princess in pigtails who had his eyes and who clung to his side.

This wasn't the first time I had seen this particular dad at the bus stop. In fact, this guy was there every morning, rain or shine, to see his little girl off. The thing is, it's not unusual to see suburban, stay-at-home moms standing at the bus stop with their kids. But to see a dad standing there… well, I guess you could say he stood out. And on this particular morning, I witnessed something that struck a chord inside of me, inspiring me to preserve it in ink.

When the yellow school bus arrived, the small circle of children swirled into a wild flurry of energy around him as they clumsily (and quite shrilly) climbed onto the bus. I watched as the burly dad, an unassuming man, blew kisses at his daughter while she managed to march her little legs up the large steps.

He watched her patiently as she made her way down the long, skinny aisle until she — his pretty little princess — finally settled into her seat somewhere in the middle of the bus. She didn't spare a moment, pressing her pink nose up against the cold glass window, smiling at him confidently. From the sappy expression written all over his face, I was certain that this dad was smitten. She had him — this brawny man who stood out like a sore thumb in the middle of suburbia — tied hopelessly around her little finger. And, judging by her confident expression, she knew it.

This little girl's dad took two gallant strides forward and with two gentle strokes, he drew a heart in the condensation that dampened her window. His little girl's smile radiated the kind of certainty every little girl should have. And as the bus drove away, the two waved goodbye. I continued to watch as this dad stood with his hands dug deep in his pockets, sturdy as a knight, until the bus rounded the corner and drew out of sight.

This scene was affirmation to me of how significant the role of a dad is in the life of a little girl. He is the first man that she will ever love and the last man to determine how she will continue her pursuit of love. This particular little girl will know what it means to be loved by the man in her life. She will know what it is that she deserves, nothing short of butterfly kisses, heart shapes drawn and the infinite knowledge that he will be there to love and protect her, far beyond when she has rounded the corner from his sight.

So many little girls grow up in a sea of disappointment, never knowing that initial safekeeping and adoration from their dads, and they spend their entire lives on a futile search for it. Hats off to those dads who are brave enough to draw lasting impressions in the hearts of their daughters, and who stand solid as knights in their duty as daddy — giving truth, love and quiet confidence to the women who will always feel like Daddy's little girl.

~Natalie June Reilly

Thanks Dad

Lessons for Life

13

This Is How We Practice Not Quitting

Perseverance is the hard work you do after you get tired of doing the hard work you already did.
~Newt Gingrich

I'll never forget the day my then fifty-something professional sports executive dad became a marathon runner. After he finished his first race, the Disney Marathon in January of 1995, I watched him walk through our front door limping, battered, and bruised. He looked like he had been in hand-to-hand combat and was dragging home from the war. I remember wondering what in the world was fun about that. But a few years later when I watched him cross the finish line at the 1997 Chicago Marathon, I caught the bug. Whatever it was that made him want to do this, the satisfaction I saw on his face told me I wanted it too. So I started training for my first marathon. To date, I've run in nine of these epic events, seven of them right alongside my dad.

The first time we did the Boston Marathon together, I had trained hard for months, and Dad and I were both pumped. The first half of the race flew by, and I was on fire. I had energy like a madwoman, but Dad was struggling... so I did my best to keep him going. Kind of like Frodo and Sam, you know? Though the plan had been to stay together, Dad kept saying, "Go! Get a better time if you can... go ahead!" I debated it, but decided to stay with him. After mile thirteen, we stopped for a bathroom break—and that's when I cramped up really bad. Dad came to life after that, so for the second half of the race, he had to "carry" me! Miles thirteen through twenty-six were brutal, and sometime during mile twenty-one, as we were making our trek up the aptly-named "Heartbreak Hill," in agony and almost in tears, I looked up at Dad and cried, "Why in the *world* are we doing this?"

"People ask me that all the time," Dad said, "but you know why I do marathons? Because this is how I practice not quitting."

Wow! What a *great* perspective. Needless to say, it gave me a jolt of energy and we finished the race with smiles on our faces, hand-in-hand as we crossed the finish line.

I have reminded myself of that statement many times since that day and it has "carried" me through many situations. I still don't know what's *fun* about marathons, but I know the immense sense of satisfaction I feel after running one. It's a great "I did it!" moment. One more time, I forced my body to keep going long past the moment it wanted to quit.

Rich DeVos, cofounder of Amway and a family friend, likes to say that perseverance is stubbornness with a purpose. I think that is a terrific quote, and it reminds me that if you quit once, it makes it easier to quit the next time. After you start quitting, it's hard to put the brakes on.

I hear people say all the time, "Oh, I could *never* do a marathon!" And you know what my response is? "Sure you could! Most of it is in your mind." People look at me like I'm crazy, but trust me, marathons are as much a mental challenge as they are physical. Basically, from the moment you start, your body wants to stop. But then your powerful mind kicks in and says, "You started this thing… you're *gonna* finish it!" There really is nothing like that feeling—the rush—of knowing you've just beaten those twenty-six miles.

I don't have the kind of dad who will sit on the porch and drink beer with you. My dad is the one challenging *you* to keep up with *him* in a marathon. How cool is that? Because of his "not quitting" attitude, he's inspired me to take up the challenge too.

Today, whether it's running a marathon with Dad or finding my way in the country music world, I know I may not be the best, but I *can* guarantee you this: I will work the hardest, I will persevere the longest, and I will strive for lasting quality in my field, no matter what. Thanks, Dad, for one of the most powerful lessons I have ever taken away from you.

~Karyn Williams

14

Okay, Fine, My Father Was Right

When I was a boy of fourteen, my father was so ignorant I could hardly stand to have the old man around. But when I got to be twenty-one, I was astonished at how much he had learned in seven years.
~Mark Twain

For most of my life I refused to admit that I was wrong, especially when it came to advice given to me by my father. I now see, with naked clarity, how right and caring and sensible my father's cornerstone advice has been from the very beginning.

Perhaps the most consistently contentious issue between fathers and sons is the question of work and how to be successful in the real world. Right from the get-go, I thought I should start at the top. I was a talented young man and I thought everyone around me should realize this. With an air of entitlement and a growing grandiosity, I did not believe that I should have to pay my dues like other people. As a result, I constantly tried to find a short cut to the big time.

The baseball metaphor my father always used was that I was trying to hit a home run rather than focusing my efforts on getting to first base. In fact, I expected to hit a game-winning grand slam in my first major league at bat, resulting in immediate enshrinement in the Hall of Fame. As most of us have come to learn through the lens of life experience, such ridiculous expectations lead directly to strikeouts and dead ends, failures that take place without the honesty of a nuts and bolts beginning. But my father and I came from very different backgrounds, and that is the genesis of our conflicting outlooks on life.

My father is a prototypical example of the American dream come to life, a self-made man who achieved success through hard work. In Denver, Colorado, he grew up in a middle-class family that often experienced a roller coaster ride of economic ups and downs. Focusing on the promise of college, Dad won a scholarship to Brown University. Digging into his studies while forming a close-knit group of friends, he thrived at Brown.

Upon graduation, my dad married my beautiful mother at the Plaza Hotel in New York City and obtained an entry-level position at a Wall Street brokerage house. As the years passed and children were born, Dad worked with an unswerving determination, becoming a respected partner of the firm and the head of the sales team. He worked hard, but was also innovative, and eventually became a renowned expert in raising capital when others failed.

His most famous effort was captured in the book, *Behind Closed Doors: Wheeling and Dealing in the Banking World*, by Hope Lampert. Dad is a central character in a chapter on the challenge of raising money for the initial public offering of the computer company Compaq. Nobody thought anyone could go up against IBM at the time. But after interviewing the founders of Compaq, Dad found an angle to use to sell the company to the investors. By 1992, Compaq was the biggest supplier of personal computers in the world.

In contrast to my father's hard-earned success, I grew up as a privileged Upper East Side New Yorker who expected everything to be handed to him on the proverbial silver platter. Like my father and both of my sisters, I went to Brown where I majored in literary theory, and partied until the wee hours of the morning. After college, I headed out to Los Angeles where I fed into the dream of selling a big screenplay. Although my partying became habitual and out of control, I always thought the next big script sale would change everything. If only I could hit the legendary game-winning grand slam home run, life would fall into place and the prison cycle of addiction would end.

Seeing my attitude firsthand, my father told me that there were no short cuts, and that everyone had to pay their dues. I never listened, always trying to convince him and myself that the next big thing was waiting just around the bend. Eventually, I lost my house and my marriage and wound up at a drug rehab facility. Never listening to the sound advice of my father and insisting on following my own path toward self-destruction, I ended up in a terrible place.

My father, however, never gave up on me and has been remarkably supportive throughout my sobriety. When I helped start a nonprofit investment company, my father accepted a place on the company's board and did everything he could to help us get off the ground. Since I had never worked in the past, I made a lot of mistakes. But with the faith of my family and the support of my father, I have been able to pay my dues and help get my career as a technical writer and a website optimizer off the ground. Unlike some old friends, I have not won an Academy Award or produced hundred-million-dollar films, but I have discovered my own sense of personal dignity and integrity.

What remains so amazing is that so many of the lessons I have learned have come directly from my father. Listening to him, I have come to realize that none of my successful friends were ever given a golden ticket to Willy Wonka's Chocolate Factory. Rather, all of them, whether they were lucky or incredibly gifted or both, paid their dues and worked hard to achieve their success. Like my father tried to teach me from day one, there are no shortcuts. No matter how talented or fortunate you may be, success is the product of sweat in the form of hard work—showing up each day and doing your job to the best of your abilities.

This may sound like a bunch of awful clichés from a self-help manual. But each of these so-called clichés has been proven to work in the real world. My father still works hard, even after all of his success. Every weekday, at an age when many of his contemporaries have retired, my father wakes up early in the morning and sits down at the computer to see how the market is doing before launching into hours of networking and conference calls. I have such gratitude that my father has stuck by my side and believed in me even when I was unable to believe in myself. Learning from his example, I have finally embraced the challenges of being an adult. Without my father's consistent love and support, this might never have been possible.

~John Lavitt

Living in My Heart

Oh heart, if one should say to you that the soul perishes like the body,
answer that the flower withers, but the seed remains.
~Kahlil Gibran

I can still remember standing at the edge, the sensation of uneasiness as I looked down at the water below me. It beckoned me to jump in, but I couldn't move.

In my seven-year-old mind, I told my legs to bend, my body to rise up and leave the platform, but they stubbornly refused. I remained motionless on the edge. It was the day of reckoning. Everyone in the class had jumped off the diving board but me. Sooner or later I would have to take my turn. My later had become now. I backed up a little, as if that would somehow make the inevitable less likely. It was then that I heard his voice.

"Jump," I heard my father's voice. "Just jump in."

I refused to look up and kept my gaze at the water below.

"Jump, Mijita, jump. You can do it!"

I finally moved my eyes away from the water. My father was on the sidelines. He had a huge smile on his face. There was no doubt on his face that I could do it. He threw an encouraging wink. Not wanting to disappoint him, I jumped. Before the sensation of falling and hitting the water registered in my brain, I was already floating up to the surface. My dad was waiting with a towel as I climbed out of the water.

"You did it! You jumped in!"

That was my dad's life philosophy. Just jump in. Anytime I was afraid of anything, he'd tell me to envision the worst that could happen, make a plan and then go for it. Just jump in, he would say, and with his help, I would. The little girl who was afraid of the diving board soon joined the swim team. That same shy girl danced in the school play and played guard on the basketball team. Often insecure, I was always sure that everyone else was smarter than me. Refusing to let me think like a failure and expecting only the best from me, I brought home A's.

My dad encouraged me to jump in all my life. When I was a shy teenager, he forced me to speak my mind and defend my position through debates at the dinner table. As I grew older, he constantly reminded me there was nothing beyond my reach; nothing I could not accomplish. He helped me to dream and make my dreams become real. I counted on him to be my strength, my cheerleader and my support. And no matter what, he was always there.

So when he was diagnosed with cancer, I had a hard time believing it. That previous year he had suffered a heart attack and a stroke. The diagnosis seemed an unfair blow to a man who was already tackling so much. But the man, who should have been bitter, never was. Like so many times before, he encouraged me to make peace with it. "I'm fine," he would say. Even in his weakened state I depended on him for my strength. I wanted to believe that all would be okay, that nothing was impossible.

So when the cancer was diagnosed as incurable, his acceptance floored me. I wanted him to fight the doctors, tell me they were wrong. Surely he wouldn't give up. There was still a lot to do. He was supposed to teach my son and daughter Spanish, and be their cheerleader when they learned to ride their bikes or learned to swim. He needed to be here to help me teach them to be strong, to persevere and to dream. I wanted him to teach them to jump. I wanted his spirit to make them the kind of people who would take risks, reach out for the impossible. I wanted him to give my children all the things he had given to me.

Much too quickly, his body gave in to the cancer. We knew it was coming soon, so my sister stayed with my dad and mom. We had decided to take turns holding vigil. But it turns out he didn't live long enough for any of that. I got a call one morning that the end was near and raced over to my parents' house. Death is not like it is in the movies. In the movies, people have last moments to say goodbye, say what you never got to say or were holding back, or at the very least, say a last "I love you." Unlike the big screen, I didn't get there in time for a last goodbye and final words. He was gone moments before I arrived. That fact still haunts me. My dad would have laughed at the idea that I think about it at all. "Wasted energy," he probably would say.

One romantic thought about losing someone you love is the notion that they are always with you in your heart. So when my father left this earth, I searched my heart to find him. I wanted to be able to feel his presence, especially when I needed his strength. For a long time, all I felt was emptiness. The sensation of him being beside me eluded me.

Then, one summer afternoon, the searching ended. My daughter Sarah and I were watching my son during swimming class. He was only three and he was shy, a sharp contrast to my outgoing, exuberant daughter. So when the instructor asked if anyone wanted to jump off the diving board, I was surprised when my son (with strong coercion from my daughter) said yes, especially when all the other boys in the class had responded with an adamant shake of the head.

Once he was up there, however, he had second thoughts. He stood on the edge of the platform. He didn't want to jump. Standing, looking at the water, he froze. Instinctually, I wanted to tell him it was okay. I wanted to tell him to turn around and come back down the stairs to where the rest of the class was waiting. In fact, I opened my mouth just to say those words. But instead of telling him to come down, I found myself telling him to jump.

Sarah and I yelled out from the sidelines.

"Jump Adam, jump. You can do it!" we called out.

Adam caught my eye and I sent him a wink and a smile.

"Jump in, Adam. Just jump!"

My dad was there with my daughter and me, encouraging Adam

and cheering him on. My dad was sure Adam could do it, and so was I. Adam moved closer to the edge. I could hear Dad's reassuring voice, harmonious with mine.

"You can do it!"

Then, sending a quick smile our way, my little boy, the same one who was afraid of his own shadow, did just that. He jumped in!

~Teresa Armas

16

His Final Lesson

If I thought I was going to die tomorrow,
I should nevertheless plant a tree today.
~Stephan Girard

"**M**eg, we need to talk."

"Sure thing, Dad."

My father and I had been sitting on the couch watching TV together, and I knew he meant business when he muted the TV.

"As you know, I have been to the doctor several times over the last few days, and well Meg, I have a brain tumor."

"Okay," was all I could say.

"Just okay?"

"Yep, just okay."

Of course he proceeded to explain to me the generalities, to which I offered only a nod. Looking back on that conversation, I didn't know then what a big impact that moment would have on my life. At the time I thought to myself, "Brain tumor—no biggie for Dad. If Mom can beat cancer, he can beat this." Now I look back, thankful for my innocence.

It was the second half of my senior year, that time in a girl's life when all the really big exciting events are happening. Senior prom, my final play performance, my eighteenth birthday and his fiftieth, baccalaureate, and graduation were all scattered about in just two short months. My parents were in and out of the hospital, and I was in and out of the house. Sure, I went to see him—like five times—but I was busy and I had all my events to go to.

By senior prom Dad was bald; he couldn't really concentrate on my final performance, but he was there. He gallantly sat through both of our birthday dinners even with his nausea, and he fought like hell to get out of the hospital for my graduation. During those months, we both were concentrating on the same thing... me, but this story isn't really about me. His doctor said that by focusing on all my future events, it kept my dad alive longer. I guess they really do know what they are talking about because nine days after my high school graduation, my father died.

For the next two weeks after his funeral, I didn't leave my room, not even to shower. Finally, my mom stormed in, opened my blinds and said, "Enough is enough, Megan. Get up. I have something for you to read." My father's doctor had sent my mother a letter. It contained the typical "I'm sorry for your loss" sentiments. But this one was far from typical. It was tear-stained. I could physically see the pain this loss had caused him. In his letter he wrote about how my father inspired him to change his life and the way he worked. My father had not been just a patient to him, and for the first time he actually saw the person he was treating.

> He cared more for the people around him than he did his own pain. I have never met someone who put everyone else first. He was the type of person I desire to be. In his short time here, he touched everyone that worked with him and quickly became the eighth floor's favorite patient. His memory will forever live on in the hearts of doctors and nurses here at Saint Thomas and my life will never be the same.

After I finished reading it, I went and found Mom. With a steady and level gaze, she told me, "Go and get out of this house. Your father is gone. We all miss him, but living in the dark of your room will not bring him back. Live your life. Get a job, hang out with your friends, do something, anything, but don't waste the life you have been given."

I took her words to heart. Two weeks and three days after my father died, I got a job as a summer camp counselor. I worked from the time I got up to the time I went to bed every day that summer. I was giving everything I had to these little kids, and slowly they helped to heal me without even realizing what they were doing. Their innocence had helped me rediscover some of mine.

Too soon, it was the end of summer and I sat in the middle of my bedroom floor packing my things to start college. I began to think back over the last few months and all the changes that had taken place in my life. I thought of my father and how he wouldn't be able to help me move into my dorm room, but also about my summer spent as a camp counselor. Then out of nowhere I remembered the letter his doctor had written. That's when I realized the biggest change that had occurred in my life that summer. I had become an adult.

My summer mirrored parts of the life my father led in his last few days. I had spent the summer months giving of myself to children. It was not the senior summer I had always envisioned. It wasn't all about me. I had learned the final lesson my father was teaching me, that in order to lead a fulfilling and happy life, you must learn how to give of yourself to others. By helping them you really are just helping yourself.

~Megan Tucker-Hall

17

The Car

*The willingness to accept responsibility for one's own life is the source
from which self-respect springs.*
~Joan Didion

I wanted a car. No, I NEEDED a car.

I'd just graduated from college and had moved back into my parents' home while I looked for gainful employment. I had some nice interview clothes, a new pair of dressy sandals, and a handful of résumés. I was all ready for job-hunting, except for one tiny glitch. I didn't have a car.

I'd never had a car. My parents had sent me off to school and paid for my education. They paid for my room and board on campus, too. But they didn't think a car was necessary, and to be honest, it wasn't. Everywhere I went was in close proximity to my dorm. And if it weren't, I'd get my boyfriend to give me a ride.

But I could hardly expect my boyfriend to drop everything and drive me all over Georgia to find a job. When I mentioned this fact to my dad, he was not concerned. In fact, he was downright blasé about the matter.

"You can borrow your mother's car to look for a job," he said.

"But what if I get a job?" I asked. My mother was a schoolteacher, and her vehicle was available, most of the time, during June, July, and August. But when school started in the fall, not having a car was going to be a problem.

"You can worry about that when you get a job," he said.

Hmmph. I sulked for a day or two, but my sulk was not having the desired effect on my dad. If you knew my dad, you wouldn't be surprised. He was not the type of father to just give his kids whatever they wanted. He could have done so. But he was very big on responsibility, which meant that he expected his children to invest their own time and money on important purchases. And a car was tops on his list of "Important Purchases."

My oldest brother was the only one in the house who'd bought his own car. He'd worked like a dog the summer after he turned nineteen, saved his pennies, and paid for a VW Beetle. My other brothers and I were jealous, of course, but not so jealous that we wanted to work like dogs during our summer vacations.

So there I was, a college graduate, stuck without a car and without a job. And with a dad who refused to budge on my car predicament.

I was ecstatic when I finally got a job at a local radio station. It was only part-time, but it was a job! Now, I'd HAVE to have my own car. It was July, and my mother had no intention of giving up her car every day, even if only for a half-day. So, I pleaded my case before my dad.

"Dad, I need a car."

"You should start looking for something you can afford," he said.

Well, that was easier said than done. We lived in a small town; there was one car dealership. No way could I afford a new car. I'd need a used car. And the only way to buy a used car was to know someone who knew someone who'd heard about someone who wanted to sell a car. I didn't know a soul who fit that description.

Ah, but my dad did. He came home the next day, talking up an Impala that had been owned by an older woman. No joke. The car cost six hundred dollars, and my dad thought we should check it out immediately. A car like that wouldn't be around for long, he said.

Once I saw the car, I could see why. Not that the car was unsightly. It was in immaculate shape. But I didn't think too many twenty-two-year-olds were going to jump on this deal. The car was a tank. And it drove like a tank. I'd envisioned myself in a red sports car. Not this dirty-white, "older person" car. I said I'd have to think about it.

The more I thought, the more I figured beggars can't be choosers. "Let's buy the car," I said.

"I'm not buying that car," replied my father, a look of surprise on his face.

"But, Dad!" Now it was my turn to be surprised. I'd barely worked one week, and hadn't been paid yet. I didn't have a cent to my name. Besides, the car was only six hundred dollars. Dad could easily afford that. But he continued to look at me, calm, cool and collected.

"You could buy the car, and I could pay you back," I said, finally. Maybe after a month or two, Dad would forget all about that arrangement.

"Or you could go to the bank and take out a loan," he said. Which was Dad's way of saying, "Get a loan."

Ooooh, I was so put out with my father! A loan! I was barely out of school a month, and now I'd be in debt! I'd have to pay back that loan, for sure. I refused to speak to Dad on the drive to the bank. I was too busy feeling put out. The injustice of it all!

My father did agree to co-sign for the loan. But he made it very clear that he wouldn't make the payments if I quit my job. I agreed to the bank's terms, as well as my father's. What else could I do? I got the check from the bank and we drove directly to the owner's house. Easy come, easy go. I drove home in my Impala, fuming and figuring out car payments.

That was years ago, and I've had quite a few cars since, some used and some brand-new. But there was something special about that Impala. Not the crummy color, or the way it chugged along, and certainly not the way it ate gas. But I was proud of that car.

No, I was proud that I'd bought that car. I had made every single payment on my own. I'd invested my time in a job and my salary was invested in that car. That was quite an achievement for a twenty-two-year-old who'd never had such an adult responsibility. And when the next summer rolled around and I moved out of my parents' home to a new job, I was sure I'd manage just fine. After all, I'd bought a car, all by myself. Thanks to Dad.

~Cathy C. Hall

Getting Back to Abnormal

As we express our gratitude, we must never forget that the highest
appreciation is not to utter words, but to live by them.
~John Fitzgerald Kennedy

My father comes up with amusing yet surprisingly
sensible aphorisms all the time. Because of their
innate wisdom, I have begun compiling them over
the years on yellow stickies. Usually said with a straight face, these
paternal sayings never fail to make me smile—and ponder. "It's getting back to abnormal," he told me the other day on the phone after
dealing with a large family holiday dinner.

"Getting back to *ab*normal?" I replied.

"Yeah, you know what I mean."

One time, I was visiting him in Pamplin, Virginia, and we were
having a father-son talk. He paused, sighed, looked into the distance
and then said, "Well, you can't live two days at once. That's for sure."
Like some sort of southern Yogi Berra, Dad comes up with the right
thing to say all on his own.

When I was younger, I somehow missed the essence of these
maxims. Now, as an adult, I grab a stickie and jot them down. I
even find myself using them when I give advice, echoing my father
without realizing it.

Dad encouraged me to stay in the now with, "The past can kill
you… if you let it." Useful advice for not obsessing about things you
can't control anymore.

His admonition against drinking was not, "Hey, drinking's bad for you," but more along the lines of personal distaste. "I don't know," he said, shrugging. "I just think beer tastes like horse pee."

Perhaps his most valuable counsel to me came when I struggled as a teacher over the years. While loving writing and literature, and conveying it to my students, I felt inundated by superfluous meetings and stacks of heart-numbing grading. I called Dad one evening to tell him about my frustrations. He thought for a moment. "You know, son," he offered, "you don't always need to be in a classroom to teach."

In fact, the best teachers carry their knowledge with them effortlessly and dole it out only when the student is ready. That is my father. He never lectures. A small phrase said kindly seems to be enough.

Over the years, he gave me twenty dollars every time I received straight A's. He offered to buy me a car if I didn't drink or smoke through high school. He vowed to send my two brothers and me to the college of our choice—and did (with my mother of course). During my time at college, he decided to go back to school and finish his own degree. We often compared grades at the end of our semesters. Not only did he put me through college, he himself returned to complete his BA as an example.

Polonius had a long list of advice when his son Laertes was leaving home in *Hamlet* "Neither a borrower nor a lender be," and so on. Here are a few of my other favorite phrases from Dad:

On religion: "Praying is someone else to talk to."

On relationships: "If you are going to love somebody, you'll need to learn to live with faults."

On living together: "Some people just shouldn't."

On jobs: "Just about every job in the world is clerical to some degree."

On secrets: "Not everybody has to know everything about you. It's all right to keep some things to yourself."

It is a father's duty to offer such wisdom. When "son" is added, these mere words can endure a lifetime. "I'm real proud of you, son," is the one I love to hear most. A father's pride has a certain power.

Some people might hear his phrases and merely chuckle, but I have taken many of them to heart, as if they came from the Buddha himself.

The other day I was on the phone with a friend, listening to more about the Great Recession. After some chatting, I was asked how I was doing. "Getting back to abnormal," I replied, smiling to myself.

~Mark Damon Puckett

Blind Determination

Oh, my friend, it's not what they take away from you that counts.
It's what you do with what you have left.

~Hubert Humphrey

"**H**ow's my little girl?" my uncle asked as he pulled his daughter close to him and smothered her with kisses. I watched as my heart hungered for the same affection. At age ten, I cried out in silence for a little of that tenderness. Words of endearment never slipped from my dad's lips. I never, ever heard a single "I love you."

Years swept by, and respect and distance characterized our relationship. Until, that is, I learned that I did receive something from him—the thing that would drastically change my life.

When I turned thirteen, my parents took me to an ophthalmologist. Seated in the examining chair, my face firmly on the chin rest and pupils dilated, I stared forward. Shining a bright light, the doctor looked into my eyes. "She did inherit it," he said. "You need to be prepared. There's no cure for this retinal disease."

My father carried the retinitis pigmentosa gene, which causes a deterioration of the retina. Its effect often brought on complete blindness with no hope of cure. Although my brother's retinas seemed fine, I'd inherited the gene.

The doctor cleared his throat. "But she might not notice any effects of the disease until she reaches the age of sixty."

Sadly, the hope-filled prognosis turned out to be grossly incorrect. Night blindness put a damper on my activities when I began my teenage years. The need for assistance from my friends in order to navigate through dimly-lit areas magnified my humiliation. Night blindness threatened to shatter my fragile teenage self-esteem.

I thwarted my apprehension and dread as I finished college and later married the love of my life. My world shone with happiness—a husband who loved me, three sons to fulfill my longing to be a mom, and general good health.

But that happiness evaporated like dew in the morning sun when, in addition to my night blindness, my peripheral vision began to close in. Slowly at first, then more noticeably with each week.

By coincidence, or perhaps by cruel irony, my father's vision began to diminish at the same time. Dad was fifty-five years of age, but I was only thirty. In a matter of two years, we both lost our sight completely.

I sunk into a pool of self-pity with despair threatening to drown me. My world crumbled as the physical darkness destroyed the dreams my husband and I had for us and our three little boys. With no treatment available or hope of a transplant, desperation and despair filled my days, and bitterness accompanied my sleepless nights. When I finally turned to faith for answers, I saw that I could embrace hope and find peace. Although my physical sight was gone, my heart had 20/20 vision. My attitude had changed, my perception had cleared and my outlook had sharpened.

The most dramatic transformation was in the relationship with my dad, who I now saw with my heart instead of my eyes. True, he wasn't the expressive type, with tender and cuddly words to sweeten my world, but what he'd given me went beyond words and warm caresses. He had given me the example of strong will and determination.

At thirty-five, he'd made the decision to move the family from Bolivia to the United States. He battled doubt as his friends and relatives criticized his perceived foolishness. Ignoring their criticism, my father pressed on. Once in the United States, he overcame humiliation, intense loneliness, helplessness and uncertainty. He endured ridicule due to his lack of fluency in English. Working the night shift unloading trucks, he managed to save enough money for the basic necessities—rent, used furniture, and a down payment on a car. Nine months later, he sent airline tickets for my mom, my brother and me.

Now that I see differently, I am grateful for what my father gave me. He showed me the determination to move forward when facing adversity. He demonstrated the commitment to family and the importance of setting priorities.

Looking back, I know that I had the perfect dad—perfect for me. He stepped from the comfort of our hometown in Bolivia to the unknown in a foreign land. I did the same as I stepped into the unfamiliarity of the sightless world.

And though Dad's love lacks words, his subtle actions give it a sweet voice. I heard its sound when my first book came out. Mom said he clutched it to his heart and tears flowed from his blind eyes.

~Janet Perez Eckles

Life Coach

No game in the world is as tidy and dramatically neat as baseball, with cause and effect, crime and punishment, motive and result, so cleanly defined.
~Paul Gallico

I grew up in Florida. There was always a league, always a practice, always a game. My father made sure of that. There was no getting around it. Not that I had a huge problem with playing team sports, though through the grade school years I much rather preferred unorganized sports (sandlot baseball, front yard football and driveway basketball). Of course, the thing about being a kid is that you don't have much of a choice. Except on the sport itself. I played baseball throughout most of my youth, and for many of those years, my father never sat in the stands. No, he was in the dugout.

My father grew up in the Cleveland suburbs during a time when it was okay for kids to take the bus by themselves to go see a baseball game at the stadium. Which is exactly what he did. He also played ball growing up and was very athletic. I've seen pictures. He was a freaking stud. He also had the added task of helping to raise his four younger siblings. I'm sure that stress had something to do with his love for fitness. Eventually it led him to the military, where he served in the Navy.

Growing up with a love of the game of baseball, it was only natural he'd pass it on to my brother and me. It must be noted however, neither of us were super athletic growing up. Sure, we loved to play outside, but there wasn't any hope we were ever going to go pro. Well, maybe there was. Everyone can dream, right? Instead, sports offered particular lessons that could be applied to any portion of adult life. Working as a team, dedication to a task, and so on. The problem was, as I mentioned before, my father was the coach.

Now that I coach my own children in baseball I can see how having your father as your coach can be a frustrating experience. You are the coach's son. You are expected to do better than everyone else. You can't slack on pushups. You can't slack on ground ball drills.

It always seemed when he was yelling at us, he was yelling at me. Only me. Why me? As I see now, he wasn't. He was yelling at everyone. But as the son of the coach, you tend to take things less constructively than the other kids. You tend to get in the mindset that you are a disappointment rather than just another infielder who needs to work on the shift when there is a left hander up to bat.

This is not something I would understand for many years. This is not something my son will understand until he's coaching my grandson. I remember coaching my son in baseball and looking over at my own father with total exasperation. His face was lit up in a smirk, almost saying, "I told you so, jackass." Only, what exactly did he tell me and how in the hell did I miss it all those years?

My father was an engineer (I say "was" because now he's a babysitter) and by nature is very critical and cynical of most actions. If you said you were trying your best, he didn't believe that it was actually your best and he would push you to do better. He'd question your actions and intentions until he got a detailed answer as to why and how. Then he'd want you to break down what you did wrong and what you planned to do to fix things. This made every process in sports a tedious learning experience, not to mention extremely annoying.

However, this is another life lesson I wouldn't pick up until I was coaching my son and drilling him on the same mistakes I had once made as a child. As an adult I had a different perspective on the game and understood certain fundamentals that had been lost on me in my youth. So was my dad being too hard on me? Or was he just pushing me to be my best?

Either way, his pushing me led to me pushing myself. With or without him, I would be in the yard practicing grounders by bouncing a tennis ball off the side of the house and catching it off the ground. I'd be running around in the yard, tossing the ball high in the air to practice tracking down fly balls. I'd be in the front yard, hitting aluminum cans into the street to work on the mechanics of my swing. Now my son uses pinecones. It looks nutty, but this kind of focus and willpower on a particular task has translated well into adult life. I don't think I would have had that kind of drive without sports, and without my father I wouldn't have had sports to give me a reason to be better.

Clearly without his influence, I don't think I'd be where I am today. I see situations and process them differently. I "break down the play," as they say in football, to solve problems. This is something my father instilled in me, not only by teaching me how to play baseball, but how to understand the game as well.

Many children watch and play baseball, but there are a rare few who are taught to have a complete understanding of the game. From the strategy in certain pitches in particular situations, to the way the catcher controls the game—these are things he made sure I understood. Baseball is a game of minute decisions and infinite possibilities and scenarios. It's impossible to figure out each one, but it's not improbable to understand them when they come up.

We used to go to the minor league games in town quite often, and after a batter would hit a sacrifice fly or bunt towards third my father would turn and ask me if I saw that. I would always answer yes, but then he'd ask me if I knew why the batter took that particular action. It was that interaction and method of thinking that I'm passing on to my son. So thanks Dad, for showing me that baseball is more than just a game—it's an allegory for life and beyond.

~Curtis Silver

The Power of Encouragement

Anyone who ever gave you confidence, you owe them a lot.
~Truman Capote

While my dad has been a tremendous influence on me throughout my life, it was a few simple words of encouragement that have stuck in my mind for thirty-five years and guided me at crucial moments along the way. I doubt that Dad would remember uttering these words, but for me, those words meant everything.

When I was in grade school, we held season tickets to a series of cultural performances in Springfield, Illinois during the winter season. We only had two tickets, so whichever parent had less work would take me to the event while the other stayed home and prepared to teach the next day.

Since my dad had no papers to grade that night, he was the one who accompanied me to the ballet. I've long since forgotten the name of the company, but it was a traditional ballet in which the men wore leotards and the women wore toe shoes. Dad and I had seats along the side of the balcony close to the stage. More importantly, we had a bird's eye view of the orchestra pit where twenty musicians peered into their music stands.

I had started taking violin lessons a couple of years earlier in the fifth grade. My parents painfully listened to me practice, no doubt wishing I had chosen any other instrument. They had already taken me to hear a few orchestras by that point, but what the musicians were doing in the pit below was different. They were accompanying dancers to the strains of Tchaikovsky or Chopin or Mozart. They weren't the center of attention, but they were the backbone of the performance. As their bow arms flew back and forth across their instruments, I was mesmerized.

When it was time for intermission this one memorable night, Dad and I roamed the halls of the high school where the performance was taking place.

"What do you think of the dancers?" he asked.

"The musicians were really cool," I responded. Not being old enough to focus on boys, I was unimpressed with male musculature. And having taken dance lessons long enough to have tried toe shoes myself, I thought the women were enduring torture. I was also opposed to those silly leotards.

During the second half of the performance, I spent more and more time focusing on the musicians. Their heads lifted in unison at crucial junctures of the music, and they craned their necks to watch the conductor, a wiry young man whose glasses seemed at the point of falling off his nose and whose tuxedo seemed to be made for someone much larger than himself. Then suddenly he laughed, and his right hand flew to cover his mouth. Several of the musicians turned around to look at the stage, and I did too. One of the female dancers had tripped, and one of the men was offering a hand to help her up. Embarrassed, she hurried back into a pirouette.

The mirth among the musicians was obvious. The dancer was unhurt, so their laughter wasn't malicious. They were merely relishing the beauty of live performance where anything can happen and small details distinguish each evening's effort. Because the musicians weren't the focus of attention, they could enjoy a special camaraderie as they silently communicated among one another. They were part of something special.

After the final applause, we lingered. My dad gave me the chance to clamber down to the orchestra pit where I could see the black folders of music and the dust on the lights of the music stands. I was too timid to talk to any of the musicians, but I watched as they wiped off their instruments and chatted, satisfied, I assumed, by a job well done.

"You could do that if you wanted to." I hadn't noticed that my dad had come to lean over the rails alongside me.

"What do you mean?"

"You could become a musician and travel along with a ballet company yourself. Do you think you'd like that?"

At the time I was still struggling to play an A scale with all three of its sharps.

"Sure. That would be fun."

"Well, you'll have to keep practicing."

I don't remember the rest of the conversation or the drive back home. What stood out in my mind was the simple phrase: "You could do that if you wanted to." My dad was actually telling me that I could grow up and be as proficient as the musicians we'd just heard and become a part of something just as wonderful. For a girl of thirteen, it was a heady thought.

At the time I had little confidence in myself, so my dad's words shook me. That night I thought of his comment over and over again. "You could do that if you wanted to." Hadn't he heard my awful violin practicing? I knew darned well he had. Didn't he know how hard it was to play an instrument well? Of course he did; he'd been a trumpet player throughout school. Yet he had faith in me even though I had none in myself.

This one comment did not cure my self-doubt, but my dad's belief in me has served as a guiding light ever since. When I was struggling as an undergraduate to learn German and Italian and Spanish at the same time, the comment morphed to, "You can do this if you want to." It stayed with me as I learned to cope with teaching fifth graders in Mexico and learning mariachi music by ear. It stayed on my shoulder while I wrote my dissertation. No matter what I chose to throw myself into, I knew the task wasn't beyond me. It was simply up to me.

As things turned out, I grew up to become a writing teacher, but music has always been a favorite part of my life. Today I play with a local orchestra so that I can enjoy the beauty of classical music, and I moonlight in a mariachi band, where camaraderie is as important as performance. I may not have become an itinerant musician, but I've always been grateful for those powerful words of encouragement that are still with me today.

~D.R. Ransdell

How to Build a Sailboat

There's a long, long trail a-winding into the land of my dreams.
~Stoddard King, Jr.

When I was young, a few books were neatly stacked on the end table in our family room. One of those, about how to build a sailboat, always intrigued me. Its glossy photos of sleek craft cutting through turquoise water spoke of adventure. The step-by-step guidelines were written to convince readers like myself that building such a boat was as easy as following the directions on the back of a cake mix box. Yet I always opened that book with the same sense of puzzlement. My mom had given it to my dad for his birthday one year, and I guess the implication was that he wanted to build one. The puzzle was my mom thinking that dad would ever do it.

My dad was handy, no question. But growing up, he and my grandpa owned three department stores in our small town and the surrounding communities, and he worked Monday through Saturday every week that I could remember. On most evenings, he set up his bookkeeping at the kitchen table. Sunday was his only free day, and usually involved yard work or upkeep on our house, the three store buildings, or, as they aged, my grandmothers' houses. He built many practical things over the years — cabinets, shelves, a playhouse — but never a sailboat. I concluded, as I flipped the pages in that book, that though my dad dreamed of building such a masterpiece, he just wasn't in a position to act on his dreams.

Dreams, I was sure, were things that one attained in the short term. I dreamed of a new bike, getting my braces off, or making the cheerleading team. My idea of a "long-term" dream back then was getting my ears pierced when I turned fifteen. It didn't occur to me that dreams could, or should, lurk for very long.

As malls and new highways were built in our rural communities and people found it easier to leave town to shop, my father's stores struggled. With my grandfather gone, my dad worked harder to keep it all together. Though Dad never let on, I'm sure his dreams at the time concentrated on just making payroll. Swept up in my own world of proms, graduation and college classes, I barely noticed that his fifty-hour weeks had increased to eighty.

As a married adult, I began to learn that some dreams, like saving for our first house, take time. About this time my dad announced that he was selling the stores and retiring. Looking back, I wonder why I was surprised. Preoccupied with my own life, I guess I hadn't noticed it had gotten that hard. "Dad," I remember asking with concern, "what will you do?" Now it was his turn to be surprised. Didn't I realize, he asked me, that there were so many things he'd just been waiting to do?

Dad dusted off those many dreams, prioritized a list, and never looked back. He's learned to scuba dive, has built local renown for his duck decoy carvings, hammered for Habitat for Humanity and recently ran as the only fifty-year graduate in the 5K Alumni race at his alma mater. He and Mom have traveled the world, taught English as a Second Language to new Americans and welcomed six grandchildren into the world.

It turns out that Dad knew a lot about dreams. He knew that sometimes, like it or not, they are shelved for the rigors of life. He taught me that as long as you have the courage to pull them back out, they can be as glossy and vibrant as ever. Dad never did build that sailboat. He swapped that dream for a more practical option in the landlocked Midwest, and got his pilot's license the year after he retired. He is now putting the finishing touches on a Starduster II bi-plane he has built from a starter pile of metal. I learned many things from my dad, but one of the most powerful has been the hope and happiness of reaching for life's dreams—even if they take time to build.

~Gail Wilkinson

Thanks for Letting Me Fail

Few things are more satisfying than
seeing your children have teenagers of their own.
~Doug Larson

Whether you've got kids or not, everyone has watched another parent and thought, "Okay, I wouldn't do it that way." It all seems easy until you actually have to do it yourself. For me, the hardest thing about being a father is watching my kids fail without interfering.

This is a tough one. I thought I'd just give them the space, watch them struggle, watch them cry and get frustrated, then I'd give them some magical tip and they'd succeed. Ta-daaaa! No problem. I didn't realize that my heart would break for them while I watched. I didn't realize that I wouldn't always have the magical tip. I didn't realize that sometimes they wouldn't even want it; that they actually might want to do it wrong.

Now that I'm experiencing this, I've been thinking back to when I was a kid. I would tell my dad about my hair-brained ideas, and he would just smile and say, "Hmmm, sounds interesting. Let me know how it turns out." If I was really struggling with something, he would ask me a bunch of questions, and usually I would come up with my own answer.

How did he resist the urge to talk me out of stuff, to help me before I failed? It must have been painful to watch, because I tried a lot of stuff, and I failed at a lot of it. And yet, Dad was always there for me, the ultimate coach and supporter. He never tried to talk me out of things, or coach me in the right direction unless I asked. He gave me the room to screw up on my own. Maybe one of the best things he did for me as a father was to have the strength to stand by and watch me fail — to let me figure it out on my own.

It has occurred to me that this was a huge factor in the fact that, for the most part, I don't fear failure. Don't get me wrong, I don't like failure, but the risk of it never stops me from doing anything. I have had a life rich with travel, adventure, and widely varying experiences and friendships, most of which can be attributed to going out and trying things that somebody should have told me would fail. It was a gift my dad gave me — the confidence to screw up on my own, to attempt anything and see what happens.

I want to give that same gift to my kids. When they're coloring outside the lines, putting tape on crooked, or trying to jam the Barbie shoe on the wrong foot. Kids are in a perpetual state of learning, so that means they're screwing up constantly.

Today at cross-country ski training, Cassidy, my seven-year-old, was falling repeatedly trying to get up a hill. I kept taking a step forward, closer, closer… thinking, "Okay I'll help her… no I better not. Okay, now I'll help her… no, let her do it!" Then, finally, she figured out a way to crawl up, and it looked silly and she giggled loudly as she did it, full of excitement that she had conquered that hill. It wasn't good skiing form, but mission accomplished, and my lip still hurts from biting it.

I have a lot of work to do on watching the failures with a smile. Maybe I'll come up with some plan, some way to deal with it. Maybe someone I know already has some good ideas. Maybe I'll bounce them off my dad.

He'll probably say, "Hmmm, sounds interesting. Let me know how it turns out."

~Tim Brewster

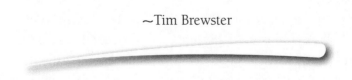

24

The Preacher's Kid

To speak and to speak well are two things.
A fool may talk, but a wise man speaks.
~Ben Jonson

The preacher's kid. Ah yes, the stuff of movies and stories and jokes: the PK. I'm also a mother, an author, a wife, a friend, even a nurse, but I have been this one thing since I was born and will be when I die: my father's daughter.

Sometimes we don't know why we love someone or something or somewhere—we just do. Love that is. It's okay not to know all the reasons why, but I do know at least part of the reason I'm now a novelist, a piece of the reason I love stories: telling them, listening to them, reading them, taking them apart and putting them back together, and that reason is the preaching. All those sermons. All those Bible studies and Wednesday night services and parables and youth group bonfire lessons. There were too many to count.

There are the harder things that come with this PK title: moving towns, being watched by a thousand parishioners, going to church four to five times a week, enduring religious confusion. Then there are also gifts, and mine was this: I learned the power of story. Because really, what does a preacher do? Tells the same story over and over in as many ways as possible. The bottom line in every sermon is always the same: God loves you. He sent his Son to die for you. That might get a little boring after a while, right? So the preacher must find new and interesting ways to get to the same endpoint every single time.

Sure, there's variation in the characters and disciples and plagues and sins, but it's always back to this: God's redeeming, relentless love.

Who really wants to sit in a pew for an hour and listen to a lecture except by the best preachers, the ones people come to hear, who tell us a story? Does it matter if the story is true? Well, yes... sort of, but maybe not always in the most literal sense. What are parables but truth hidden in story? What really matters is The Truth, not whether the particulars of the story are facts. Dad would get so carried away with the story that he'd teach the congregation the Greek word for the English word (as if they cared) and then what that word *really* meant. He wanted everyone to know what it all *really* meant, and he somehow knew that this Truth was inside all those words. He might have failed in other avenues of life, but here he never wavered—wrapping words around faith and trust in an unfailing God.

And there it is. The power of story.

His other gift of story to me is less obvious. When I was twelve years old, God apparently told my dad to move the family from Philadelphia to Fort Lauderdale and start a new church (I didn't hear this particular marching order, so I still doubt it). Now God and I didn't exactly agree on this subject, so we had a long talk (God and I, not Dad and I) and with me God was silent on the subject. So we moved. In the process of finding the right place to live and the right place to plant the church, I attended four different schools for seventh, eighth, ninth and tenth grades until we finally landed where we stayed, in Coral Springs, Florida.

The desperation born of adolescent loneliness sent me into novels and stories. Libraries and small quiet rooms with a book in my hands became my sanctuaries. These books were my best friends, my confidantes. These stories understood the world beyond south Florida, beyond loneliness and into dreams. These books carried my heart and me to better places.

Then there were the days I'd be bored while the cool kids (meaning they had friends) were driving around in their Firebirds and T-top Camaros, while they had dates and went to football games. This is when I'd browse through Dad's library. Here is where I found

C.S. Lewis. Not literally, of course. Mr. Lewis had departed from this world the year I arrived. But his words were there just as if he sat with me. I read *The Screwtape Letters* and understood the truest power of story—how sometimes the thing that needs to be said is best said with fiction.

When I finished my first novel, *Between the Tides*, the last person I had in mind to thank was my dad. I'm the one who rose at four in the morning to write while my babies slept; I'm the one who toiled away for years on the art and craft of words to write a single novel. I'm the one who fell in love with words, and the way they sound and move and come together.

But there is a beginning for all loves: a first encounter; a first moment; a beginning. There is always a beginning. And my love affair with story and words began with and because of my dad.

So let me thank Dad for not only showing me the power of story, but also offering me the chance to lose and then find myself in its magic.

~Patti Callahan Henry

Thanks Dad

Dad to the Rescue

25

A Father's Persistence

The difference between perseverance and obstinacy is that one comes from a strong will, and the other from a strong won't.
~Henry Ward Beecher

Whenever I was distraught as a teenager, my father, like most parents, shared in my pain. Nothing, however, could compare to his agony when my life was dramatically changed forever.

I was at the wrong place at the wrong time, an innocent bystander at an armed robbery. I was shot in the head execution style by one of the thieves. Very few people thought I would survive, much less be a productive member of society. In the hospital waiting room, my father believed that I might die and his thoughts were of the past. What could he have done differently? Could he have spent more time with his son?

My parents met with the neurosurgeon in the morning, who told them that he was surprised I had made it through the night. Now that I had, he needed to operate. He then proceeded to say that there was only a 40% chance of my surviving the surgery, and if I did survive, almost a 100% chance of my living in a nursing home, not being able to walk or communicate.

My father was devastated. The surgeon was talking about his second son, a young man. An honor student at the University of Texas. He wondered when this nightmare would end. My mother refused to listen to the pessimism. She told my father, "We need to rent a storage space to keep Mike's furniture until he returns to U.T."

But my father, still stunned, replied, and reminded her of the grim prognosis. "Toby, did you hear the neurosurgeon? Mike will be lucky if he spends the rest of his days in a nursing home."

My mother quickly and angrily barked back, "That doctor does not know my son, my Michael."

My father did not want to argue, especially not at such a delicate time. They rented a storage space in Austin. My father never believed the space would be opened again. But I beat the neurosurgeon's odds and survived the surgery. I was in a coma and with each day that I showed no progress, my father agonized even more.

Then, miraculously, I woke up. I was completely paralyzed on my right side, could not speak, and was hallucinating. When the doctor informed my parents that I was stable enough to fly home to a rehabilitation hospital in Houston, my father finally had reason to hope. My rehabilitation in Houston was steady, but also (especially for my father) very, very slow. He was not a very patient man. He became extremely frustrated when he could not understand what I wanted. When my mother had no problems understanding me, my father's frustration grew even more.

Then, seven weeks after being hurt, I began to utter some words. My father thought this was the perfect time for him to work with me. At first he would drill me on simple things, such as pointing to a 1, then a 2, then a 3. He was so happy when I accomplished each goal, only to be devastated the next time when I was unable to repeat the task.

As time progressed, I continued to improve. My verbal skills grew steadily each day, and after my father's busy day at work, he would come to the hospital, ready to work with me. I still remember his bag filled with flash cards. He drilled me on math and spelling. He stretched my limp leg. Anything and everything that might help.

The hospital staff worried that he was working me too hard, that I would grow frustrated working with them all day, and with my father all evening. None of that mattered to my father. He knew what was best for his son and no one would be able to persuade him otherwise. Very few of the medical staff at either hospital believed that I would ever be able to return to college. But that is exactly what I did almost a year and a half after the shooting. I could not have made this recovery without my father. He always encouraged me to look for the positive, even when there was very little to feel positive about. He held me up mentally and physically, pushing me as hard as he could and believing that I would have my life back.

Four years after returning to school, I graduated at the top of my class with many honors, including *Phi Beta Kappa* and *summa cum laude*. I was one of twelve students named as a Dean's Distinguished Graduate.

As I limped up to the stage to get my diploma from the Dean, I received a standing ovation. One of the many thoughts racing through my head was of my father — the man who helped me throughout my ordeal. The man who has always been there for me, no matter what, and who believed I would one day reclaim my life. Even though I could not see his face in the huge auditorium, I knew he was smiling at me. I will always love him.

~Michael Jordan Segal, MSW

Always at My Back

What a child doesn't receive he can seldom later give.
~P.D. James, Time to Be in Earnest

My relationship with my father is complicated. It always has been. We are alike in many ways and this only adds to the complications. But there was one time when it was simple, when I was just a daughter and he a father, and it is this one time that I remember with great affection.

I was in college, probably my freshman year. I attended school only two hours away from my parents' house, so I came home every break I got to see friends from high school, or to sleep and eat free groceries. Occasionally, I brought friends with me. It was a great place to escape the many pressures of college and growing up, and to be someone's child again.

On one break, I came home early to catch up with my best friend from high school. My mother's sister was visiting, so I camped out in the basement bedroom—which was just fine by me because it made for easy entry in the early morning hours. My friend's mother took us to a movie and we made it an early night. The house was dark when I came home, but David Letterman was still on. I watched some TV and then went to bed myself.

A few hours later, I woke up with a horrible pain in my gut. I didn't know this at the time, but it was similar to labor contractions—only it didn't come and go in waves of torment. The torment was constant. I tried to get comfortable and fall back asleep, but that wasn't happening. So, clutching the walls as I walked, I made my way up two flights of stairs to the bathroom medicine chest. I scoured the shelves for anything that might help—antacids, Tylenol, Motrin. My aunt, who was sleeping in the next room, heard the commotion and came out to see what was going on. She had been a drug counselor at one time in her life, and had keen hearing for roaming teenagers. By the time she found me, I was doubled over and getting dizzy. She rushed down the hall to my parents' bedroom, and by the time they arrived, I had passed out on the floor.

I woke up in the nearest bed with all three of them around me. They immediately began questioning me. Where had I been? What had I done? What had I eaten? Did I take any drugs (that one from my aunt)? The answer was, simply, movie and popcorn. They checked for signs of appendicitis and gave me some Motrin. I can't remember whether I fell asleep again or just waited out the night, but in the morning the pain was still there, full on.

My father was dressed for work, but he called in to say he would be late, then bundled me in the car and drove me to the emergency room at one of the local hospitals. It was the usual scene—crowded, chaotic and filled with the distinctive feeling that comes from being at the mercy of a headless bureaucratic machine. We checked in and sat in the chairs waiting for our turn. The one thing about my father that is easy to understand is that he has never been a patient man, and this is especially true when someone he loves is suffering. I was far too distracted by my own pain to notice it then, but his patience was depleting as the minutes, then hours ticked by.

We made it, finally, to an exam room and that's where the waiting really began. Seeing that I needed observation, the first doctor came, then quickly left us in a line for admission to a regular room. Only the line was very long. Four hours passed. My father came and went from the room as I lay there in fetal position, breathing through the pain and freezing cold with only a hospital sheet and my father's coat to cover me. Out of everything that day, the pain in my gut, the eventual needle sticks and IVs, it's the cold in that room that I remember most vividly. Eventually, I began to shiver and my lips started to turn purple. I needed to be admitted, and soon.

Typically, my father's lack of patience resulted in, let's say, fervent advocacy. But not on this day. On this day, there was no arguing with nurses or yelling at desk clerks. Instead, my father asked someone if they were prepared to admit me that moment. When they couldn't give him an answer, he simply grabbed the bag with my clothing, draped his coat around me, and carried me — out of the room, past the hospital staff that tried to stop him, through the security doors, the room with the chairs, out the front door and into his car.

With me dressed in a hospital gown and his overcoat, he drove to a second hospital, a second emergency room. He carried me again to the admitting desk and within an hour, I had been admitted to the hospital for observation. I stayed there for two days, at which point the pain was gone and written off as a stomach bug. But that's not why I remember the story.

People who know me well know that I am no shrinking violet. Had I been capable of removing myself to a second hospital that day, there is no doubt that I would have done it and that my father would have encouraged me to do it myself, taking pride in having raised a strong, independent woman. But on that day, I was not a strong, independent woman. I was a child rendered helpless by pain. I was a daughter in need of protection. There was no one in the world I needed more than my father, and he was there.

It's not often that people are put to a test. Indeed, it is precisely those rare times that make the headlines — heroic firefighters storming a building, pilots landing planes under extreme duress, bystanders pulling a stranger from the train tracks. I can't imagine any comfort greater than knowing there is someone in your life who will never fail to have your back and do whatever is needed to protect you. I had that in my father.

I am a mother now, and I know what it feels like on the other side of that equation. I can feel it inside me, this likeness I have to my father. Some of it presents an ongoing struggle. Lack of patience probably tops that list. But I gladly take it all to have that one thing of his that I can bestow upon my own children. There are times when I can see it on their faces, this knowledge that I am strong, and that no matter what, I have their backs.

~Wendy Walker

27

Words of Wisdom

A father is always making his baby into a little woman.
And when she is a woman he turns her back again.
~Enid Bagnold

My heart was broken for the very first time when I was four years old. The neighborhood boy I adored told me that he didn't want to be my friend anymore and that was that — the first scar on my heart on the road to everlasting love. My dad fixed it with an ice cream cone from Dairy Queen. He always knew what to do, my dad.

I managed to make it to the age of fourteen before another scar was added. My cherished boyfriend of two weeks dumped me for my friend. My dad fixed it with a funny tale about how weird my ex-boyfriend's ears were. He always knew what to do, my dad.

I slugged it out through my teen years, avoiding the big heart-break that can strike during this treacherous time. My father had made me believe I could do anything and that I was smart, funny, and pretty, and I didn't need a boy's arm around my shoulder to know that. He taught me to like everyone, but love only a chosen few.

He always knew what to do, my dad.

When I turned twenty-one, I met THE ONE. The one who flipped my heart, touched my soul and made every day a day worth singing about. We dated for two years, got engaged and started to plan the wedding. My dreams were coming true.

We picked the date, starting looking into halls, limos, catering, the works. It seemed like all we had to do now was finalize the date, send out the invitations and just like that we'd be married and living happily ever after.

Until the day he called me at work, from my cell phone, while driving my car, to tell me he was in love with someone else.

I stood there, transfixed, mouth gaping, and unsure of what to say. I managed to get him to pick me up, for no other reason than to return my car to me. We argued, fought, I cried and he was bitter about having to talk to me at all. He left me alone, crying in the parking lot. He was about to start his new life with the other woman who, according to him, he had loved forever.

I went through the usual stages of grief. I cried. I cried some more. My girlfriends rallied around me, trying to cheer me up, make me laugh, whatever was needed to get me through the first horrible weeks of the break-up and then returning the ring and telling my family there would not be a wedding this year.

I moved back home for two weeks to get my head together and to allow my friends to remove all traces of him from my apartment. One night as I was sitting on the back porch, my father came outside with a bowl of ice cream. I smiled through my tears.

"Dad, I'm not four anymore."

To which my father replied, "No kidding, you're old enough to get your own ice cream now." He just sat with me, eating his ice cream. We stared at the stars in silence. When he began to speak, he just repeated the same mantra over and over about how special I was, how I would recover and move on and although I would always remember the hurt, he told me not to let it cloud my judgment and make the same mistake again. He warned me not to jump into anything right away, to allow the hurt to heal and remember that I didn't do anything wrong and time really does heal all wounds. He went on and on until he finished his bowl and once again we sat in silence and listened to the sounds of the evening.

After a while, he asked me, "Did anything I say help?"

I smiled sadly and answered honestly. "Not really, Dad. At least not today."

He put down his dish and looked me in the eye, asking sincerely, "Do you want me to go and beat the crap out of him?"

The laughter began deep in my belly and erupted from my mouth. For five very joyous minutes, I could not stop laughing. My tears of pain turned to tears of laughter as I thought about my father getting into the car, tracking down my ex, and slugging out a twenty-five-year-old man. Truth was, because he had the rage of a father behind him, he had a shot!

After the laughter slowed down to a giggle, I told my dad, "No thanks Dad, but I appreciate the offer." He smiled at me and ended the conversation with, "Well, it's never really off the table, just so you know."

I smiled as he went back inside and for the first time, I knew I would be okay.

He always knew what to do, my dad.

~Tracy Cavlovic

28

Just Wait

Good things come to those who bait.
~Author Unknown

"**I**f I have to come in here again, you're going to be in trouble. Now, go to sleep!"

I heard my bedroom door slide shut. I guess Dad wasn't kidding this time. After the sound of his footsteps grew silent, I peeked out from underneath the blankets. With my flashlight on low beam, I read the hands on my desk clock: 12:55 AM. Whew—a close one. Dad had made three walkthroughs already this evening. How did he know I was still awake? I had taken the usual precautions: door closed, curtains pulled, nightlight unplugged, no squirming around on the bed. In fact, I was hardly making a sound. Maybe all fathers have X-ray vision or something. But sleep now? No way! In a few hours we would leave for a week's vacation at my favorite place: Palomar.

Palomar Mountain State Park in Southern California offered my family the perfect getaway, with its majestic sugar pines, observatory, and fish that were always hungry. The best camping spot was the one closest to Doane Pond, where I only had a short hike to the fishing hole. This little pond provided the best trout fishing I'd ever seen. Well, that's what my dad always said, and I agreed with him. We always filled our stringers when we fished at Palomar.

Dad even allowed me to explore the park by myself, as long as he or Mom could see my location. Besides, there was no way to get lost. I could view the trail, campground, and pond from almost any angle. Although I was only seven at the time, I couldn't have felt more secure.

One afternoon, I rushed down to the fishing hole to stake out a good spot for Dad and me before the evening crowd showed up. I had made the trip from the campsite a dozen times without any problems, so I hardly needed to look twice. Catching a limit of fish was easy for a disciplined angler like me. My Eagle Claw pole and Mitchell reel assured my success. With any luck, I would have a stringer full of fish by the time Dad showed up.

About the time I should have passed the meadow, I realized something was wrong. The pond was nowhere in sight. When I glanced back over my shoulder, I noticed the campground had disappeared as well. Now I had a problem. I was lost!

I knew better than to keep walking. My father had always said, "If you ever get lost, just stay where you are and wait. I'll be along directly." Using a nearby post as a backrest, I sat down and waited. I was still waiting as the sun dipped low on the horizon and the evening chill crept in.

Finally, a forest ranger drove by in his patrol truck. He stopped in front of me.

"Hey kid, have you seen a boy about your age?" he asked. "Well, he's missing and his family is worried about him."

Smiling back at the ranger, I shook my head in a silent "no." Before I could think of anything else to say, the pickup rambled down the road and disappeared into a trail of dust. Since I considered myself lost already, it was fortunate the ranger didn't enlist my help with the search. Still, I wondered why he never asked if I were the boy for whom he was searching.

It was almost dark when a big man rounded the corner with a slow but steady pace. It was Dad. My father came looking for me just as he said he would. I felt so secure that night as we headed back to camp, his arm wrapped tightly around my shoulder.

I found out later that the park ranger didn't believe anyone could get lost sitting by a signpost that read "Doane Valley Campground." My dad only grinned when he saw me by a sign pointing the way back to our campsite. He never laughed about it though, because I had patiently waited as he instructed.

Dad is gone now, and I never got to thank him for rescuing me that night. I guess some cancers work that way, taking fathers away unexpectedly. The chaplain at the funeral service said my dad went on to a better place. I'm no expert on all this hereafter stuff. Still, from what I hear, Heaven is a pretty big place. It might take a while for newcomers to get their bearings sorted out. So Dad, if you're feeling a little lost up there, just sit down by one of those pillars and wait. One of these days, I'll be along directly.

~Charles E. Harrel

29

Daddy's Little Girl

A daughter may outgrow your lap,
but she will never outgrow your heart.
~Author Unknown

When I was very small, my father would dance with me, singing a popular song of that era called "Daddy's Little Girl." I would stand on the top of his shoes as we glided around the living room floor, pretending we were in a grand ballroom.

How I loved to dance with my father and pretend I was the belle of the ball. But suddenly, one day I could no longer dance. One spring day, in 1955, I awoke to raging fever, pain, and muscle contractions. My father scooped me up into his arms and rushed me into town to our little hospital. The diagnosis was one that struck fear in the hearts of every parent and child at the time. Polio had come to our little ballroom and life would never be the same.

As we lived far from any major city, our hospital was ill equipped to deal with polio patients. I rapidly began to decline. Although I was outwardly unconscious, I can remember hearing the doctor speaking to my parents and telling them I would not live through the night. At that moment, my little eight-year-old mind began to pray. *There are four corners on my bed; there are four angels round my head. Now I lay me down to sleep, I pray the angels my soul to keep. If I should die before I wake, I pray the Lord my soul to take.*

The next thing I remembered was my dad sitting beside me and singing to me. "Daddy's Little Girl" became his fight song—a song to cheer me up, to help me make it through the night. And most of all, a song from his heart that echoed to mine through all of the pain.

Finally, I began to recover from the worst of the illness and was sent home, crippled but alive. We could not afford for me to remain in the hospital, so our little home was quarantined. Through it all, my father never left my side. Hour after hour, day after day, my dad was beside me. He read everything he could find about polio and treatments that might strengthen my ravaged legs. From our small town library, Dad found a book that was to change the course of my life. It was the autobiography of Sister Elizabeth Kenny, entitled *And They Shall Walk.*

Dad contacted the Sister Kenny Rehabilitation Institute to learn how to do the therapy and doggedly began working with her methods to bring my legs back to life. The therapy consisted of stretching exercises and hot packs, which burned like fire. I can still remember his big strong hands red from the heat. And as I would cry out in pain, Dad would cry with me and promise me it would be better, all the while singing our battle song to keep me strong.

When I could not stand the pain of having even light covers touching my body, Daddy built a special cage from chicken wire which formed a frame around my bed so I could stay warm without the blankets touching me. He slept on the floor beside me and never let me see his exhaustion or his worries. His ever-present laughter was our constant companion throughout that terrible summer.

Finally, his effort began to make a difference. Slowly but surely I could once again stand. Now we began our little ballroom dance in earnest. Balancing me on the top of his feet, he would teach me to walk once again, just as he had taught me how to dance. And of course the song was always the same. "Daddy's Little Girl." The day that I stood and walked into his arms unaided, I know that song was in both of our hearts.

By the time school rolled around again, I was able to walk and return to a normal life. My dancing legs would never be quite the same, but the muscles had come back with only minor weakness in one leg.

Polio is still a part of my life, since I later developed post-polio sequelae, but I will keep on dancing and remembering my father's strength, and unyielding faith. My father will always be my favorite dance partner.

~Christine Trollinger

30

The Cape of Good Hope

Courage is being afraid but going on anyhow.
~Dan Rather

We tumbled out of the gold minivan like a troupe of clowns. Thirteen family members were on vacation together and had arrived at the Cape of Good Hope in South Africa, the southwestern-most point of the African continent and the place where the Atlantic Ocean meets the Indian Ocean. Around us the waves raged, the wind was crisp, and the rocks off the coast held steadfast against the water.

Signs on the entrance road announced: "Beware of Baboons" and "Don't Feed the Baboons!" Our tour guide told us not to approach a baboon even if it looked friendly. He explained that the baboons loitered near the parking lot because it was close to the restaurant and the garbage cans. He said if a baboon approached us we should be still and stay in place.

The sun shone brightly, and I put my hand to my forehead to admire the view and block the powerful rays. Along with the land, sky, and sea, I saw numerous baboons scattered around us. I was amazed there were so many. They were sitting, walking, playing, and picking fleas off each other. They were like the many gray squirrels scampering around my backyard—but one hundred times the size.

Our group started spreading out, amazed by the vista and wanting to explore. I turned slightly and noticed a baboon loping up a hill with a bag hanging from its mouth. The bag was my dad's. I looked back at our aging minivan and saw that the sliding door had been left open. Our last clown had forgotten to close it.

"Hey," I yelled. "That baboon has our bag!" I pointed for all of us to look, and then I started walking toward the baboon to get the bag back. The baboon turned around and looked at me. I could see then that it was a large male baboon. He dropped the bag and charged. He sprinted toward me, his mouth open wide and his large, pointy teeth bared. He screeched loud, angry baboon noises.

I turned and ran. I didn't know where I was going, but I knew that the baboon wanted me and I wanted to be as far away from that baboon as I could get. Despite the recent reminder to stop and stand still, not once did it occur to me. Adrenaline tore through my body. Panic spread to every nerve. I turned my head and saw the baboon coming closer. I tried to run faster. I turned again and saw he was right behind me. He raised his clawed hand and took a swipe at the back of my leg. I screamed.

I was aware of a movement off to my right side, and, as if on command, the baboon stopped. With a quick glance I saw my father. Crouched down in a football tackle, arms outstretched, Dad was rushing the baboon. In an instant the baboon understood. He knew this man was the father. He knew this woman was his daughter. Quickly retreating, the baboon loped, hands over feet, back up the hill, abandoning the bag where he dropped it.

Relief flooded my body. Tears wet my cheeks as the released adrenaline slowed. Dad gave me a long hug while the rest of my stunned family tried to digest what they had seen. One by one we looked back up the hill at the baboon whose attention had quickly been diverted.

In the days following, we shared many laughs thumping our chests and imitating the baboon's behavior. No one bothered to imitate Dad's behavior, but I know that if he hadn't done what he had done, we would all remember that day a little differently.

~Jennifer Quasha

A Shorts Story

He is a wise man who does not grieve for the things which he has not,
but rejoices for those which he has.
~Epictetus

Like many elementary school students, I didn't have much of a work ethic. I never studied anything, and I don't recall ever using a textbook. I coasted through Odem Elementary School on the "Gifted and Talented" track through sheer osmosis and a healthy dose of *Full House* reruns.

In third grade, Mrs. Stovall assigned our class a big project — we had to make a sock puppet of our favorite author. I remember choosing between Beverly Cleary and Judy Blume and blithely tucking the assignment instructions into the front of my folder and the back of my mind.

Days passed until Mrs. Stovall mentioned that our sock puppets were due the next day. Where did the time go? I knew my puppet could never be as beautiful as that of my classmate, Betsy. At eight, the girl was more together than I probably am now. Also, her mom stayed at home and had a hot glue gun and fuzzy pompoms.

Though my sock puppet couldn't compete with Betsy's, I didn't think it could be that hard to make. We had yarn and permanent markers at home. I'd be fine.

My mom worked, so my stay-at-home dad always oversaw homework completion. Sock puppetry turned out to be harder than I'd anticipated. I don't remember if I had a tantrum or asked my dad for help, but he started wracking his brain to come up with some way to make a more presentable puppet. At the very least, we needed to find some red fabric to make the inside of a mouth for Beverly or Judy.

No such luck. My mom never sewed; she only mended on occasion. My dad was better at repairing the innards of a car than sewing on a button.

Things were getting desperate. My dad scolded me for using one of my dress socks and gave me a large, white one of his own. He rummaged through his dresser drawers and found a source of red material—his favorite pair of shorts.

They were Ocean Pacific board shorts that he wore around the house. Very retro cool, I guess. If you knew my dad, you'd know how little time or energy he puts into his clothing, and how rare it is when he does get attached to an item. One time he thought he'd lost a beloved, tattered gray jacket in a movie theater and looked for the same design on eBay. It had long gone out of style.

The red shorts were like that, too. But somehow, my dad didn't wince when he cut into them to make a mouth, or when he sewed the red scrap onto the sock and saw how bad it looked. He eventually called my step-grandmother, Betty, as a last resort. She agreed to help, so we went to Walmart for a new sock and then to her house. Betty made eyes and a perfect red mouth for Beverly or Judy. She even added eyelashes.

I thought Betty was the hero when I went home with a puppet that didn't look anything like my favorite author, but would easily earn an A. When my mom got home from work, she shook her head at my dad's favorite shorts lying in the trash in pieces. She asked why he'd sacrificed the only piece of clothing he cared about.

"Because that puppet needed a mouth," my dad answered.

Surely, Betsy's mom didn't do that.

~Amanda Green

The Hero
Who Broke the Rules

You are remembered for the rules you break.
~Douglas MacArthur

Drip. Drip. Drip. I sat in my classroom chair watching raindrops fall onto the windowpane. Tiny rivers of water trickled down the glass. Dark skies, thunder crashing, and moments of brilliance from lightning made it hard for me to focus on my second-grade teacher.

"Turn around, Brenda," Mrs. Garrison said.

"How are we going to get home?"

"Don't worry about that now. Face the front, please."

I turned around to face the front of the class where Mrs. Garrison was teaching a history lesson. She was my favorite teacher, although some of my friends feared her rotund, intimidating body and her stern look. I wanted to please Mrs. Garrison by appearing to pay attention, but thoughts swirled in my head: "I don't have an umbrella. How will I get home in this downpour? Will Mom be mad if my papers get wet?"

The bell rang and we jumped up from our chairs like popcorn. Scooting sounds from chair legs against the tiled floor signaled the end of school. We grabbed backpacks, books and papers that Mrs. Garrison tried frantically to distribute as we scrambled toward the door. I hustled into the crowded, noisy hallway toward the building's exit door.

Classmates pushed and shoved as they swung open the door leading to the school's enormous, pillar-lined front porch. The massive porch was met by three steps leading down to ground level where a flagpole stood. From the flagpole, a long concrete path led toward the street curb and crosswalk.

We huddled together watching the storm dump rain on buses that were waiting by the curb. Each bus had its doors open to welcome students. I didn't have a dry bus waiting for me. Instead, I could look across the street to my house. Dad told us he wanted a home close to his kids' school so they wouldn't have to be bussed.

This day, it would've been nice to board a bus. I didn't know what to do. "Do I wait it out?" I fretted. "Maybe the rain will stop and then I can walk home."

Although I could see the safe haven of my house, I knew it was too far away to not get soaked. I could never run fast enough with my books and important homework. Lightning flashed again, revealing heavy, dark clouds. Rolling thunder echoed overhead. Some of my friends screamed and others dashed for their buses.

I turned again to look at my house where Mom was waiting for me. Safe. Dry. I wanted the comfort of home. Then I saw a familiar figure tromping through the school's flooded lawn. It was my dad. "What's he doing?" I wondered. "We're not allowed to cut across the grass." He didn't wait at the crosswalk either. I fixed my eyes on him as he plowed ahead, unaffected by the rain, thunder, or lightning.

He came up to me, stretched out his husky arms, and scooped me off that school's crowded porch. Right in front of my friends, he grabbed me, held me tight against his chest and retraced his steps. I looked back at my friends still standing on the porch. They became smaller as my dad and I neared my house. I don't remember anything more—not our dog wagging her tail to see me, Mom waiting, how wet we were, or the familiar smell of our house. What impressed me and remains in my mind's eye was Dad… my hero who broke the rules to rescue me.

~Brenda Nixon

Saying No to No

Success seems to be largely a matter of hanging on after others have let go.
~William Feather

For as long as I live, I will never forget that phone call. I was twelve years old and it was the day after Christmas. Early that morning, my grandmother found my grandfather unconscious in the bathroom. He had been there since the previous night and she didn't realize it until she awoke. My father went to follow the ambulance and my mother and I were left waiting for news.

The phone rang, and my mother got to it first. I picked up in another room, though, and I don't think anyone knew I was on the line.

"They said he's going to die," my dad said. "But he's not!" I had never heard my father fall apart before. He went on like a crazy man, tripping over half-coherent, tear-laden thoughts about how the doctors were wrong, and my grandfather couldn't die. He was too stubborn to die. Too capable. Too alive.

He'd had a seizure and lapsed into a coma. Since he had been comatose for so many hours before anyone found him, the odds were against him ever waking up.

The hospital emergency room was short-staffed because of the holiday, and there was only one doctor available. He noticed that my grandfather's blood pressure had spiked so he gave him medicine and waited. There was no response. The doctor advised my father to call the rabbi. It was time to accept that my grandfather wasn't going to wake up.

But there was one small problem: my father flat-out refused to accept anything of the sort. "You're not going to stand here and watch him die," he yelled. "I want him transferred to another hospital immediately!"

Unwavering in his determination, my father then called his childhood family doctor for help. The doctor recommended a hospital in New York City a full hour away.

Faith is usually expressed in beliefs. My father's faith was expressed in his total disbelief. He refused to listen to the doctor who told him hope was gone, and he took action with the single-minded drive that only comes from within. This was his father, and he was going to be fine. Period. Anything else was unthinkable.

Taking a comatose, dying man out of the hospital and putting him into an ambulance for an hour-long ride was just short of plain ridiculous, but my father insisted. He called a private ambulance, and the hospital told him they would make sure a doctor was waiting for my grandfather when he arrived. The doctor flew his own plane to the hospital to meet that commitment.

During the ambulance ride, the miracle began. My grandfather was regaining consciousness, but he was very delusional. The moment they arrived at the hospital, the doctor looked into my grandfather's eyes and declared, "I know what's wrong and I can operate."

What was wrong, he explained, was a meningioma tumor lodged between my grandfather's brain and his skull. As he finished the examination and took the history, the doctor said my grandfather must have been exposed to mustard gas in World War II in England—he had seen many of these slow-growing tumors in war veterans before. They were going to stabilize my grandfather, then operate immediately.

Unfortunately, there was another surprise in store.

When my grandfather regained his faculties, he began hallucinating. No one is sure what he thought he saw, but whatever it was, he stood at the edge of his hospital bed and dove off. He now had a gash under his eye that meant a postponement of the surgery. He was going to have to make it through one more day before they could risk anesthetizing him.

He didn't recognize my father, and he had no idea of the date or year, but he knew when D-Day had occurred, and he remembered who was President during the war. The son he didn't recognize was going to keep this man grounded—literally.

Since he didn't have any string handy, my father tore up a sheet and wound it into a rope. He tied my grandfather's arm to his own to be sure that he couldn't take another dive.

My grandfather made it to the operating table, and he survived. But it was anyone's guess whether he'd regain his mental capacity after such an ordeal. My father stayed with him in the hospital, keeping that sheet tied to his arm for two weeks. The outlook was grim, and relatives came to relieve my father from time to time. The doctor had drilled three holes into my grandfather's skull to remove the tumor, which had been larger than a lemon.

He was seventy-eight years old, and had lived a full life. He had married the girl of his dreams, even though their relationship had been forbidden. She was Catholic, he was Jewish, and in those times, that was that. Still, he didn't give up and her parents' blessing was granted on her father's deathbed. My grandfather was a hard-working man who had only recently retired. He loved to swim and go to the beach, and he kept up with the news and followed politics. And all this time he had been living with a deadly tumor that had gone undetected for several decades.

Five years after the surgery, my grandfather held up a champagne glass.

"This is to my wife, my bride of fifty years," he said, toasting his wife at a restaurant in Florida where we'd all gathered to celebrate. "I was supposed to be dead five years ago. But here I am."

Five years. Five years, and no one had ever suggested that my father call in the rabbi ever again. The tumor was gone, and he had slowly and completely recovered from the stroke.

That was nine years ago. He's ninety-one now, and still going strong, thanks to a devoted son who wouldn't take "no" for an answer.

~Jenna Glatzer

Mooning Misfortune

Every survival kit should include a sense of humor.
~Author Unknown

1:12 AM November 28th, 1988.

My mother burst into my bedroom.

"Get up!" she shrieked.

Before I had time to respond, she grabbed my arm, dragging me down the hall. It was pitch black and so loud I could hardly hear her screaming. "What's going on Mom?" I yelled, scared. Her answer was inaudible.

We passed my sister's room. I saw the night sky where her ceiling was, and her bed… now gone. I looked above us in the hall only to see the night sky. I was pushed down the stairs and shoved under them, where my sister and father were waiting. I will never forget the horrified look on my sister's face.

We huddled together for what seemed like an eternity, glass breaking, doors flying off their hinges. Our family's china had turned into high-speed shrapnel; the entire house was shaking as it moved off its foundation. I felt rain on my face. My father sat stoically, physically holding the staircase up above our heads.

"What's happening? What's going on?" I asked, wind whipping through my hair. I had never been this scared in my life.

"It's a tornado," my mother answered. Another French door flew in our direction but we were shielded by the staircase my father held to protect us.

"It's going to be okay," my dad said.

Then we prayed.

The funnel cloud, an F4, took only about five minutes to pass. It touched down twice to destroy our home and two others, leaving the rest of the neighborhood homes unscathed. The tornado took four lives in its course of devastation and destruction. Our entire roof and second floor walls were ripped off, except for a small portion over my room, which had been shielded by a huge oak tree that had fallen upon it. That tree saved me from being sucked out by the storm when it hit the first time as my mother was still running down the hall to get me.

We lost almost everything. The house was totaled. The attic and all of its contents were gone. Our house, our new house, was only a shell. All of our possessions were broken or damaged by the 210+ mph winds and rain. It was three and a half weeks before Christmas. I was seven, my sister eleven.

We stayed with neighbors for a few nights, but our house couldn't be locked. We needed to secure the few possessions we had left, so my father bundled up the best he could to fight the cold North Carolina winter and slept alone on the frigid floor of our garage with only a shotgun and our Siberian Husky.

There he slept for four nights, in a lonely skeleton of a house, to protect us. To protect what was left of our home, to protect our family. He had no heat, no electricity and no running water. He had a little cooler with water and food that we filled up every day before dark. One night, he heard scratching at the garage door. When my dad went outside he found our neighbor's cat that had been missing since the storm and hadn't eaten in a few days. After my father shared his dinner of chicken nuggets with our dog and the hungry cat, he got out his milk ration for his morning cereal and fed it to the cat.

My father doesn't really like cats because he is very allergic, but he still put that cat before himself. And when he realized the kitty was freezing in the forty-degree garage, he put the cat in the sleeping bag with him, even though he knew he would break out in hives and itch all night.

My parents were both so strong. They did everything to make Christmas special for us. I remember my sister cried because the Christmas present she bought me had been blown out of her room. I was just glad that she too had not been sucked away by the tornado.

One cold day my parents were standing in the kitchen of our destroyed home, which had now been looted (robbers took all the kitchen appliances). Snow had fallen on everything that was left. My mother starting sobbing, completely overcome with the loss of our home, of our memories that had been made there.

"I'm so sorry," my father said. "I always promised I would give you everything. I would give the sun to make you happy, the stars for you to dream and THE MOON for you to gaze upon."

At this my mother, who thought it was the most romantic thing my father had ever said, looked up to see my dad's pants around his knees and his bare white butt glistening against the snow!

It was at that moment my mother said she knew everything was going to be okay and that we were going to get through it as a family.

So thanks, Dad. Thanks for always showing me the light in the darkness. Your humor has gotten me through many things in life. Thank you for teaching me to laugh even when things get rough. And for being the protector through every storm.

~Ashlan Gorse

35

Watching Over Me

We can only be said to be alive in those moments
when our hearts are conscious of our treasures.
~Thornton Wilder

There is nothing more wonderful than the smell of the Adirondack air! It fills your lungs with a purity and freshness that invigorates and motivates a love for living. Every weekend in the summer, my father would plan a trip from our home in upstate New York to one of the magnificent lakes nestled among the tall pines and thick forests of the Adirondack Mountains. There were no favorites; instead, each lake was an adventure to explore and enjoy.

One trip that I will never forget was a visit to Oneida Lake at the foothills of the mountains. After arriving at the lake beach area, we emptied the car of our picnic supplies, towels, blankets and beach chairs, carrying them through a wooded path that seemed like a forever distance. Once we located the perfect picnic spot, my dad, sister and I ran into the splashing waves with our beach ball, leaving my mother behind to "set up." In the lake, we immediately played "monkey in the middle" for at least an hour, and then after retiring the ball, my father let us dive from his knee, throwing us up in the air and flipping us like flapjacks on a grill. This timeless game went on and on as our begging for "more, more" never ceased.

When we finally tired of our games, my dad stopped to watch my older sister. She loved synchronized swimming and started practicing skills that her team used in competition. My father, being an athlete himself, became engrossed in her demonstration. I was sad that no one was playing with me; no one was watching me. I became bored and jealous watching her show off. Sulking, I decided to swim by myself and try some of my sister's stunts on my own in deeper water, far from both of them. The waves were getting stronger, but I didn't care. I just wanted to do what my sister could do so that I could capture my father's attention.

As I tried a jackknife dive from my tiptoes, a huge wave engulfed me just as I took a breath to submerge. I unexpectedly swallowed water, and a huge undercurrent swept me deeper beneath the waves. I panicked under the water, lost buoyancy and any hope for a breath. I remember trying to stand up, but the sandy bottom had disappeared. As I came up searching for the surface, struggling for oxygen, sputtering to clear my lungs, I felt a firm grasp on my arm and a pull to safety. It was my dad! He hugged me tightly and carried me back to a place where I could stand. There was no scolding, no interrogation, just a big hug and smile because he knew I was all right.

What a great feeling I had at that time; I will never forget it. He had been watching me all along! He had never taken his eye off me, even as he had the other eye on my sister. He had protected me. Being told by someone that you are loved is great, but experiencing that love is awesome. So thank you, Dad, not only for the love of the outdoors that you instilled in me from those summer adventures, but also for the sense of security and well-being. Your unrelenting love has helped me through life's challenges. Without your caring, without your watching over me, without your loving me, I would not be the strong woman I am today.

~Terrilynne Walker

36

Daddy to the Rescue

To bring up a child in the way he should go,
travel that way yourself once in a while.
~Josh Billings

I was usually the first one to greet my father every afternoon when he came home from work. I would throw myself into his arms and revel in the best bear hug in the world.

But not today. Today I was hiding, buried under the covers on my twin bed in the room I shared with my sister, Kelly.

I heard Daddy come into my room and I felt him sit down on the bed next to me. "Hey, no hug for me today? What's going on?"

I started to cry before he even finished the question. I sat upright in bed and threw off my covers. "I can't skip!" I wailed. "Everybody in the whole first grade can skip except me!"

Daddy understood the gravity of the situation immediately, as he always did. "Oh, that's not good. What are we going to do?"

"I'm never going back!" I cried. "Everyone made fun of me!" And they had. Even my gym teacher had said, flustered, "Who doesn't know how to skip?"

"I'm the only one in the whole school who can't skip," I said. "I'm never going back!"

"I'm so sorry," Daddy murmured, drawing me into his arms. I started crying in earnest and Daddy held me close. He talked to me softly as I cried. "It'll be okay," he said. "We'll figure something out."

When my crying subsided, Daddy and I talked. I loved first grade. I loved my teacher, Mrs. Howell. I loved my principal, Sister

Mary Margaret. I loved reading and spelling and recess, and I even loved Chris Miller, the blond boy who sat next to me in the reading circle and who held my hand at recess.

I did not love gym. Gym was loud and messy and intimidating and I hated it. I much preferred to be in the classroom. Now gym class on Tuesdays had become a nightmare because I didn't know how to skip.

Daddy came up with a solution, though: "I guess I'll have to teach you."

I did not notice the hesitation in Daddy's voice as he made this decision. I didn't even notice that he put off my lessons every day until the following Monday, the day before my next gym class. By then, I was a wreck, worrying about what I would do when my gym teacher and classmates made fun of me the next day because I still didn't know how to skip.

After supper that Monday evening, Daddy took me out into the front yard for my first lesson in skipping. "Okay," he said. "I guess the first thing I need to do is to watch you skip."

"But I don't know how!"

"Just show me what you do in gym class."

And so I did.

After a minute of watching me struggle, Daddy said, "I guess I should show you how I do it now." He began tentatively and finally just gave in to it. He skipped and skipped, all over our front yard and even out into the street a little, trying to show me how it was done. He yelled things as he skipped. "See how I sort of hesitate right there?"

I did not see at all.

Neighbors rode by on bicycles and waved at us. The three boys from down the street were walking past on their way to the ball field and sat down on our porch to watch Daddy and me instead. Before long, we had an audience of twelve or thirteen people.

Daddy's form was flawless. The neighborhood boys and their dads made frequent comments about that, so I knew it was so.

Everybody laughed, too, when they said these things, but Daddy was serious.

It didn't seem to matter just how good Daddy was or how much the neighbors enjoyed his performance, I still couldn't figure out how to skip.

"It isn't the same as running," Daddy said. My gym teacher had said the same thing. But Daddy added, "There's a little hiccup in there."

"A hiccup?"

"Yeah," Daddy said, realizing he was on to something. Now he started skipping around the yard again, this time yelling out at odd moments, "Hiccup!" At first everyone watching just laughed harder, but soon they were all yelling "Hiccup!" with Daddy as he skipped around the yard.

I watched Daddy carefully. I started to notice the hiccup ever so slightly. I tried with all my might to see the hiccup everyone else could see.

The sun was starting to go down when Daddy said, "I have an idea." He was sweating profusely and panting hard. "I can carry you."

After he rested just a minute and had a nice glass of water, Daddy picked me up and put me on his back. "Ready?" he called.

"Ready!" shouted the huge audience.

"Ready!" I shouted back. I held on tightly. Daddy started skipping around the yard for maybe the hundredth time that day. Everyone standing or sitting around watching yelled "Hiccup!" in unison as Daddy's body made a jerky hesitation.

"I feel it!" I screamed.

After just a few minutes I said, "I think I know how to do that!"

Daddy stopped dead. He looked back over his shoulder at me. "Really?"

"Really!" I said. "Can I try?"

"Of course you can." Daddy set me down on the ground gently and I didn't even care that half the neighborhood was in our front yard. I immediately started to move. At first, it was just an awkward sort of run. After a few seconds, though, I remembered the feel of the hiccup and I tried it. I closed my eyes a little and kept moving. Hiccup. Hiccup.

"You're doing it!" Daddy yelled loudly. "You're skipping!"

And I was. "I'm skipping, Daddy!" I screamed back. "Look at me!"

Everyone laughed and applauded. I was, indeed, skipping. I skipped until it was too dark to see anymore and everyone had gone home. I skipped until I was exhausted, while my dad sat on the front porch and drank sweet tea.

"You see," Daddy said, as we walked inside hand in hand. "I told you we would figure something out."

He had said that very thing.

What Daddy hadn't said, and what I never knew until years later, was that he was going out of his way, risking humiliation in front of all his neighbors and friends, to teach me how to skip. He loved me that much. He would risk a lot of things for me all the rest of my life.

The next day in gym class my teacher applauded me heartily. "You learned how to skip!" she sang.

"Yes," I said proudly. "My daddy taught me."

~Marla H. Thurman

Thanks Dad

Making Gray Hairs—
Fathering Teenagers

37

Wrong Way Reuscher

Son, you outgrew my lap, but never my heart.
~Author Unknown

One of my earliest recollections of how proud I was to be Conrad Reuscher's son was when I realized that he was responsible for creating the Cavalier basketball program in St. Mary's, Pennsylvania. I was born in 1965 and a year later he formed a basketball program for sixth-, seventh- and eighth-grade boys from all three local Catholic grade schools. It served as a feeder program for the Catholic high school. He created a very successful program. Thinking back on what he accomplished with a shoestring budget and limited talent was incredible.

Dad made his teams successful through hard work and discipline. I can remember when he would take his teams to play in Erie, Pittsburgh, Philadelphia, and against a bunch of other teams he had no right challenging and yet they won or came close trying. The highlight of the season was the Thanksgiving Tournament held at the high school, Elk County Christian. Crowds packed the place to watch an eighth-grade basketball tournament, heady stuff for a little boy. I always remember saying to myself, "That's my dad."

One of the happiest and saddest periods of my childhood occurred in a span of two years. The happiest was when my father took over as head coach of the Elk County Christian Crusaders, the Catholic high school team. I remember sitting on the floor of the living room, with Dad lying on the couch, on a Saturday afternoon with the announcers describing the action from the night before. I thought it was so cool to sit and listen to the game and ask Dad questions on strategy and why he subbed this guy and why he did that or why he didn't take a timeout. To his credit, he would answer my questions patiently and honestly.

The saddest time was when he got fired. I'll never forget when he came home and told me he wasn't going to coach the Crusaders anymore. I was sitting at a card table working on a puzzle and Mom had already informed me of what had happened. Dad came in behind me and told me the news and I broke down, sobbing uncontrollably. To his credit, he placed his hand on my shoulder and gently started squeezing and said, "It'll be alright Eric. This won't be the worst thing that happens to me in my life."

But a dream of mine died that day. It's a dream that every little boy has, playing for his Dad. I joined the Cavaliers in third grade and didn't want or expect to receive special treatment because of who my father was. I tried hard, but I wasn't very tall or talented enough to crack the starting line-up or second string. I was a pine rider. As I progressed to eighth grade, I had formed a tight bond with my two teammates, Dino and Rodney, because we were the last three players to be put in the game. We called ourselves the Bomb Squad. People knew the game was well in hand when the three of us took off our warm-ups and walked to the scorers table.

Three years after my dad was fired as the head coach at ECCHS, when I was in eighth grade, he came to see me play. Although he taught history at the high school, to my knowledge this was the first time he had been back in the gym. It was the final game of the Thanksgiving Tournament. Our toughest game had come the night before when we had won by two points. Our opponent in the championship game wasn't going to give us much of a challenge. Dad was a good friend of the head coach, Pete, and Pete had mentioned that we had a very good chance to win and that Dad might like to be there to see the first team in Cavalier history win the prestigious Thanksgiving Tournament.

We fired on all pistons and by halftime we were comfortably ahead. I remember seeing Dad come into the gym right before the half and I watched him as he took his seat at the top of the bleachers. The place was packed and people seemed to move so Dad could walk, reminding me of Moses parting the Red Sea. With four minutes remaining in the fourth quarter, we were well ahead. Coach Winklebauer barked, "Bomb Squad, get ready." I remember sitting at the scorers table getting ready to check in and how excited I was that my father was there.

There was a timeout and I don't remember a thing that Pete said. We ran an in-bounds play right at center court. I faked left and broke right. The ball was thrown to me and I remember being all alone. I drove hard to the hoop on cloud nine and I remember thinking, "It can't be this easy. I am all by myself." I was pumped and thought for a split second I could dunk, but I decided not to risk it and laid in a beautiful left-handed layup. "Dad's going to be so proud. I can't believe I broke free so easily."

As I turned to head up court the whole gym was laughing. Pete had his hand over his eyes and when I got to half-court it dawned on me — I scored at the wrong basket! I immediately looked at my dad and he was smiling. I pleaded with my eyes for Coach Winklebauer to pull me out of the game, but he didn't. The last three minutes lasted an eternity.

After the game, my teammates were very understanding, as eighth grade boys can be.

"Hey wrong-way Reuscher, I bet your old man is proud of you tonight!" All I could do was sit in my locker and take the ribbing, but I was on the verge of either fighting or crying. I waited until everyone had left and then I stood in the shower all alone thinking, "How could I have embarrassed my dad like this? We are the first Cavalier team to win this tournament, and his son scores at the wrong basket." I was devastated.

I finally dressed and slowly descended the stairs that led to the gym. When I opened the doors the only light was from the red and white exit signs at the far end of the court. Dad sat on the bleachers at center court. I walked up to him with tears in my eyes and as I was about to speak, he said, "That was the finest left-handed layup I've ever seen."

In a moment he wiped away all the shame I was feeling. He put his arm around my shoulders and we walked out of the gym with my head held high.

~Eric T. Reuscher

38

Johnny

A young lady is a female child who has just done something dreadful.
~Judith Martin

My parents were not cool. They did not try to be my friends. They did not keep up with the latest trends or host teen drinking parties. They were very well practiced in the art of saying "no." Most of the rules and the "no's" were issued by my mother. My father was the more easy-going parent—the parent from whom I asked permission first and who would invariably respond: "Go ask your mother."

However, there was one area of parenting where he took charge: dating. His only stated rule was that my date must always come to the door when picking me up. The rule seemed harmless enough—an opportunity for a father to make sure the young man escorting his daughter for the evening was enough of a gentleman to make the twenty-yard trek from the driveway to the front door, shake my father's hand, look him in the eye and compliment my mother. However, my father was never just evaluating handshakes and date night plans. And I knew it.

The summer before my senior year of high school, I had just turned seventeen, was working in a deli and had a huge crush on a coworker. The coworker, Johnny, was twenty-two and in college. Apparently, Johnny was not completely oblivious to my dopey giggles and smiles because toward the end of the summer, about a week before he had to return to school, he asked me out. I was thrilled, excited and I immediately concocted a way to avoid having Johnny come to the front door. My parents might recognize Johnny and I knew they would not approve of me going on a date with a college guy five years my senior. Meeting him out was not an option; I wanted this to be a "real" date, meaning he would drive.

Luckily, Johnny chose an early movie for us and would have to pick me up well before the time my father returned home from work. I told my mom that I was going with some friends from school and one of them (I gave her my friend Marc's name) was giving me a ride so that when Johnny pulled up she would allow me to run out to the car. I phoned Marc and told him not to call my house the rest of the evening. Then, I waited by the front door ready to dash to Johnny's car before he could get out.

This was my plan until my father came home early from work. Johnny pulled up to the curb as my father was standing just inside the door going through the requisite "how was your day" interrogation. "My ride is here!" I interrupted him and ran out the door. My father managed to ask who was driving before I could get safely out of earshot and I yelled "Marc" without looking back. At this point I didn't think I had a chance, but I jumped in Johnny's car anyway. My father was already bounding down the front steps after me.

I'm from New Jersey, land of the dreaded U-turn. My parents' house happens to sit within a "U" so that the back of our house is facing the main road, a six-lane divided thoroughfare, and the front is facing a much quieter street used only by the neighborhood residents and the occasional lost and confused out-of-stater. There is only one obvious way to get from the house to the traffic light in order to make a left onto the thoroughfare that would put us in the direction of the movie theater. In order to evade my father, who clearly intended to follow us, I directed Johnny to make a right at the traffic light and then double back through the neighborhood once we were further down the main road. My father was not to be seen anywhere behind us and I began to relax as we drove back toward the light.

My ease quickly grew to anxiety when I saw my father approaching in his car, not from behind as I had anticipated, but from the one direction I wasn't looking for him: directly in front and head-on. My father stopped his car within a few yards of Johnny's and in such a manner that there was no getting around him — not that Johnny would have tried. Before I even saw him get out, my father was yanking open the passenger door. The look on his face was wild, yet he calmly told me to get out of the car. I tried to explain that it was just a friend, but now my father interrupted me, "That's Johnny from work. Get out of the car." Full of fear, I responded, "no." Then it was Johnny who spoke: "Robin, get out of the car." I suppose my father's red face, crazy eyes and eerily calm voice were not lost on him. I had no choice.

I got out of the car and drove the hundred yards or so back to the house with my father. I truly believed that nothing could be more humiliating. How wrong I was. When we got home, my father immediately called my boss to explain that I would not be returning to work until Johnny was safely back at college.

To this day, I am still mortified by the scene my father caused. However, I am also profoundly grateful. Although nobody but Johnny will ever know his true intentions in asking me on a date during the last week he had home before returning to college, I think it's safe to assume they were probably no more (or less) virtuous than most young men closer to my age. Despite this likelihood, my father was absolutely right to intervene in the date. My crush, as most crushes are, was intense, and Johnny's experience in dating and social life in general far surpassed mine. The possible outcomes for that night, had I been allowed to go on the date, are endless. But there was only one outcome once my father interceded: I would not be taken advantage of by an older guy with vastly greater life experience.

Despite whatever I may have said to him that night, I will forever be grateful my father was willing to risk a little humiliation — mine in front of Johnny and his in front of the entire neighborhood — all to ensure my safety and emotional well-being.

~Robin Pepper Biasotti

39

Dud and the Catcher's Mitt

Baseball is the only place in life where a sacrifice is really appreciated.
~Author Unknown

I should have been a boy. Boys climb trees and fall out. They play sports and get black eyes. Boys break bones. I did all of those things, and more. It was hard on my mom, but my dad had the best of both worlds. All wrapped up in the same package, he had a little tomboy to romp with and a little girl to sit on his lap.

Somewhere along the line, I started calling him "Dud." It wasn't a reflection on his abilities, just a pet name that happened over time.

One day, when I was about thirteen, an unexpected package arrived for me from my Uncle Mike. "Wow! A package for me? Mom! Dud! Come look!" As my folks came in to watch, I grabbed a pair of scissors, cut the twine and ripped open the box. Nestled inside was a brand-new, top-of-the-line catcher's mitt.

Dud looked at the gift. "That's an expensive glove. Uncle Mike must have noticed you needed a new mitt when he played catch with you."

I took it out of the box and tried it on. "Perfect fit!" I declared, even though my fingers didn't reach very far inside and the glove could have fit Dud better than me. I handed the glove to Dud, anxious to share the joy. "Try it."

He slipped it on and pounded his fist into it several times. "Now, the first thing you need to do is break it in." Dud handed it back to me and I looked at him, wondering what that meant.

"You break it? Won't that ruin it?" I asked.

Dud smiled, his eyes crinkling at the corners. "Breaking it in means you soften the leather and give it a pocket."

I frowned slightly. How would you go about making leather soft? Put hand cream on it?

Dud looked pensive for a second, as if making sure he had his facts correct. "You spread special oil on it, which makes the leather supple. I'll pick some up on my way home from work."

Dud brought home a can the next day. We lovingly rubbed the oil into the glove with an old rag and put a softball into the pocket. We wrapped the mitt closed with twine and placed it in a warm oven to cure.

I waited, conjuring visions of me tagging a runner out at home plate using the best glove on the team. I could almost hear the thwack of the tag, and smell the dust in the air from the runner's slide at the plate. My mind cheered as I pictured myself making the out and saving the most important game of the season.

Then, a little devil sat on my shoulder and brought me back to reality by whispering thoughts in my ear. "What if your glove catches fire in the oven? You'll open that oven door and a black cloud of smoke will belch out. All that will be left is a charred lump of something that used to be a catcher's mitt!"

I looked at Dud and clasped my hands. "You're sure it won't get ruined in the oven?"

"It'll be okay."

The earthy smell of oil and leather drifted from the kitchen. The glove beckoned me, but still I waited. When I thought I couldn't stand it any longer, Dud finally said, "I think it should be ready."

I reached into the oven and pulled out the mitt. It wasn't burned, but my throat tightened as I realized something had gone wrong. Concrete reinforced with rebar would have been softer and suppler than that glove. The thing could've been used for a doorstop.

"What happened?" I cried in dismay. Even after untying the twine, the mitt stayed frozen in position, wrapped around a ball that we had to pry out of the pocket.

Dud picked up the can of oil and read the label. "I bought the wrong kind," he said with chagrin. "You're supposed to use Neatsfoot oil. This is linseed oil and it hardened the glove."

My heart sank as I blinked back the tears. We hardly had enough money for groceries. I knew we couldn't buy another mitt. It was back to using my four-fingered, hand-me-down glove. My adolescent mind was convinced that the old mitt had been around for centuries.

Dud set his square jaw, the jawbone working back and forth with determination, and said, "It was my fault. I'll buy you a new one."

I never knew where he got the money (I suspect he took on extra work to earn it), but he kept his word. When the season started, I played catcher with a new glove.

That day, Dud taught me a lot about honesty and taking responsibility. He showed me that when you do something wrong, you have to make it right. He taught me fairness and kindness to others, no matter what their age or position in life.

The principles that I learned from that experience have stayed with me long past my softball days. They've guided me when it would have been easier to let someone else take the blame, and given me the determination to make restitution, even when it was hard to do.

Dud is a great-grandpa now. I've never told him what I learned that day, but I plan to before it's too late. I'm going to thank him for being the kind of man that he is, and for the lessons he taught me with the wrong can of oil and a brand-new catcher's mitt.

~Cindy Beck

Showing Up

*Love is absolute loyalty... You can depend so much on certain people,
you can set your watch by them. And that's love.*

~Sylvester Stallone

As a stay-at-home dad, my father wasn't exactly a traditional father. He made us breakfast in the morning, packed our lunches, and had dinner on the table when Mom came home from work. He drove us to sports practices, chorus concerts, and dance recitals. He built us the tallest swing set we'd ever seen, taught us how to shoot a slingshot, and played video games with us on days we were sick and stayed home from school. At our Halloween parties, he dressed up as Igor and developed a limp and hunchback. Dad was always there for the fun stuff, and the tough stuff, too.

He was the one to break the news to me that I hadn't made the high school basketball team. As an avid fan of the WNBA and the Connecticut Huskies, I'd had my heart set on it. But at just over five feet tall, significantly lacking in coordination, and dedicated to my academic studies (I would go on to graduate salutatorian of my high school class), I should have realized that making the team wasn't exactly going to happen. My father broke the news to me in my bedroom on a Saturday morning with his hand on my back. But he had good news too. My father had asked the coach if I could still practice with the team. Although a part of me would always want to wear the uniform and be on the court when there were fans in the stands and the scoreboard was lit up, practice was a privilege I'd willingly take — and my father was the one who'd made it happen.

He drove me to every last practice, even those 6 AM ones that had us leaving the house long before the sun rose. While I wiped sleep from my eyes and packed my bag, he'd be scraping ice from the car and getting it warmed up so that by the time I slipped into it, it was warm enough for me to catch a few more minutes of sleep before we arrived at school. He could have said no to any of those practices, particularly the 6 AM ones. We both knew I'd never set foot on the court during a game. I'd never even suit up. But my father understood how much those practices meant to me, and that was enough for him. It didn't matter that my lay-ups all went hard off the glass or that I could never get any spin on the ball when I took a jump shot. It only mattered that I wanted to be there.

At the end of the season, I was granted the chance to warm up with the team and wear the black wind pants and the maroon shooting shirt. My father came and sat in the bleachers while I ran out of the locker room and onto the court. Music was pouring from the speakers and jolting adrenaline through my body. He didn't have to come. I wouldn't play in the game; I'd sit on the bench keeping stats. But he did come, cheering and clapping when I hit one of my warm-up shots. Though my dad rarely said too much at once, somewhere along the way he managed to teach me how important it was to show up. I always showed up for practice and he always showed up for me.

I'm in graduate school now and my father still shows up, still calls to ask about my intramural basketball games. When I tell him we've lost to a bigger and more athletic team of undergraduates, he says that's all right. He knows we showed up. He knows we played hard. And that's what matters the most. Dad taught me that.

~Rachel Furey

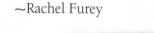

41

Cool Dad

*I would maintain that thanks are the highest form of thought;
and that gratitude is happiness doubled by wonder.*
~G.K. Chesterton

My stomach dropped. There was nothing I wanted to hear less than the words coming from Mrs. Nelson's lips.

"This is just a reminder that Shadow a Student Day is tomorrow!"

"Dear God, please, oh please, help Mom to be free tomorrow so Dad will not have to come!" I prayed. What would people think of him? I put all negative thoughts aside with the determination that Mom would be able to come, and that was the end of it!

The bell finally rang and relief swept over me. This was one of my favorite days, when soccer practice was cancelled and I could go home, having extra time just to relax.

I walked in the kitchen door and smelled fresh bread. It was one of Mom's baking days! She met me with her usual warm greeting.

"Well, hello there! How was your day?" That along with two hot slices of bread with butter hit the spot. Junior high was turning out to be a little worse than my expectations.

"Oh, it was all right," I mumbled.

"Anything exciting happen?"

"Not really. It was just another day...."

Her face showed her disappointment, but then at the same time her eyes kept probing mine trying to read if I was being truthful. It worked. She saw there was something on my mind.

"Heidi, are you sure you have no news for me?"

I explained that Shadow a Student Day was tomorrow. And go figure, Dad was walking in the back door just in time to hear the news. I quickly asked Mom, "You are free, aren't you?"

"Well Heidi, I have lots of errands to run and commitments I've already made for tomorrow. Maybe Dad will be willing to go."

"You better believe I'll go!" Dad grinned. I loved Dad's upbeat spirit and enthusiasm. He had made life so exciting and adventurous for the family and I adored him for it. But would people see him the way I saw him?

His thin body and practically bald head, with a weak attempt at a comb-over, was not exactly what my friends would consider a "cool dad."

Dad was also much older than most of my friends' dads, who were closer to the age of my older siblings.

Their dads would be professional businessmen, doctors, dentists, or engineers. Dad was a draftsman and he worked in an office at home.

His choice of clothing was not anything close to stylish. Faded jeans with an old T-shirt was his daily outfit, so he could juggle the farm and handyman jobs around the house as well as draw plans in the office without changing clothes. Dad was very efficient and would do the most practical thing that would save him even the slightest amount of time throughout the day.

"Do you want me to come with you Heidi? I would really love that!"

"Sure, Dad. That would be cool." He was either a really good faker or he really did not notice my lack of enthusiasm as his face brightened and he started talking about how much fun it was going to be. I did my best to make up for my rude reaction and smiled. Don't get me wrong, I really would have been stoked about the idea of spending a day with Dad, just as long as my friends and their dads didn't have to meet him and spend the day with us.

Well, whether I liked it or not, the next morning came. Dad was ready long before I was. He was sitting in his usual position in the kitchen, as he always did when anxiously waiting on someone in the family to go somewhere — usually Mom. He perked up as I came up the stairs from my bedroom.

"You all ready to go?" He was smiling from ear to ear by then. My half smile didn't quite compare. The car ride to school was practically an interrogation.

"Who are all your friends? What do you like to do at lunch? Do you like all your teachers?"

Dad was doing his best to get a sneak preview of the portion of his daughter's life he was about to see.

Walking onto campus, Dad led with his confident brisk walk. I realized now where I had learned to walk so fast, but today I lagged behind.

We walked into my first period science class with Ms. Hall. My predictions were not too far off, as Dad definitely stood out visually and vocally. As soon as he entered, he was making friends. The once awkwardly silent room soon began to buzz with conversation. Dad had some way of relating with each of the parents there. Whether he knew them, their cousin, or their brother's wife's dog, he made the connection.

I looked around the room, checking my friends' expressions and reactions. All of my classmates looked at Dad with such wonder. But it was not the confused, freaked-out wonder I had expected. They liked him!

"Your dad is so cool!"

"I love your dad!"

"Your dad is so awesome!"

My classmates actually liked him! I was in shock!

Dad and I walked in sync, side-by-side to my next class. Pride surged through me just to be walking beside him. My friends were actually interested in his crazy stories of catching the skunks that frequently stole eggs from our farm, and how he put an owl box up in the old cottonwood in our backyard! How had I been so oblivious?!

The things that I was most embarrassed for my friends to see in my dad were the same things that made me love him the most! I turned and looked up at him.

"I love you, Pops!"

~Heidi L.R. Zúñiga

42

Driven

Adolescence is a period of rapid changes.
Between the ages of 12 and 17, for example,
a parent ages as much as 20 years.
~Author Unknown

When I was a junior in high school I was convinced that I would be the last member of my generation to obtain my driver's license. Even though I turned sixteen the summer before my junior year, I was scheduled to take a driver's education course at my suburban Chicago high school during the fall semester, which meant that I would not be able to test for my license until a few months before my seventeenth birthday. While I dreamed about having private driving lessons and a car of my own like some of my classmates, my father had other plans in mind.

Dad was a guidance counselor/college consultant at another local high school, and he wasn't about to spend my future tuition money on private driving lessons, teen driver insurance rates or my own car. As far as he was concerned, he and my mom were working hard enough to save money for a college education for my younger sister and me.

The car I would be training on was the family vehicle—a 1978 white Oldsmobile Delta 88 Royale that was at least seven years old by the time I was old enough to drive it. When the Olds was brand new, it was a powerful, gleaming "King of the Road" with spoke hubcaps, a V8 engine, and a crushed red velvet interior. By the time I was driving it, the car was a rusting gas guzzler that maneuvered as easily as a cruise ship. The engine occasionally died at stoplights, or ran on for another fifteen seconds after I turned it off. My parents had the entire vehicle repainted twice, which kept the bottoms of the car doors from rotting off; and a thin layer of rust bonded by new paint would shudder every time I slammed a door shut.

There was no way on earth that I could look remotely cool in my father's Oldsmobile, not even when I cranked up my favorite Tears for Fears song on the car's AM radio.

Of course, my father was more than happy to supplement my driver's education classes with his own behind-the-wheel lessons. He was right next to me when I first started lurching about an empty parking lot in the oversized Oldsmobile that I lovingly nicknamed Coche, which is Spanish for "car." Since Coche had a bench seat in the front, Dad had to bend his six-foot-three-inch frame to accommodate me every time I adjusted the driver's seat all the way to the front so I could comfortably reach the gas and brake pedals. For hours at a time, he would calmly advise me on the finer points of left turns and lane changes while his knees were shoved up around his ears.

I can still recall the day I obtained my license—March 3, 1986—and I remember being grateful to Casimir Pulaski, the Polish-American Revolutionary War hero who was the reason why public schools throughout Illinois were closed, enabling Dad and I to spend an entire weekday morning at the Department of Motor Vehicles. I seemed to be the only person who was happy to be there, as I anxiously awaited my turn.

My study skills served me well on the written exam, and Dad's careful instruction paid off during my behind-the-wheel test. As the DMV instructor took notes, I carefully maneuvered Dad's enormous Oldsmobile through parallel parking, a three-point turn and a trip around the block.

By lunchtime I became the proud owner of my first driver's license. I grinned giddily as a dour DMV employee took my photograph in front of a bright red background. As I showed my father the license, clearly marked "Under 21" in several places, I could see the expression of pride on his face. He handed me the car keys, which dangled from a Bicentennial keychain that was even older than his car.

When I got behind the wheel of Coche I turned to look at Dad, who was already tensing up his leg muscles as I prepared to slide the front seat forward. For the first time in my life, I realized the patience that was required of my father as he waited for this day. I thought about all those hours that he sat with me without complaining, twisted up like a pretzel while I jerked the family car around empty parking lots and navigated busy suburban roadways in hazardous winter weather, striving to gain my own independence.

Suddenly it occurred to me that after all this patient waiting, I had a lifetime of opportunities to drive ahead of me—a lifetime of places to go, passengers to transport, and cars to drive (hopefully with power steering, bucket seats, and an FM stereo).

I lowered my hand from the ignition. "Dad, you've been cooped up enough these past few months," I said. "Why don't you drive us home?"

Dad was surprised but I could already see his muscles relax. "Are you sure?" he asked.

"I'm sure," I said, handing him the keys. "It's my treat."

~Robyn Kurth

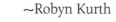

Melody of the Heart

Where words fail, music speaks.
~Hans Christian Andersen

A bit of home arrived in the small package I received around my twenty-second birthday. It was from Wyoming. I had moved away from the small town there in order to attend Arizona State University a few years before. The familiar sight felt like a cool breeze reaching its way across the mountains and into my little spot in the desert, giving me some relief from the stress and deadlines my life had become.

Full-time classes along with a full-time job at a hotel had left me little time to stay in contact with anyone from home. I smiled when I saw my name written in my dad's distinct handwriting on the package. Although my dad still lived in the same town after my parents' divorce when I was young, I didn't feel close to him for much of the time I was growing up. Opening the package and seeing a cassette tape reminded me of the journey we took to change that.

Both of my parents could see early on that I perceived myself as an independent spirit. They reluctantly allowed me to stay behind when my four siblings went to visit Dad. "I've been babysitting all the time," I would explain. "I need a break." Disappointed, Dad would ask me to reconsider. I would get even more stubborn and stand my ground.

These breaks chipped away at the bond with my dad. I talked my way out of fun camping trips. I lost the chance to take part in his family reunion in Michigan and learn about my own birthplace. I was old enough to remember enjoying listening to Dad playing guitar and singing while he still lived at home. By staying away, I missed out on the performances taking place in his new living room. By the time I was in my teens, I was performing a role of my own: Angry Teenager.

As a man who never seemed to want to rock the boat, it must have been difficult for Dad to cast his oars into these turbulent waters. But one day, he took the plunge. He was worried that we were not close. "I'm here for you, you know," he said. I rolled my eyes and inhaled deeply on the cigarette I had lit to show how grown-up I was. I performed the kind of screaming fit appropriate for the Angry Teenager role.

This fiery argument started to turn to ash as I realized that, at the very least, Dad had been an audience for my living room performance. He was right there, even as I was pushing him away. I smashed out the cigarette, not sure of my next line.

The next big performance didn't belong to me, or even to my musician father. Dad planned to take me to Salt Lake City for an eye appointment. I was excited; it was the Big City, after all. My four younger siblings stayed at home, so for now, it was just my dad and me.

During our road trip, Dad and I listened to music. He could respect a lot of what I was listening to. He may not have understood why all of the guys in bands I liked wore more make-up than I did, but he seemed to relate to my excitement about the songs that made up the soundtrack of my life. Dad would play music from his day. I realized bands like The Beatles or the Stones could be as good, or even better, than my music. I told him all about my sophomore research paper. It was about music censorship and the new parental advisory labels. I sensed Dad agreed with my tentative title, "Let Freedom Rock."

This shared appreciation of music let me see that I was more a reflection of him than I had given myself a chance to realize. Somehow, he had known this already. About halfway to Salt Lake, he told me to open the glove compartment. I reached in to find two tickets for a concert at the Salt Palace, for that night!

Hours later, I was racing up to the stage to get closer to the guys from Winger and Cinderella. I turned around to find my dad. There he was, tall enough to see above the teenage girls, enjoying the show. "Who are you here with?" a familiar voice yelled through the wailing guitars. A girl from my high school had made the trip.

"My dad surprised me. Isn't that cool?"

As I made my way through the next few years, I did see my dad more. Often, I watched him from the audience while he performed with one of his bands at local fairs or picnics. It was something he loved to do when he wasn't working down in the mine. But usually, I showed up when I needed something. I didn't yet have the emotional tools to show up "just because." He bought my prom dress. He test drove the white Mustang with T-tops that I saved up for and just had to have, even though I didn't know how to drive a stick shift. Later, that same Mustang and I became frequent visitors to Dad's Repair Shop—his garage. Maybe I was being needy, but I wasn't being turned away. We would still talk about music. But eventually I started to talk about the other important things: my plans for the future, school, boyfriends. I may have just been hovering backstage, but, somehow, I had started to find a place for me with my dad.

So there I was, at twenty-two, holding a representation of our still newfound connection: a music tape. I turned it over and read the title. The tape held just one song: "Tina Marie '73." Written and performed by my dad. When I listened to it the first time, I couldn't help but cry.

Rising through the melodic strumming of the guitar I heard my dad's voice wondering if "the bright wallpaper made her shine, the way she did"—singing about me, in that quiet time when I was a baby. Calling out to me with the magic that is music, he reminded me of more recent times when he "tried to look in, to see what was on my mind." My tears of sorrow for time lost turned to tears of hope when I heard Dad explain about how "much time was ahead" and now it was "time to dry all the tears we shed."

This song reminds me that the love my dad felt for me was essential to create the melody he had in his heart for all of his children. Even as I tried to separate myself, Dad had been willing to wait. Now, even though he is physically miles away, I can still listen to the song that bears my name and feel my dad's love surround me, causing me to shine, the way I did for him all along.

~Tina Haapala

Chicken Soup
for the Soul

My Unfair Father

Making the decision to have a child is momentous. It is to decide forever
to have your heart go walking around outside your body.
~Elizabeth Stone

"**I** don't care what time the dance ends," my dad said.
"You're leaving at 9:00." And that's how it was for every
dance I attended in middle and high school. The music
began to blare at 7:00 and I would dance to "Electric Slide" and other
hits of my era until the hour of doom chimed.

At one particular event, a St. Patrick's Day dance, I knew the
dreaded hour was approaching and I headed for cover. I walked to
the farthest, darkest corner of the room, behind the green and white
streamers, and hung out there until the very last moment. "Melissa, I
think your dad is here," my friend David chuckled.

"Really?" I asked. "I haven't seen him." Then I trotted to another
corner of the room and continued dancing to Debbie Gibson's "Out
of the Blue." In the middle of the song, I felt a tap on my shoulder. I
whirled around and there he was. "It's time to go," my dad said. And
that was it. No argument. No discussion. We left.

Those were really tough years for me. It's hard enough fitting
in with your friends when you are allowed to do what the crowd is
doing. But it's even more difficult when you are the girl who is always
the first one to leave a function. And sometimes, I was the one who
didn't get to go at all.

That was the case in seventh grade, when all of my friends would
walk around town in the afternoons. They would go to Pino's for

pizza or play pool and eat hot dogs at a local gas station. I asked my dad if I could go but I'm not sure why I bothered. It was always the same answer. "You are not crossing that busy highway in the middle of the afternoon," he would say. "It's just not safe."

So each afternoon, my friends waved to me as they ventured off to have some fun on the town. I waved back and climbed into the front seat of my parents' Chevrolet, and went home.

Most kids receive an increase in privileges as they become older. For me, it seemed like each year there was even less that I was allowed to do. This was especially true when it came to my physical appearance. All of the girls in my class were getting their ears pierced and I desperately wanted mine pierced as well.

"God didn't intend for us to put additional holes in our bodies," my dad rationalized. "Besides, why do you want metal in your ears anyway? Do you want to attract lightning?"

I don't know why I wanted pierced ears so badly. Maybe I never really wanted them. I just didn't want to be the only one without them. And I didn't want to be the last girl in my class to wear eye make-up either. But I was.

"If all of your friends were jumping off a bridge, would you want to do that too?" my dad echoed. I'm not sure exactly how many times I was asked that question. But if it were a song, it would have been the soundtrack of my teenage years.

Of course I wanted to do what the other kids were doing. I wanted to fit in. I wanted to know what they were laughing about during homeroom. I wanted to understand the one-liners that were tossed around the table at lunchtime. I wanted people to write funny "remember when" stories in my yearbook. I wanted to belong. But that was difficult when I wasn't allowed to do anything they were doing.

I also wasn't permitted to watch a lot of the TV shows that my friends watched. "Did you see *The Real World* last night?" Megan asked.

"I don't have MTV," I replied.

"What do you mean you don't have MTV? You have cable, don't you?"

I did have cable and I did have MTV. I just didn't realize it until several years later when my friend Kevin simply punched in the number nineteen on the remote control. My dad had only removed it from the main menu because he knew that I used the arrow keys. And when I did, the channels went from eighteen to twenty. No channel nineteen—no MTV.

Add to the list the fact that I couldn't watch PG-13 movies; my dad said the PG stood for "Public Garbage." And that I couldn't buy cassette tapes with "Explicit Language" warning labels. And add the fact that I wasn't allowed to have a phone or a television in my bedroom. What does that equal? A completely unfair existence.

When my friends were out walking along the railroad tracks, eating pizza on the other side of Highway 460, or watching *Beavis & Butt-head* on MTV, I was in my bedroom. I was busy writing poetry and essays about how mean my parents were (especially my dad), how unfair my life was, and how they couldn't possibly love me or they would let me do what I wanted to do.

A teenage girl is incapable of understanding that a father's chief desire is to keep his child safe and that he isn't just being "mean" and "unfair." I was not that insightful and I didn't know that my dad was only trying to keep me a little girl as long as he could. He didn't want me to grow up too fast. I thought he didn't want me to have any fun.

Some of the most important lessons that we learn in life don't occur in the classroom. Sometimes decades pass before our lives begin to make sense. And for me, it was a lot like piercing my ears and wearing make-up; I had to "wait until I was older" to understand how much my dad really loves me.

Today, it's easy to remember the things I wasn't allowed to do. I don't have trouble recalling the times when I was unhappy. They stand out in my mind because there weren't very many of them. There were quite a few times when my dad didn't give in to what I wanted. But he always gave me what I needed.

~Melissa Face

45

Valentine's Day Ambush

The beauty of fragrance is that it speaks to your heart...
and hopefully someone else's.
~Elizabeth Taylor

Valentine dinners with my parents became a thing of the past once I was old enough to date. Still, before heading out for the evening, I always received a sweet card and possibly a small gift. Upon returning home later, I indulged in my fair share of whatever homemade, mouth-watering dessert Mother had prepared for the occasion. Typically, it was a layered cake baked in heart-shaped pans, a scrumptious treat she served each year.

During my senior year of high school, Kansas was under siege on Valentine's Day with a winter storm blasting its way across the plains. School was dismissed early and "puppy love" dates were cancelled. For the first time in a few years, I'd be celebrating with my parents. Amazingly, it made a real impression on me.

Mother had prepared Dad's favorite meal for dinner, but as the storm intensified she began to watch the clock and pace the floor.

"I'm really getting worried. With this weather I knew your dad would be a little late getting home, but not this late!" She busied herself keeping dinner warm, determined not to burn anything, but continued her march to and fro, glancing out the windows for headlights.

As a self-absorbed teenager, I continued with my phone conversation until I heard the door open and Mother wailing, "Oh, where have you been? I've just been worried sick!"

I rounded the corner to see Dad with his arms full of flowers and a box of chocolates. He smiled, "Happy Valentine's Day, Honey!" Mom threw her arms around him causing him to juggled gifts while trying graciously to accept Mom's embrace.

The bouquet of flowers took center stage on the table as we seated ourselves for dinner.

I reached for my napkin and spied a small package by my plate that had seemingly appeared out of nowhere.

"What's this?" I asked, filled with excitement and surprise.

"Just open it!" Dad's brilliant blue eyes sparkled with mischief.

I ripped the package open and could barely speak; it was a new bottle of Ambush cologne, quite a popular and affordable scent for teenagers at that time.

"Dad! Did you buy this all by yourself?" I squealed.

"Well, just kind of. It took some help from the clerk—actually it took a lot of help!"

I was stunned beyond belief. A Valentine gift purchased by Dad. I gave him a bear hug and a big kiss!

"You know I've seen that perfume around here forever and figured I could remember the name if I thought about Western movies. You know how they're always ambushing one another. Well, everything was fine until the clerk asked me what brand… I told her Apache."

"Apache!" I giggled until I had tears rolling down my cheeks.

Dad informed me it really wasn't that funny at all. The clerk insisted there was no such cologne, while he swore there was. They went back and forth until he decided maybe he had forgotten the name—but made it clear he would recognize the smell his daughter obviously bathed in. That's when the "misting marathon" began.

"It wasn't long until I started to sneeze non-stop. My nose began to run, and I almost got sick from so many smells. Just when I thought I'd have to take a break outside in the fresh air before continuing, the clerk suddenly hit on it!"

Dad said he smiled at the clerk through the sneezing. "That's it, that's it! Thank you for your time ma'am." Then he charged out the door toward his car through an all-out blizzard.

Never once have I asked Dad what possessed him to buy me a gift that year. I suspect it had something to do with the realization that my days under his roof were quickly coming to an end.

Roses, teddy bears, and cupids abound each February, creating fond memories. As for me, I have comical but precious memories of my Valentine's Day Ambush! They reside in a special niche in my heart.

~Kathleene S. Baker

46

Runaway Letter

Mother Nature is providential.
She gives us twelve years to develop a love for our children
before turning them into teenagers.
~William Galvin

I was born on Father's Day, Sunday, June 18, 1950. Until I reached my terrible teens, I had always been "Daddy's Baby Girl." But then, everything changed. At 250 pounds, life was a struggle. I saw myself as the family outcast. My sister was valedictorian, head cheerleader, prom queen and a size eight. My brother was athletic, good-looking and the town sports star. I wish now that I could go back and relive those years, for I would never choose to be a high school dropout and runaway—especially back in the late 60s in the small town of Clarksville, Missouri where nobody did such things.

Now that I am a retired high school teacher having dealt with many students with similar problems, I realize there was not as much help available when I was a teen. Not only did I not have any coping skills back then, neither did my parents. They tried everything they knew to do, including taking me to counselors and child psychiatrists, but nothing seemed to help.

The following letter was written in 1968 by my precious, loving daddy when I was a senior in high school. I didn't get it until twenty years later when my mother told me she had been saving it for "just the right time."

January 1968

My Darling Baby Girl,

    I write this as you have threatened to run away again. I am leaving this on your pillow with the hope that you will get it before you leave. I know at seventeen you are a young woman now and we can't stop you from going. Your mom and I have asked ourselves a thousand times where we went wrong... where we failed you. I would give anything if we could go back to the days when you were Daddy's little girl and would snuggle up on my lap and bring all your hurts and wounds to me to "make better." I only blame myself for all that has gone wrong and would give my very life for another chance to make it right.

    I didn't see soon enough how much you were hurting. Mommy and I have prayed and cried for you more than you will ever know and have asked if we were too strict or too lenient, too giving or not giving enough. All we know is that we love you and want you to talk to us. Please reconsider before you leave again and let's see if we can't work it out one more time. Dearest Debbie Girl, we love you with no strings attached. God brought you to us and no matter what, you will always be my precious baby girl. When you read this, no matter how late, please come talk to me.

Always,
Your Loving Daddy

I never received the letter that night as I had already run away again and wouldn't return for six weeks. However, my parents saved the letter for more than twenty years, anticipating the "right time" to present it to me. It was the night of the 1990 Missouri State Teacher of the Year banquet at the state capitol. I had been designated as one of the top five teachers in the state who were being honored along with our families and school administrators. Having survived those terrible teen years by much prayer and faith, I did finally graduate from both high school and college, became a teacher, lost 100 pounds, got married, and had my own wonderful family. Unfortunately, I had also become filled with pride for all that I thought I had accomplished.

Before my big acceptance speech that night, my parents gave me a beautifully wrapped present to celebrate the occasion. Thinking I was opening a little gift box with perhaps a pendant or medal with the inscription "Teacher of the Year," or "Wonderful Daughter," I instead opened the box to find nothing but a yellowed, crinkled, tear-stained, faded twenty-year-old letter. As I read it, I was transported back to my teen years and wept uncontrollably. I not only realized for the first time all that my parents had gone through, but also how pride had kept me from sharing with others my troubled past, and the road that we all must travel to achieve success.

With mascara streaming down my face, I gave an entirely different speech from the one I had planned. I thanked God that my parents were finally able to see the fruits of their labor. All their past struggles, the sleepless nights, the times they insisted I stay in school and in church, had finally been worth it all. The real gift, which they had been giving all along (and still do), was the priceless gift of unconditional love! Those words written by my father so long ago will now remain with me forever. Thank you, Daddy, for showing me this unconditional love.

Now that I am a radio talk show host and speaker, I always share this letter with my audiences, as I did with my students and fellow teachers after that eventful night. Often my parents will accompany me, and my dad always has to blink away tears, as do I, when I read his letter.

We recently returned from taking my parents to Europe for their sixtieth wedding anniversary where we had a hard time keeping up with such active eighty-year-olds! When Dad was asked the secret of his youthfulness and vitality, he teasingly said, "If I could survive my daughter's teen years, I can do anything!" Daddy recently had a stroke and though he can't walk very well, he still shuffles over to hug me every time I enter the room. He says he always knew how special I would be when God gave him the best Father's Day gift he ever received nearly sixty years ago—his baby girl!

~Debra D. Peppers, Ph.D.

Thanks Dad

Through Thick and Thin

Crazy Curtains

A daughter is a gift of love.
~Author Unknown

It is a moment in time, engraved into my mind: The time my father ironed my crazy curtains.

My father and I are both only children, kind and tenderhearted with big, radiant smiles designed to put others at ease. Perfectionists with strong work ethics, we put our hearts and souls into each and every endeavor we undertake. And with our similar dispositions, we both have lifelong struggles with depression. Yes, I am my father's daughter, and I wouldn't have it any other way.

A year or so ago, life just felt crazy. I could feel those all-too-familiar clouds of depression rolling in. I needed a pick-me-up and decided that making new curtains would be just the thing to distract me and lift my spirits. Wanting to bring hope and happiness into my living room, I bought some crazy, quirky, bright-and-shiny fabric. During a weekend when my husband and children were out of town, my parents came over to help me make the curtains. When they arrived, my mother, optimism personified, entered the room as a woman on a mission. Sewing machine in hand, she was ready to tackle this project. Behind her stood my father. Now I will tell you, my father can relate to me unlike any other person on the planet. I looked into his eyes, and he knowingly nodded.

For hours, we worked on the curtains. Measuring and cutting. Sewing and hanging. And ironing. I recall the moment with clarity. Noticing that my father had not spoken in a while, I turned to find him ironing my curtains with painstaking precision. And I watched. This retired Special Agent, with his great tales of high-speed chases and espionage cases, of breaking organized crime rings and being on Secret Service detail to protect presidential candidates, ironed my crazy curtains.

As kindred spirits, prone to the same affliction, we've spoken before about the ways we get out of our moods. Exercising, reading, napping, and journaling have all been known to alleviate our symptoms. Reaching out to others, focusing on gratitude, and retelling funny stories are also some of our favorites. Yet on this day, he inspired me without saying a word. With his two hands, he tenderly worked on the delicate textile. Slowly and methodically, he turned the crumpled pile into crisp sheets. For him, it was a labor of love, and I received it as such.

For the past year, each and every time I look at the curtains, I smile. Not only because of their whimsical pattern, but also because of the memory that is evoked when I see them. I recall feeling supported, and understood, and loved... when my dad ironed my crazy curtains.

~Michelle Sedas

The Track Meet

*Every time you smile at someone, it is an action of love,
a gift to that person, a beautiful thing.*
~Mother Teresa

One of the most memorable days of my life was the day of my fourth grade track meet. This bit of information would probably shock most people who know me. You see, I have always been on the chubby side and have always failed miserably at everything remotely athletic. But the day does not stand out to me because of any medals or ribbons. It stands out as the day I saw just how much my father loved me.

Before school that morning, my dad and I went through the normal rituals of getting ready for the day. My mom was already at work and my dad had just gotten home from his third shift position at an aircraft manufacturer. As he was fixing my hair, he told me he had something important to tell me. While he was talking, I detected fear in his voice. This was something I had never heard before. He was always so strong—I didn't think anything could scare him.

He told me that his boss had called him into his office before he left and set up a meeting for later in the morning. There had been a lot of talk going around about layoffs, and my dad was almost positive he was going to be one of the unlucky ones this time around. I was completely shocked. My dad had worked for the company for twelve years, longer than I had been alive! Our family knew layoffs were coming, but we just assumed Dad's job was secure since he had worked there for so long.

After he told me about his job, he told me not to worry about anything. He said everything would work itself out and that we'd make it. I believed him, but I could also tell how worried and scared he really was.

Before he dropped me off at school, I told him he didn't have to come to my track meet. I knew he had a lot on his mind and probably wouldn't want to stand around in the heat just to watch me come in last place in all of my events. He just shook his head and promised he would be there. He told me to do my best and not worry about winning or losing. He wished me luck before kissing me goodbye.

There were a couple hours of regular school before they released us for the track meet. None of the students could focus on anything else. I couldn't focus either. I couldn't stop thinking about my dad and how scared he sounded. The teacher broke me out of my reverie with her loud announcement of "Track meet time!" I remember thinking, "Here goes nothing."

I saw my dad as I was getting ready for my first event. He waved at me with a big smile on his face. When I saw how happy he was I figured he must not have lost his job after all. The boss must have given him a raise instead! I heard him cheering for me as I ran. I didn't win the race, but I tried my best. When I finished that event I ran over to him and asked him what had happened at his meeting. He told me he had been laid off. I was shocked. He looked so happy and he was in high spirits. I couldn't understand why he was smiling. He told me not to worry about it and to enjoy the track meet.

As the day wore on, I continued to run, jump, and lose. Every time I looked over at my dad he was smiling and cheering me on. I never once saw him frown that day. I looked over at him after I lost my final event and saw him wave and smile. Seeing him smile made me smile. All day, he stood and cheered for me in the heat without any sleep after he had been laid off.

So the day of my fourth grade track meet is one of the most memorable days of my life. I don't remember all the events I participated in. I don't remember who beat me. I remember my dad. I remember his smiling face and his cheering voice. And I realized in that moment how much my father loved me.

~Fracia Heter

Pops

Adversity introduces a man to himself.
~Author Unknown

I can vividly remember standing alongside my mother's grave as her shiny, lilac casket was lowered into the ground. I was five years old. As friends and family threw flowers into the grave, I recall throwing a letter that I had written. Then I watched it descend into the open earth.

During the ceremony, my father masked his pain by holding back his tears as he received consolation from those who surrounded him. He held the three of us close in his arms, and with a knot in his throat he whispered, "I promise you girls that everything is going to be okay." Although we were too young to understand, my father tried hard to remain strong for my two younger sisters and me. My father was only twenty-five years old when he took on the challenging role of both mother and father. From that moment on, he devoted himself to providing a life of happiness and fulfillment for us as we grew up without the love of a mother.

For many years, my father worked long hours with complex and dangerous factory machinery. Although this physically demanding job consumed his energy, he always managed a smile when we greeted him at the door with open arms. He attended many of our school functions as well, events that were often painful without our mother. My sisters and I dreaded most of all the annual Mother's Day performance at our elementary school. Watching so many mothers gazing at their children with admiration made our participation difficult. But our sadness faded as we saw our dad smiling proudly by the back doors. As a grown woman, I now understand how hard this must have been for him.

His endless sacrifice took a toll. When I was a teenager, my father suffered a back injury at work that resulted in the loss of his job. We experienced a tough economic time, as he was out of work for several years. However, my sisters and I never felt deprived of anything because of the love and attention he bestowed upon us. In spite of the physical back pain and emotional stress, he used this long stretch at home to attend our sporting events and chaperone school field trips. Fully present for his children, he spent hours and hours with us inventing new silly games that always ended with tears of laughter. He even shared stories about our mother as we listened to music.

Eventually, my father regained the strength to find work, though he was precluded from physical labor. Because he had never graduated from high school, it became extremely challenging for him to find employment. Most of the job offers he received paid less than what he needed to provide for our family. As a result, my father decided to complete high school by pursuing a GED. I can clearly remember waking up at night and seeing him lying on the living room floor with his books scattered alongside as he studied and prepared for the exam. His diligence and commitment to his studies paid off when he passed the exam and was able to find a fulfilling position as a school assistant and athletics coach at an elementary school.

I am forever grateful to my father for his unconditional love and for being the best parent he could be, even during the toughest times in our lives. His endless sacrifices and commitment to putting us first have not gone unnoticed. Twenty-five years ago he told my sisters and me that everything was going to be okay, and he has kept his promise ever since.

~Lizy Herrera

50

Flowers that Never Die

The temple bell stops but I still hear the sound coming out of the flowers.
~Basho

Hospital beds are miserable places. Mine seemed to swallow me up. I was six years old and wanted to go home. My throat hurt and no one was offering me ice cream. The children's book my parents had read to me about having my tonsils removed said the hospital would give me some ice cream. Where was my ice cream? I was mad. No ice cream.

Nothing had happened that day the way I had been told. Even in the operating room. The book said I would count backwards from 100, then go to sleep. Instead, the hospital staff put a strange blindfold on me. For a moment, I saw flashes of colored light and then went to sleep. And I had practiced counting backwards.

It had been a difficult day and now I faced a long night. A long night, but as it turned out, not a lonely night. Although Mom had returned home to care for my baby sister, my wonderful, loving father was there. All night. Relaxing in his presence, I fell asleep. When I woke up not long afterward, Dad was asleep on the floor beside my bed. Not able to speak above a raspy whisper, I wondered how to wake him. I needed Dad to give me water, hug me, and comfort me. Searching for an idea, I looked around the room, stopping at the box of tissues on my nightstand. Reaching over, I pulled one out, and dropped it by the side of my bed hoping it would fall onto Dad.

My idea worked. Instantly, Dad was on his feet tending to my every need. He told me to drop a tissue whenever I needed him. I dropped a lot of tissues that night. Each time, Dad was instantly beside me. He never complained. Not once. His constant presence that long night was a gift of love.

Dad gave me another gift of love the following year when I was swallowed up by another hospital bed. This time, I was a thousand miles from home and flattened by severe cystitis, a bladder infection.

The infection had developed during my family's annual visit to my grandmother's house. I hated going to my grandmother's house. There simply wasn't anything for a kid to do. Now, on top of being bored, I was in pain and confined to bed.

Before I became too depressed over my lousy summer, a series of special gifts lifted my spirits. My mother gave me the gift of her loving presence, rarely leaving my side. My grandmother sent me a large portion of the "thank you" bouquet her Sunday school students had sent to her. My aunt and uncle presented me with a batch of peonies and snapdragons. Peonies to remind me of Peony Park, the city's amusement park. Snapdragons because I enjoyed squeezing them open and shut.

The most beautiful flowers were yet to come, however. Dad brought them—a tiny vase of plastic flowers.

"These flowers," he said as he handed them to me, "represent my love for you. Not that it's artificial but that it will never die."

I hugged the vase to my chest.

Over the next few years, Dad continued to envelop me in his boundless love. Then, one day, he was gone.

I was sixteen.

I lost Dad's physical presence that day but his gifts of love have never left me.

When my eight-year-old nephew, Andrew, underwent a tonsillectomy, I sent him a Pittsburgh Steelers box of tissues along with the story of my tonsillectomy, the hospital box of tissues, and the grandfather he never knew.

Andrew still has the tissue box.

The tiny vase of flowers sits in my bedroom. And sitting on Dad's grave, there are always artificial flowers. Always. These flowers represent my love for him, not that it is artificial but that it will never die.

~Kathy Irey

51

Dad's Secret Ritual

Underneath prayer disappears adversity.
~Pepper Giardino

When I was a child, my family had a nighttime routine. After dinner, my five siblings and I would play outside and then gather around the TV with our mom and dad to watch our favorite shows. But later, as we all brushed our teeth and got ready for bed, my dad would mysteriously disappear. After fifteen minutes, he would emerge in a more peaceful state and quietly walk from room to room to say goodnight and tuck his little ones in. For many years I wondered where he went during those stolen moments, which seemed to get him through even the toughest of times.

My father lived a very stressful life, and twenty years after leaving home I am still in awe of him. Not only did he have a wife and six children to support working as a mailman, he also built our family's house with his two hands and a 1950s tractor. We had outgrown our trailer home so my dad took it upon himself to build us a new one. This undertaking nearly killed him, and also led to my discovery of his secret.

I remember that Saturday afternoon well. My dad had spent the entire day shoveling cement for the foundation of the house, while my siblings and I played kick the can in the backyard. Suddenly, my mom came running. "Kids!" she hollered as she peered around the trees looking for us. We weren't sure if we should stay hidden or emerge to find out what she was yelling about.

But her next words made me come running. "Kids, your father is hurt! I need to take him to the hospital!" We all stood around her, wide-eyed, as she held my six-foot-tall dad at the waist.

"Stay here," she continued as she looked over her shoulder to my teenage brother and sister. "Dave and Debbie, you're in charge," she ordered.

We all watched as my mom helped my dad into the front seat of our family van. He was bent over at the waist and struggling to take off his tool belt. He tried to hide his eyes, but I could see he was holding back tears as he sat doubled over, grimacing in pain and clutching his chest. "I'll be okay, kids," he whispered. "Just hang in…." His voice trailed off as my mom reclined his chair, then waved a quick goodbye. We all stood dumbfounded. I started to cry as my older sister tried to reassure me. "Everything will be alright," she said. But I didn't believe her.

Our neighbor, Sophie, came over an hour later to check on us and bring dinner. But we were too upset to eat. Time seemed to stand still as we paced around our small living room, waiting for the phone to ring.

Finally, the call came. My sister answered. "Oh, thank goodness," she said after listening to the voice on the other end. She gave my mother assurances that we would be fine until morning and then gave us all the news. "Dad has a collapsed lung, probably from all the lifting and shoveling he's been doing."

I remember being so thankful that my dad didn't have the "heart attack" that my brother and sister had been whispering about. When he returned home the next day, he bravely told us that he was "good as new." Though he had to rest, he still read us stories at night, made us his famous chocolate milkshakes before bedtime, and when we were getting ready for bed, resumed his mysterious nighttime ritual that gave him such peace of mind.

His near-death experience made me acutely aware of how difficult his life was, and increasingly curious about his secret ritual. Finally, when I was twelve years old, I gathered the courage to find out his secret for myself. I tiptoed down the hall, opened his door just a crack, and peered in.

What I saw was my dad kneeling down at his bedside, his head bowed, whispering. He was praying. I got down on the floor and strained to hear him. With his hands clenched together, he listed each of his children's names and made one specific request for each of us — all six of us. For me, he prayed that I would have the strength to stand up to the peer pressures of junior high, and that I would always do the right thing.

He ended with a prayer thanking God for all of his blessings, particularly my mom and her incredible strength. To this day, I've never told my dad that I heard him pray that night, and that I had discovered the secret ritual that gave him peace as he struggled to raise his family.

Until now.

~Victoria LaFave

Coach Dad

Whether you think you can or think you can't—you are right.
~Henry Ford

Thanks to my dad, I learned to intercept life's fumbles and turn them into winning plays. Decades later, I still use his guidance when I overcome obstacles with my optimistic outlook.

"It's how you respond that counts," he coached. "Have a positive attitude. Do your best. Enjoy life. Do your part. Be resourceful. Believe in yourself. Believe in others."

Dad lost his youthful dream to coach football when he couldn't afford college. Yet he didn't let disappointment bench him from a productive life. He held varied jobs until the end of the 1930s. Then he founded and ran Parks Sand and Gravel Company until he retired.

By the time of my birth in 1951, my parents had been married twenty years and my sister had celebrated her thirteenth birthday. We lived in Emporia, Kansas, where my dad had earned respect as a hardworking businessman who mentored others.

Dad boosted floundering souls and freed the daring spirit in those around him. He set reasonable expectations. He offered support and feedback. He created opportunities to build strengths and demonstrate competencies. I heard stories about his kindness from those who stopped to say, "Wes, thanks for believing in me and for giving me a chance."

Dad had become a coach after all: a coach about life, a model of strength, courage, and integrity.

As his daughter who had hearing and voice impairments, I bene-fited from the same "believe in yourself" approach. Coach Dad taught me that we become stronger when we face our setbacks. We shape our strengths and sharpen our compassion. From his viewpoint, the disabilities and challenges I braved became scrimmages to train my coping muscles to manage the ups and downs of life.

I had the typical childhood tasks to master along with tough medical issues to tackle. My ear malformations and hearing loss in both ears required several surgeries. Lifesaving throat surgery at age twelve damaged my vocal cords and nerves and muscles to my face and tongue. I had countless sessions of speech therapy due to my hearing loss, and later for problems I had using my tongue and voice.

My parents encouraged me. They made a terrific team with my dad's inventiveness and my mother's faith that all things worked out in one way or another. Growing up under their "I can" philosophies, I gained the strategies I needed to face my challenges.

Dad focused on finding solutions, not whining. He didn't let fear, failure, or worry immobilize him and rob him of innovative ways to solve problems. He expected no less from me when I grappled with frustrations during my younger years.

Sometimes I didn't hear crucial information at school. When I tired, my face drooped. My weak voice gave out. I disrupted class with incessant coughing spells. I ate at a slow pace to avoid choking. Sometimes I got weary from studying hard to make up for missed information. Even though I practiced relentlessly to improve my speech and my voice, I often felt my progress was too slow.

With his head cocked to the side, Coach Dad listened. Then he'd ask, "Did you do your best?"

"Yes," I'd say. "I tried."

"Well then, that's all you can ask of yourself."

He'd pause then continue, "What did you learn?"

To him everything—good or bad—provided a learning oppor-tunity. A chance for self-improvement. A clue to solve a problem. A way to help others.

Coach Dad didn't cut me any slack. He held me accountable for making positive contributions. When the church high school youth group elected me president, I didn't want the leadership role. I thought it would tax me with my hearing loss and voice limitations.

"I can't do it!"

Coach Dad listened. "Sounds like others have faith in you."

"That doesn't matter!"

"I wonder—what would it take to make it work?" He nudged me to list ideas. Then he stepped back to allow me to take charge.

I learned resourcefulness by using my strengths to find solutions. I observed, listened attentively, carefully chose my words, and facilitated ways to help all feel included. I taught others to keep background noise to a minimum, to talk one at a time, and to look at me when they spoke.

Coach Dad followed up. "How did it go this time?"

"Great, Dad!"

"What did you learn?"

"I can do it!"

He smiled. Point made.

During an eventful year, Coach Dad stood by me as I graduated with my master's degree in social work, moved to Iowa to start my career, and subsequently survived a medical emergency and two grueling surgeries. When I recovered and returned to my job, he knew his coaching had paid off. I bounced back despite the serious setbacks that had blocked my path. Most importantly, I had conveyed confidence in my ability to tackle tough times.

Before the end of that year more turmoil arrived when Coach Dad was diagnosed with pancreatic cancer. He knew he couldn't control the existence of the cancer, but he could control his response. As he faced life's last game with dignity and grace, the core truth of his coaching became clear: He had taught me and many others the skills we needed to direct our own lives.

I was twenty-four when Coach Dad died. That was over thirty years ago. Every day since, I've been grateful for his legacy of values and lessons about resilience.

He taught me to believe in the irrepressible quality of the human spirit. He empowered me to learn from both the joys and challenges of life. He coached me to use my strengths to respond in positive ways to life's fumbles. He instilled in me the kindness of sharing my hard-earned wisdom.

Today Coach Dad cheers from the grandstand of my heart. I continue to call upon his wisdom to tackle whatever life throws at me, an inspiring tribute to his lifelong influence and the relevance of his lessons.

~Ronda Armstrong

The Constant

Love is the condition in which the happiness of another person is essential to your own.
~Robert Heinlein

My parents divorced when I was seven years old. My dad moved out of our house and into his own place and we began our memorable routine of weekly visitations on Wednesday nights and sleepovers every other weekend. It was the characteristic and predictable court-appointed agreement for divorced families. My dad's idea of visitations and parenting, however, was vastly different from the Court's. He made a promise on the day his divorce was final that would change the course of my life forever.

My dad promised that he would be more than just a "weekend dad" who fulfilled his obligatory parental duties with limited visits. He wanted more than anything to be a significant presence in my life even though we were not living under the same roof. To this day, I am so grateful to him for overcoming the many obstacles that face divorced dads and cementing an unbreakable bond with me, his youngest daughter.

Throughout my life my dad made me a priority and everybody knew it. He would stop by my house every day, usually after school, to chat for a minute and tell me how much he loved and missed me. I waited on most days with eager anticipation for his shiny, yellow 1976 Stingray Corvette to turn the corner of our block and meander slowly toward my house. When I spotted my dad with the T-tops off and the windows down, I just knew my day was going to get better. Sometimes he would take me for a ride and sometimes we would just sit in the car and talk for a few minutes in the driveway while he learned about what went on in my day.

I felt like the luckiest girl in the world to have someone so interested in what was happening in my life. If he could not see me in person he would call on the phone. For the next eleven years until I left for college, I talked to my dad every single day.

During the weekends that I spent at his house I can remember him grilling the best pork chops I've ever tasted. He made scrambled eggs for breakfast every morning and cooked pot roast to perfection on Sundays. He always let me help because everything we did, we did together. He rarely accepted any party or dinner invitations on our weekends together because he cherished our time alone as much as I did. We played catch or Frisbee in the yard and rode bikes or took walks to find secret treasures. My fondest memory of those weekends, however, was when my dad would turn on the stove after dinner and I would hear the slow crackle and smell the unmistakable aroma of Jiffy Pop popcorn. I can remember like yesterday the excitement I felt as the tinfoil pouch began to rise and steam poured out from the sides of the pan. My dad would shake and jiggle and pop those kernels to absolute perfection every time.

My adolescence was a typically confusing time, but the bond I had with my dad was the constant in an otherwise chaotic life. After the divorce, and during all of the tumultuous times that the divorce brought to our family (remarriages, stepfamilies, bitter ex-spouses etc.), he always listened patiently. He never discounted the sometimes complex feelings of a young girl. He just listened. And he remained the only reliable, stable presence in my life. I could count on my dad to take me to every doctor or orthodontist appointment, watch every softball game, attend every conference and be present at every significant life event. He always lived up to his promise. I cannot say that about anyone else.

All of my life lessons I learned from my dad. He taught me that you must keep your word. Period. He taught me to be kind, fair and just. He taught me to take the high road, give 110% and never let 'em see you sweat. He taught me that success is a journey, not a destination. But most importantly, he taught me by example.

Conventional wisdom says that to be successful you should simply develop the traits you admire in other successful people. As I figured out what to do with my life and how I wanted to live I didn't have to look too far for inspiration. My dad is, by far, the most successful person I know. Ever since I was a little girl, I have admired his sense of humor, determination and integrity. He taught me that my only limitations were those that I imposed on myself. I will always be thankful for having such an encouraging and loving teacher in my father; something that many young women of divorced families never get to experience with their own fathers.

Even though I recognized and appreciated my dad's love, it wasn't until I had my own children that I realized the profundity of our bond. The closeness we share has always transcended space and time, but I am even more in awe of our relationship because now I can fully appreciate his sense of purpose. To comprehend my dad's unconditional love for me I need look no further than my own children. When I look deep into their adoring eyes and promise to love them forever and ever, I see the reflection of pure happiness and joy staring back at me. I know my dad must have seen that same blissful reflection in my eyes.

The confidence and security I possess today as a person and a parent is directly related to the man who vowed so many years ago to be more than just a "weekend dad." He made good on his promise in more ways than I can convey in one story. However, I am most thankful for the father who took in his arms a scared, confused and angry seven-year-old and whispered in her ear, "I love you and I will never leave you."

~Kimberlee Murray

54

An Orphan's Daughter

Adversity enhances this tale we call life.
~Ever Garrison

"**D**ad," I said, "can you help me with my homework? The assignment is to make our family tree."

After supper, we settled at the kitchen table. I gripped my pencil, ready to take notes.

"I was adopted," my dad said.

I swallowed hard and gazed at my father. "You were?" I was stunned, but full of questions.

"In 1923, your Uncle Harry and I rode a train from New York, and Grandpa and Grandma Gray adopted me."

"What about Uncle Harry?" I asked with a fourth grader's curiosity. Uncle Harry and his family lived in a nearby town.

"He was adopted by a different family, named Pistole," Dad said. "My brother, Marshall, died in World War II, and I don't know what happened to the others."

I stared wide-eyed. "How many others?" I asked.

He paused in thought. "Well, I also had two older sisters named Greta and Hattie. And I remember seeing a baby who died." He shook his head. "Once when Marshall came to visit, he said there were others. But I don't know how many or anything about them."

I listened quietly, trying to absorb this amazing story.

"I was born in Constantia, New York, in 1915. My father was

fifty-four years old and my mother was twenty-six. They named me Ethel Franklin Wright."

I squirmed in my chair, counting in my head the forty-four years since Dad's birth.

"I hated my name," he said. "It was pronounced Ee-thal, but kids teased me and called me Ethel."

"Sounds like a girl's name," I admitted. He showed me his birth certificate where he'd scratched his first name from the paper with a penknife.

"We lived in an old house with two rooms and a pantry. The plaster was coming off the walls and you could see through the roof. My dad kept his bicycle and camera locked in the pantry."

"What about your mother?" I whispered, almost afraid to say anything for fear he'd quit talking.

"My mother took us kids hunting for greens and leeks in the marshy wetlands near our home. We also hunted bullfrogs and dug clams and ate whatever we found."

I tried to picture five children scrambling along a riverbank looking for food, but all I could see in my mind were the cookies my mother had baked that afternoon. Their sweet, chocolate scent still lingered in the air.

"We moved, probably because we were evicted, and lived in a large tent. We had a stove but slept on the ground."

He paused again, and I knew he was thinking about those long ago days. I sat still, waiting for him to go on.

"Before winter, we moved back to the house with the hole in the roof, but life was no better. All spring and summer the bread man threw a loaf of bread on our doorstep each day when he made deliveries."

"Is that all you had to eat?" I asked, thinking about our family favorite of fried chicken with mashed potatoes and gravy.

He nodded. "Sometimes we went to bed hungry."

I sat back in my chair and chewed my lip. "Didn't your dad work?" I asked. "Why were you so poor?"

"He worked at a sawmill," Dad said, "but he didn't have steady work. Times were really hard back then. New York was full of immigrants, and many died from the influenza epidemic. There were always black hearses in the streets."

I saw lines crease his forehead at the recollection, and I buried my head and made notes on my lined, yellow pad. When I looked up, he spoke.

"My father liked to sit on the back stoop and smoke a small clay pipe." He indicated the size of the pipe with his thumb and forefinger. "He let me smoke from it, too. That's nearly all I remember about him, except he had red hair and a couple of fingers missing from a mill accident." He smiled. "And he was really stern."

I tried to picture the parents he described, but it was difficult, except for the red hair. Dad, my older brother and I were all redheads.

"When I was five, I was placed in an orphanage run by the Children's Aid Society," Dad paused and took a drink of root beer. "My brothers went, too, but my sisters went to private homes."

A lump formed in my throat. I'd never been away from my family. I wanted to cry.

"I had my first bath in a real bathtub with hot water and plenty of soap, and got clean clothes, shoes and socks. They were good hand-me-downs, and each item was numbered for identification."

I glanced down at my new pajamas and remembered the dresses Mom bought me for school. I'd never worn hand-me-down anything.

"We ate burned toast, hot chocolate, jelly, cooked oatmeal and mush for breakfast," he said. "Definitely a much different menu than I was used to." He patted his stomach.

"We only saw our parents once in the orphanage." He paused a moment. "Then we moved to the Brace Farm School. Marshall ran away and returned to our parents. He eventually changed his legal named to John Ryan and joined the Army."

I turned to a new page of paper and scribbled the names.

"Nearly two years after leaving Constantia, Harry and I were among a group of children involved in a 'placing out' process for relocating orphans from New York State to the Midwest. J.W. Swann and his wife, of Sedalia, Missouri, were our sponsors and traveled with us. We curled up on the hard seats of the huge train and slept during the long trip.

"We had a sack lunch and the clothes on our backs," Dad said. "When we arrived in St. Louis, we were cleaned up and given a brand new set of clothing." He smiled. "The first new clothes I ever had. They told us the Maryville, Missouri, newspaper had advertised our visit. We arrived at the First Methodist Church on a freezing November day in 1923, and stood quietly while townspeople heard our stories and looked us over.

"I worried when I wasn't chosen that first day," Dad continued, "and I stayed a few days in the Jake Wiley home. Mr. Wiley tried to reassure me, but it was scary. Kids that didn't get picked rode the train to the next stop.

"I was lucky," Dad said. "I got the best parents in the world. They named me Oliver and I never looked back."

I nodded as I thought about my loving grandparents, Orville and Erma Gray, yet I found it hard to see my dad as the small boy born into the impoverished, undisciplined lifestyle. Dad learned tenacity and compassion, not laziness or bitterness. He always believed the future held promise.

"I always felt obliged to make the Grays proud of me, not because of who I became, but in spite of my background. They took a stranger into their home and family, and I was never treated like an outsider."

That incidental, fourth-grade assignment was more than a study in genealogy. It filled me with appreciation for a man who worked hard to be a model citizen, devoted husband and son, and loving parent.

To me, that westward train movement of "placing out" orphans was more than a piece of history or the addition of a limb on my family tree.

I inherited an incredible legacy.

~Karen Gray Childress

55

Always a Winner

He didn't tell me how to live; he lived, and let me watch him do it.
~Clarence Budington Kelland

T he doctor's grim diagnosis sent a collective shudder through the family. It looked as if Dad had cancer. The X-ray showed a large mass inside his brain.

Prognosis: Bad, really bad. Treatment needed to begin immediately. According to the doctor, my father was in for the fight of his life.

Literally.

But if anyone expected Dad to launch into histrionics or some display of denial, they were soon proven wrong. After taking a deep breath, my father lifted his head, looked the doctor straight in the eyes and said, "Could be cancer, huh? Well, either way, I'm a winner."

The physician's office filled with silence.

No doubt, Dad must have felt a dozen bulging eyes fixed on him as his family sat, incredulous at his reaction to the horrible news.

Either way, I'm a winner?

What kind of response was that? The doctor said this was probably cancer — brain cancer!

Although stunned, we should've anticipated Dad's stoic response. After all, hadn't he always faced the unknown with this calm, yet fierce resolve? Not once in forty-odd years had I heard him ask "why me" or rail against God, blaming the Almighty for any setbacks or tragedies. Instead, he tackled life's cruel disappointments in a quiet, dignified manner. The severity of the situation didn't matter. Whether it was financial problems, conflicts at work, even a health crisis, Dad wrestled the issue calmly, always shielding his children from the awful truth.

Only then, as I looked back, did I realize how strong my father was—and how others leaned on him for support.

No doubt he found his strength at an early age. My father was born to an immigrant family. His dad hailed from Portugal and eventually Brazil while his mother came from Mexico. From his earliest days, he had to help his parents—usually as a translator.

The road wasn't easy for Dad. Eventually, he started to work after school to contribute to the lean family income. As a result, he didn't have many playmates or close friends. When his father died, Dad became the sole provider for his family. As a teenager, he attended school while working a stream of thankless jobs in the evenings and on weekends—a balancing act he continued until he graduated.

After a short stint in the army, Dad landed a good position with California's largest grocery chain where he eventually met my mother. His relentless strength was evident throughout his married life, raising children while still assisting his mother and various family members over the rough spots. During these years, he helped my mother take care of her parents as well.

As usual, there was no complaining, no wallowing in self-pity. Dad simply accepted the many challenges thrown at him and soldiered on. In fact, I never heard Dad complain about his childhood, which he always described as a happy, normal one.

His biggest test of strength came as an adult when my mother battled cancer, eventually succumbing to the disease. After Mom's death, Dad found himself alone for the first time in thirty-odd years. They had made such a strong team in life that my siblings and I were worried about Dad's ability to carry on without his spouse. Surely he wouldn't be able to make it on his own. The grief, we assumed, would take its toll on him.

The first few months proved to be his worst period as he lost weight and seemed a bit withdrawn. During my visits, I noticed the refrigerator and cupboards were not as fully stocked as they once were. Nor was the house as clean as I remembered it. He watched a lot of TV and seldom ventured beyond the living room.

It was obvious: Dad was depressed; life had finally beaten him. Or so we thought.

Dad's recovery began a few months later as he returned to work and started to socialize again. He attended all the family functions and even met some new friends who helped him over the sadness of losing a spouse. Before we knew it, he had cleaned the house from top to bottom and even replaced some old furniture and appliances.

The message was clear: Dad had rebounded and was ready to move on. Somehow, he had found that quiet, unshakeable resolve and had risen from his grief stronger than before.

Ironically enough, I hadn't realized the magnitude of Dad's fighting spirit—or how much he had inspired me—until that pivotal day in the doctor's office. Only then did I understand the breadth of his philosophy that nothing in life was a safe bet, that struggles and setbacks will always follow us. In the end, we simply must know how to deal with them—and to fight with all the strength we possess. His life was an example that although there would be agonizing moments of quiet questioning, that we must accept whatever God throws at us and learn how to be thankful.

It was true. Either way, we're all winners.

My debt of gratitude for all the lessons my father taught me may never be fully realized in my lifetime. However, I have come to understand the priceless gift he has given me—the strength and will to survive, and maybe, just maybe, serve as a rock for others to lean on.

Thanks, Dad, for teaching me how to be a winner.

~Al Serradell

The Final Gift

When you are sorrowful look again in your heart, and you shall see that in truth you are weeping for that which has been your delight.
~Kahlil Gibran

Today started like any other weekday. I got up at 5:30 AM, dressed, showered and drove to work. Grabbing a cup of coffee, I settled into my chair to begin my day. I wasn't prepared to be thrown into the past by an e-mail.

My cousin had forwarded a photograph of my father from 1944. In it he is twenty-two years young, cocky and handsome in his Army uniform on his way to serve his country in France and Germany. Like many men headed to war, he had married before he boarded the ship to Europe, and there was a baby on the way. I looked at the photograph, one I had never seen before, and I felt the tears sting my eyes. I wondered why this was hitting me so hard. Then I realized his birthday was the next day. I always think the grieving is behind me, but there it is, creeping up silently before I am even aware of it.

My father came home from the war to a wife he really did not know. Two weeks of courtship, and then a wedding at the courthouse before he boarded his ship, didn't leave much time to discover who my mother was. He did not discover that she had a mental illness until he was struggling hard to support a young family and build a home for his baby daughter. My mother had "episodes" and in 1946 people did not acknowledge mental health issues, let alone talk about them. So my parents struggled along, presenting a happy face to the world. But behind closed doors the severe nature of my mother's mental state was impossible to hide.

My mother became pregnant with my twin sister and me in 1952. While I was born healthy and able to go home, my sister, Diane, was rushed to an incubator where she spent the first month of her life. My father worked the graveyard shift at a local newspaper setting type, but he always ended his day sitting with my twin sister in the hospital. My mother never went. A special bond grew between my father and Diane. He often talked about holding her tiny hand and watching her struggle to breathe. He knew he would care for her better than anyone, so he went every single day.

When we finally were all at home under my mother's care, things began to fall apart. My father would go to work and come home to chaos, with children unfed, dirty and crying and my mother out of touch with reality. My older sister, Connie, tried to be the mother while he was gone. Eventually, my father had to place my mother in a hospital. During this time, we moved back and forth between home and my grandmother's house. My father was like a ghost, flitting in and out of our lives as he tried to take care of our mother while keeping us from being taken from him. Whenever he could, he would give us our baths, dress us in our pajamas and tuck us into bed. He was the one constant in our lives and we loved him.

When Diane and I were ten, my father moved us to California. My mother got treatment and was able to function but was never really a mother to us. She struggled every day simply to stay connected to reality. Even though as children we knew she was sick, the true nature of her mental health was finally revealed to us at the age of sixteen after a disturbing visit to the hospital. There was a disconnection that happened that day. We realized we would never have a normal family life. My mother would always be like this. We could not talk about it to anyone and we could not have friends over to the house in case something happened.

We struggled to understand why my father stayed in a marriage with our mother when she was not capable of loving him back. We presented a united front to our father, as we demanded to know why he was putting us through this horror. He sat us down and told us how he had met our mother. "I loved your mother the moment I first saw her. She wasn't like this then. I thought we would be together forever, and when you were born, I thought if I just tried hard enough, I could fix it for her and for you. I took a vow I cannot break, for better or for worse. Someday you will understand."

So it continued into our adult lives. We left home, married and had children of our own. We stayed connected to our parents because of my father. We tried to make him proud of the women we had become. My father was never an affectionate man. The special bond that connected Diane to my father was always evident because he would whisper into her ear that he loved her. For me, the stronger twin, those words were never murmured. In my way, I understood. He looked to me to take care of Diane and to be the solid rock she could cling to when he was not there, but I always longed for the words that were not spoken.

The week before my father's seventy-fourth birthday, I called home and my dad picked up the phone. I asked if my mother was there and Dad said she'd gone shopping. When I told him I'd call back later, there was a silence on the other end of the line. Then he said, "Marsha, I love you." Startled, I replied, "Well, Daddy, I love you too." I ended the call and stared at the phone in disbelief.

The next morning I was at work when I got the call that my father had stopped breathing. I rushed to my parents' house. Diane stepped out of the door in tears and right away I knew he was gone. In the days that followed I wondered why, of all the times I had talked to my father, he had chosen that day to tell me he loved me.

Even in the most dysfunctional families, there is that bond that connects children to their parents. As children we look for love and acceptance, and even as adults, the need is always there. Going through my father's things we found bits and pieces of the man he once was. His war diaries were in the bottom drawer of his dresser and Diane and I poured through them, reading them aloud to each other, laughing and crying and mourning the man who was our father. As we scattered his ashes, we remembered his words from years ago, that someday we would understand. My father did the best he could to love his daughters and take care of the woman he had vowed to love for better or worse. To me, the stronger twin, he left his final gift with four words. "I love you, Marsha." As his daughter, that is what I needed to hear and with it I have found peace.

~Marsha D. Teeling

Handstands

*Love is missing someone whenever you're apart, but somehow feeling
warm inside because you're close in heart.*

~Kay Knudsen

Father's Day approaches and I am a little sad that my dad
lives 3,000 miles away. I would love to barbecue burgers
with him and pepper our conversation with reminders of
the stellar job he did raising three daughters as a widower.

I was eight when my mother died. My sisters, Mary and Kim,
were nine and eleven. My mother fought cancer for two years, and
during the battle my father made my life amazingly cheerful. He
tucked us in by shining a flashlight on his hand, casting shadows of
bedtime creatures on our wall. He took us candlepin bowling and
easily convinced me that renting used shoes was luxurious. His endless cheering as the only spectator of my underwater handstand act
at the beach made me proud. His idea of after-dinner entertainment
was holding the transparent lid of a pastry box against his face and
performing a one-man television program.

My mother was nursed by her sister and my father while cancer diminished her abilities to walk, think and remember. When my
father — a social worker at the time — was not at work, he spent every
available moment at my aunt's with my mother. I cannot imagine
how he salvaged a fulfilling childhood for us. But he was there, dia-
gramming sentences, working on book reports, reading, and taking
us to movies. I have memories of my tired father half-smiling through
a trip to Disneyland, a *Monopoly* marathon and several jigsaw puzzles.

I recall taking a business trip with him to drop off two foster kids at their temporary home after getting them ice cream. There was always spaghetti, soup or something simple at the end of the day.

Then there were our teenage years when our mother was gone and the questions of female pubescence abounded. My father attempted to act casual in the dreaded health and beauty aids section. I wonder how he managed to get time in his own bathroom.

Last Father's Day, I flew to Kim's home in Pittsburgh and we drove to Boston, meeting Mary and my dad. It was the first Father's Day in years that my father had all of his "babies," a nurse, a reporter and a freelance writer, with him. Kim's teenage son, who is my father's favorite person lately, was with us. My dad had tears in his eyes when Kim and I appeared at his door after his day of work at the post office. He will have another weepy moment when he meets Kim's newborn son later this month.

This Father's Day, I cannot travel to Boston. I will celebrate by phoning my dad to talk about books and tell him for the millionth time what I will do in the event of an earthquake. And I will finish celebrating at the beach where I will honor my father's support, unconditional love and survival by doing the best underwater handstand I can muster.

~Amy Lyons

Manhood 101: Having Your Masculinity and Your Marriage Too

Housekeeping ain't no joke.
~Louisa May Alcott

When it comes to macho, you don't get more manly than my father. Air Force fighter pilot, Air National Guard Hall of Famer, Golden Gloves boxer. Happily married to the same woman for sixty-six years, still willing to match anyone drink for drink and insist on picking up the tab for the whole bar. He has a gruff voice, refuses to mince words, and radiates an athletic energy that's served him well throughout his life.

So far, so good. You're with me.

But here's where the story goes off the beaten track. When the going got tough, he went shopping. Literally.

My father was stationed in Alaska when he mastered the art of braiding my sisters' hair, changing my brother's diapers and doing laundry. No, it wasn't some early version of *Wife Swap*, but a much grittier reality show, one you've not seen on TV.

The first indicator of trouble was a phone call he got in the midst of scheduling flight runs. It was my mother's doctor. "Your wife has a spot on her lung that indicates tuberculosis." In those days, not only was TB highly contagious, it was also a death sentence. Perhaps it was the fact that the doctor hadn't yet told my mom her own diagnosis that made my father hang up the phone with a brusque, "I've got to talk to my wife!"

When my mother's tests came up negative for TB, she was released from the hospital until shortly before Christmas, when she began coughing up blood. At that point in time whole hospitals were filled with patients dying of "consumption," and because it was so contagious, my mother was immediately quarantined in a hospital fifteen miles away.

In 1950, hospital rooms didn't have phones. Arranging a call ranged between rare and impossible. Thus my folks' sole contact came in the form of daily visits, first thing in the morning when Dad and my siblings, bundled up against the severe weather, stood outside in the snow waving up at my mother who smiled back from the third floor window. It was a comfort, I imagine, for all of them.

Meanwhile, Dad's commanding officer was able to get Mom into a promising new treatment program in Denver. Two weeks after Christmas, she was on her way, strapped into a gurney on a plane transporting wounded soldiers from the Korean War.

My father packed up the house and prepared the children for their "compassionate transfer." It took nearly six weeks to reach their new home, during which time they and my mother were deprived of even the scant comfort of seeing—much less talking—to one another.

Without my mother around, my father learned the hard way what it meant to walk in my mother's shoes, coming home from work to cook dinner, do dishes, bathe the kids and get them to bed before picking up the house and doing laundry. When he tells the story now, it's with characteristic self-deprecation. "I didn't have a clue. I remember, before she got sick, she wanted a clothes dryer. 'Are you kidding?' I asked her. 'Do you know what those things cost?'"

A few weeks into the Denver transfer, he saw the light—or was it a Whirlpool?—in the rivers of wash created by four children, including the cloth squares that were—in those days—not an *alternative* but rather the only barrier standing between him and much less pleasant overflows.

Diaper delivery wasn't an option, not even a gleam in an eco-marketer's eye. Deliver*ance* came in a large steel box that rendered clotheslines obsolete and turned my father into a walking-talking spokesperson for the unsung plight of the housewife.

When not hunting for perennially lost socks, he prayed for my mother's safe return. He began—as we recovering Catholics say—to "offer things up." First candy, which he loved, then cigarettes. As he tells it now, it was touch and go, because the next thing he planned to tackle on this list—right when my mother was released from the hospital—was wine. "Just in the nick of time," he laughs.

Everyone they knew saw my mother's recovery as miraculous. I wonder if she didn't think this might be God's way of getting her husband to give up sweets, cigarettes *and* the ghost of male chauvinism all in one fell swoop. Dad says he was too busy giving thanks to think much at all. Giving thanks and teaching his kids that each time they did a chore around the house, it wasn't ever menial. "Consider it a labor of love," he'd say. "If you do it, your mother won't have to."

A labor of love. When I think about it now, all they achieved, the military honors and the Ph.D. he earned after "retiring" at the age of forty-five, I'm awed. That they could do this with ten children is almost as amazing as the fact that he shared his every accomplishment with his wife. They were a team. He'd learned the hard way just how much her labor at home allowed him to excel in the world at large.

What I've learned from his example is that the honest work of love, the real "manning up," involves putting yourself, whoever you are and whatever you do, into your spouse's shoes. Marriages thrive when both partners break through their inexperience and empathize with the other's challenges, whatever they may be. That's the real lesson at the heart of my father's heroism. He can shake his head at his former self, bare his soul in unflattering light, be humble enough to admit when he was wrong, and imaginative enough to remember, long after my mother had returned to the kitchen, that love's labors—unlike socks—are never really lost, just tucked away in a place it takes a brave heart and eagle's gaze to notice.

~Sheila Curran

Thanks Dad

Stepping Up to the Plate

Finding a Friend

Recognize others, be recognized, help others, be helped;
such is a family relationship.
~Hawaiian proverb

My stepdad, Ted, and I were at the back of the school bus. Ted was instructing me on the finer points of constructing a waterproof viewfinder for a fieldtrip to Hanuama Bay. Ted was the only man on the bus other than the bus driver. He had been living in Hawaii six years before he met my mom and they fell in love. When she came to Louisiana to collect my sister and me from our biological father's home and move us to Oahu, we wondered what this "new dad" and new life would be like.

I had many friends in Baton Rouge, but second grade in Hawaii was the year I became a loner. The only white girl in class, with white-blond hair and buckteeth—I was an easy target. Classmates called me "Haole" and "stupid round eye." Having Ted with me instead of my mom wouldn't make school easier. Ted was a bartender, so while Mom worked days, he would be my representative parent for school functions and his presence would be another source of teasing tomorrow.

I tried to ignore this and focus on instructions. Ted cut the top and bottom off the can; he had thick plastic he'd measured, and duct tape. This was part of the assignment: construct a viewfinder to identify the fish we'd see at the bay. The other kids had supplies in nice paper bags with handles—tube foil, precut cardboard, and Saran Wrap. No one but me had a used coffee can.

That morning everyone had a picnic breakfast together at school before we left. The mothers sat together in clumps, but my Ted laid out a tatami mat and sat with me. He talked about all the cool things we'd see at Hanauma Bay because he'd snorkeled there many times. As he talked, I shoveled eggs into my mouth.

"What's really neat," he said, "is that the fish come right up to you—they're not afraid. Once, I saw a Honu—a sea turtle!"

He didn't look anything like the other mothers. They wore bright-colored muumuus and had tiny, hard-bottomed slippers on their feet. Ted was in shorts and an Aloha shirt.

"Maybe," he continued, "you and a couple of your friends could work together and identify all the fish faster." He smiled then, his blue eyes sparkling.

The first thing I remember about meeting Ted was this smile and those sparkling blue eyes. My sister and I ran off the plane, not even knowing who we were looking for, and Ted was there in his flip-flops and Aloha shirt. He picked up my sister with one arm and me with the other, leaned his head between our bodies to kiss my mother, and then we walked out of the airport into Hawaii. I smelled plumeria flowers and the Pacific Ocean. It was easy for me to fall in love with my stepdad, just as Mom had done. He spent a lot of time with me that summer, having committed himself to teaching me two very important things: how to surf and how to speak pidgin.

After school started, the lessons were relegated to weekends. When my sister and I got home, Ted had already gone to work. Now, two months into school, I still hadn't made any friends, despite my five months of learning pidgin to prove I was Kama'aina—local.

As the bus pulled into a row of parking spots at Hanauma Bay, I held the coffee can with both hands. Ted measured plastic against the jagged bottom of the can and I secured it with duct tape. We all exited the bus and trudged down the hill with our flippers, towels, and mats.

My teacher, Mrs. Takabayashi, passed out laminated papers with pictures of sea animals. We were given grease pens and instructed to wade into the water and identify fish. As the mothers settled themselves on the sand, Ted removed his shirt and flip-flops.

"Well," he said, "which of your friends do you want to work with?" Other kids had partnered up and were walking into the bay with their viewfinders held on top of the water.

"I can do it by myself," I said.

The sun shone just above the top of Ted's head. "It'll be more fun with your friends, don't you think?" I had to squint as I looked up at him. "Kiddo," he continued, "don't you have any friends?"

I looked at the sand and felt hot, fat tears fall. Ted crouched in front of me.

"No one likes me," I whispered. "Everyone calls me a round-eye."

Ted put his hand on my shoulder. "Well listen," he said, "they just don't know you yet. Come on — we'll do it together."

He stood and took my hand and we waded into the bay. Ted handed me the coffee can and I held it on the top of the water. The glare of the sun went away as Ted moved to block the light. Through the sealed, plastic bottom I saw a row of lime-green sea urchins against orange coral, and also saw blue fish, spotted starfish, and pink anemone. We checked five off the chart right away.

I looked up at the other kids. Many were exiting the surf and running to their mothers, their cardboard viewfinders soggy, limp, and unusable. I looked back down through my coffee can and saw the black spindles of a sea urchin. I saw green sea cucumbers too.

"Ted," I said, "look at that!"

He reached his hand into the ocean and picked up the sea cucumber, careful to keep it underwater. I put my hand down and he helped me softly poke it until it spit sand. He put it down then gave me a starfish. When I held it, it sucked itself onto my palm.

"Cool. Right, kiddo?"

A girl named Lani was watching us, and came over when my Ted lifted a sea urchin above the surface of the water.

"Wow," she said. "That's cool!" She patted me on the back. "Your dad is so cool!"

Other kids came over too, and soon Ted and I had a circle around us, all of us marking fish off our sheets, and kids taking turns looking through my viewfinder.

Later that afternoon we sat on the beach and unpacked our bag lunches. Lani sat next to me and we giggled and laughed the whole afternoon and the whole bus ride home. I had a new friend.

The weekend after the field trip, Ted and I walked to the beach for another surfing lesson.

"So," he said, "how was the rest of your school week?" He was laying out our mats and anchoring the corners into sand. I was holding my board.

I thought about my friend Lani, and my new friend Laura. "Dad," I said, "it was the best week of school I ever had."

"That's great, kiddo," he said. And then we walked to the ocean and we both dove in.

~Kirsten Ogden

A Real Dad

We must be willing to get rid of the life we've planned,
so as to have the life that is waiting for us.
~Joseph Campbell

From the age of eight, I had yearned for a father. When I was seventeen, my mother married for the fifth time and I expected this man, Steve, to be a poor father like his predecessors. But I was wrong.

The walls I had built to protect my heart did not come down easily, and this time, my new "father" did not attempt to tear them down. Instead, little by little, he weakened them with patient and loving kindness.

This became clear to me as he helped me catch the wild kittens that hid in our garage. They darted in between boxes, yowling, hissing and scratching. Determined to escape, the tiny fur balls fought like lions. Steve's arms bore the bloody scratches of their escape attempts. He never complained.

During the golf lessons he brought me to, I did my best to watch my stance and avoid slicing the ball. But golf was not my "thing." Steve didn't care. He patiently guided my strokes. His big grin and bushy eyebrows framed a face of mirth, never frustration. "Nice try," he said, encouraging my pitiful attempts to follow his instruction.

"Steve, your fettuccini is better than Mom's," I raved one night.

"You think? I'll make it more often." He beamed with pleasure.

"Thanks." I savored a mouthful.

Steve shook his head. "It's just a package." He flushed from my praise.

I loved the fettuccini, but more than that, I treasured sitting on a barstool talking with him as he made the fettuccini twice a week. Even when I grew tired of it, I enjoyed the time we spent together while he prepared it for the family.

He held me while I cried about never knowing my father. I held him when he cried, because he had not been able to spend enough time with his daughter after his divorce.

The fact that I quit high school never swayed his belief in me. He gently nudged me to seek higher goals. Throughout junior college, he tutored me in algebra, economics, statistics and philosophy. Grinning from ear to ear, he clapped and cheered the day I walked across the stage to receive my Bachelor of Arts degree in history. The words, "I'm proud of you," meant more than the degree I had earned after five years of study.

Finally, when I was twenty-one, I told Steve I had an important question to ask him. I trained my eyes on the ground, still uncertain about asking it. What if he said no? So much of myself would be laid bare. With one word he could break my heart. Dare I ask? He took my chin in his hand and brought my eyes level with his. "You can ask me anything. You know that, don't you?"

I knew then, as much as ever, that this was a man I could trust without exception. I plunged ahead.

"Will you adopt me?"

Tears slid down both of our faces as he hugged me and said, "I'd love to."

Five years after he adopted me for my twenty-first birthday, I had a brainstem stroke and became a ventilator-dependent quadriplegic. Four months after my stroke, Steve was diagnosed with cancer and had his right lung removed. He tried to continue working, but found it physically impossible. After Steve was deemed permanently disabled, he assumed my care.

I had caregivers from eight to five each weekday, and during those hours he caught up on sleep, ran errands, scheduled my medical appointments, filed insurance claims, cleaned the house and cooked dinner. In the evenings and on weekends, he fed me and gave me fluids every two hours, and cleared my lungs at least every three hours to help me breathe.

He slept in the extra bed that was placed in my room in case I needed help during the night. Many times when I was sick, I woke him every forty-five minutes to assist me. When I was well, he still got up with me once or twice a night, giving me a smile, making me feel loved.

I was unable to speak, so I made a clicking sound with my tongue to call for assistance many times each evening and throughout the days on weekends. Regardless of the reason I summoned him, he came, whether it was to straighten my covers, adjust my shoe splints, apply lip balm, clear my lungs or tend to me in any one of a million ways.

Out of the endless nights Steve took care of me, I rarely heard him complain, even when he was exhausted. Frustrated. He has never shown resentment or anger.

Still, an immense amount of guilt weighed me down as I watched him grow older from my wants and needs that consumed his every minute. These were the years he should be relaxing and enjoying retirement. I expressed these feelings once and he answered, "Don't you know I don't begrudge even one minute I've spent taking care of you?"

Whatever I wanted or needed was his top priority. When the days were long and my spirit became defeated by the vagaries of my disabilities, Steve selflessly wiped away my self-pity and made me feel wanted and deserving of his love. He made the unbearable bearable by simply being Steve. I call him Steve even today. You might wonder why I don't call him Dad, Daddy or Father. He was and is so much more than that. He's Steve. Today, tomorrow, and always, I will cherish the gift of his love. I can only say thank you, but the words could never express all that I feel.

~J. Aday Kennedy

The Christmas Present

A little girl, asked where her home was, replied, "where mother is."
~Keith L. Brooks

On this beautiful October morning my aunt's spacious farmhouse was brimming with excitement. I was eleven years old and had been living with her and her large family since I'd lost my mother a year earlier. My dad, who was working out of state and could only see us occasionally, was on his way. I'd been counting down the days since his last trip six weeks earlier. Now that the big day had arrived, I was so excited I didn't think I could wait another minute to see him.

When he still hadn't arrived by late morning, my cousins Bonnie and Ruby and I wandered into the kitchen where my aunt had been cooking for hours (as she did each time her younger brother came). The large, sunny kitchen was filled with the tantalizing aroma of roasting chickens and deep-dish apple pies my aunt had just taken from the oven. As my cousins eyed the pies, I asked my aunt for the sixth time that morning, "Shouldn't he be here by now?"

Though normally good-natured, she was becoming exasperated.

"He'll be here when he gets here. You girls scoot so I can finish getting lunch ready. He probably hasn't had a home-cooked meal since the last time he was here."

My aunt and uncle were kind to me and I loved them and my cousins, but there were times I felt incredibly lonely in the midst of this large family. I grieved for the loss of my mother and yearned for the family and home we'd had. Being fanciful, I compared myself to the fruit salad my aunt was making. The cousins were the apples, pears, grapes, cherries, and peaches that were all homegrown and belonged together. I was the pineapple that my aunt had just added. While it blended in, anyone eating it knew it was a foreign ingredient.

My steps were slow as I followed my cousins to the back door.

"If you girls go to the top of the hill, you'll see his car when it comes around the curve. That way you'll get to see him even sooner." My aunt's voice had softened at the sight of my slumped shoulders.

We'd barely gotten to the top of the hill when we heard the sound of a motor and saw the hood of my father's Chevrolet coming around the curve. As it pulled to a stop beside the front gate, I began a headlong dash down the hill. I ended my wild dash with outstretched arms ready to wrap around my father when suddenly the redheaded woman with him stepped between us. I found myself enfolded in soft arms that reminded me of my mother.

I stepped back and studied her. She stood no taller than my father's shoulder and was pleasantly rounded. When the sunlight touched her hair, it sparkled as brightly as a new penny. And when she spoke, it was with the soft accent of the Deep South. "I've been so anxious to meet you that I couldn't resist hugging you," she said. I liked her instantly. Then, along with a hug from my dad, I got the news that this young woman's name was Polly and that she was going to stay for a week so we could get acquainted.

That week was one of the happiest of my young life. I didn't want it to end. Neither did my six-year-old cousin, Virgil, who asked Polly, "Are you going to marry my uncle?"

A grin spread across her face. "Stranger things have happened."

By the time the week was up, I had made up my mind. This was the woman I wanted to be my mother. As they were getting in the car, I shyly whispered, "Please come back."

She smiled back. "I will."

As fall turned into winter, my dad, Polly and I spent many wonderful weekends together. Each one made me more certain than ever that she was the answer to my prayers. Snow covered the land around the farmhouse as Christmas approached. My cousins played outside as it fell, making snowmen and pelting each other with snowballs while my youngest cousin was trying to catch the snowflakes on his tongue. While the snow meant fun to them, to me it meant that for the first time in my life, my dad wouldn't be with me for Christmas. I knew the mountain roads he would have to travel would be too dangerous for him to make this visit.

As I moped around the house feeling sorry for myself, the door flew open and miracle of miracles, my dad and Polly blew in. While I chattered excitedly, they added their wrapped gifts to the stack already under the tree.

Brushing snow from his blond hair, my dad said, "The roads were terrible but with chains on the tires, we managed to make it. It would take more than a snowstorm to keep us away this Christmas. We have a wonderful present for you that couldn't wait."

I wondered which brightly wrapped package held this special gift. But my dad just looked at me and said, "It's not under the tree." Then he grabbed a fistful of tinsel from its green branches and draped the silver strands over Polly's red hair. As I stared in amazement at my father's peculiar antics, he made the pronouncement I dreamed I would hear. "It's Polly! She has agreed to marry me and to be your new mother!"

Polly waved her new ring in the air and said, "That isn't all! We've rented a house big enough for your dad and me and you and your brother. You two are going to come with us after Christmas to our new home." I could feel the tears of happiness spill down my cheeks when she said the words I had prayed to someday hear: "We're going to be a family!"

When I look back on the many Christmas presents my dad gave me over the years, I want to thank him for the baby dolls, the bicycle, the skates, the gold locket, the pearls, the angora sweaters, and my first wristwatch. Most of all, though, I want to say thanks, Dad, for the best present of all, the one you presented to me in the parlor of my aunt's farmhouse when I was eleven years old. It was the answer to a lonely little girl's prayers. The precious gift that lasted for more than fifty years—a wonderful mother.

~June Harman Betts

My First Bike

Christmas is not as much about opening our presents
as opening our hearts.
~Janice Maeditere

The doorbell chimed and my heartbeat lurched into an anxious cadence as I walked to the door. My stepfather Roger appeared casual in a button-down, light-blue shirt and jeans. I shook his hand and gazed into a face weathered from age and alcohol.

My mother had gone to Vegas with friends, and my wife, Quyen, suggested we invite my stepfather over for dinner so he wouldn't be alone on Christmas. I was hesitant because I knew how he could get when he drank. I really didn't think he'd show.

He entered and cast a quick glance at the Christmas tree before heading with me into the family room. Quyen came out from the kitchen to greet Roger and asked if he wanted something to drink. He eyed me nervously and said, "Maybe a Coke."

I breathed a sigh of relief as Quyen went to get him a glass. Roger settled on the couch and sighed like a man shouldering the weight of too many burdens. He looked around and asked, "So where's the baby?"

Kevin was nine months old, and this would be their first meeting. Roger hadn't come with my mother to the hospital when my son was born, and he had never accompanied her when she visited. There was a part of me that still resented him for that. I sat in a chair facing Roger and conveyed that Kevin was napping.

After some small talk, we arrived at an awkward silence. Finally, Roger said, "So how's work?"

I thought for a moment about how much to disclose. "Sometimes, it's pretty rough. There's a lot of petty squabbling at the school."

Roger leaned forward. "Raymond, twenty years." He paused as if that was all he was going to say. "For twenty years, I put up with that kind of crap in the Navy. I'm telling you; it never ends. The worst part was at China Lake…."

As he spoke, a memory surfaced. I was eight, and we had just moved to China Lake, a naval weapons center in the Mojave Desert where Roger had been stationed. It was December. There was no snow on the ground, and we didn't have a Christmas tree that year. Packed boxes were still strewn about our tiny, Navy housing unit.

Roger had just married my mother, but I didn't know what to make of him. He and I didn't talk much, a pattern that continued throughout the years. Mom told me he came from a small town called Pengilly in Minnesota. He wasn't close to his family and joined the Navy to get away from the harsh winters. That was all I knew about him.

On Christmas day, I woke to find a shiny new bike in the living room. It was a Huffy Stingray, the color of moist summer grass. The metallic frame sparkled like jewelry, and the long, padded banana seat glistened a bright, shimmering green. Even the kickstand gleamed. I marveled at the wide, Cheetah Slick back tire with zigzag treading.

At my stepfather's encouragement, I grasped the waffle handle grips for the first time, and they fit in my hands as if they'd been molded for them. The bike left me speechless.

Roger broke the silence, "Don't just stand there, Raymond. Take it for a ride!"

I shrugged because I didn't know how.

Roger said, "I'll help you."

We rolled the bicycle outside. My stepfather held the bike up, and I climbed onto the seat. I looked at him, and when he nodded, I began to pedal. As soon as we started forward, I dropped my feet to the ground.

"I've got you, Raymond; you're not gonna fall. Just keep pedaling," he said.

I hesitated, but did as he instructed. We began moving, and this time, I continued to pedal. My stepfather held my seat with his strong, steady hand and jogged behind me as we went down the street. Riding a bike for the first time, I felt like a glider pilot sailing across a cloudless sky.

We zipped all the way down our street and turned around. Then I raced back. We must've done that twenty times on Christmas Day, and Roger stayed with me every step of the way.

In the next few days, when I rode faster, he ran harder. Then, during one of the many jaunts down our street, Roger said, "Raymond, don't turn around, but you've been riding on your own."

Still pumping the pedals, I could only utter, "What?"

Roger said, "Raymond, I haven't been holding you."

He jogged with me the rest of that day, making sure I was okay before he let me go out on my own.

Now, Roger sat with me in the family room at Christmas and told me stories about the people he had worked with in the Navy. Then he talked about what it was like going to school in Minnesota. He informed me he owned a German Shepherd named Michael that wouldn't touch the food set before him until Roger instructed him to eat. Throughout Roger's childhood, Michael was his best friend, the one he trusted most. I listened and nodded, and after awhile, Quyen brought Kevin into the family room. She put our son in his walker, and he giggled and launched himself around the room, bumping into the couch and the TV before going over to Roger.

Roger peered at my son for a moment, then reached out his hand and said, "How are ya, little fella?" Kevin latched onto Roger's index finger and let out a delighted shriek.

We had a pleasant, uneventful dinner of ham, mashed potatoes, corn on the cob and my stepfather's favorite — pumpkin pie. We watched *The Grinch Who Stole Christmas* together, and I gave Roger a present from under the tree. Surprise registered on his face, and he remained silent—about as awe-struck as an eight-year-old seeing his first bike.

Later in the evening, when my stepfather stood up to go home, he looked at Quyen and Kevin before turning to me. He said, "You have a really nice family," in a soft, cracking voice. Tears welled up in his eyes.

I paused a moment and said, "Merry Christmas, Dad. Thanks for coming over," and I meant every word.

~Ray M. Wong

Finding Home

Home is a shelter from storms—all sorts of storms.
~William J. Bennett

There's an old adage that says, "You can never go home again." While I don't know the origins of the saying, I do believe it holds some truth. Leaving home changes you. It alters your perspective. It sometimes even changes the fundamentals of who you are.

When I was in college, I used to love going home for the weekend. I would visit with all of my old friends from high school, but hanging out with them seemed different. Like somehow we had all changed in that short period of time.

Halfway through my junior year, my parents sold the house I grew up in and moved to a different town. It was only thirty minutes from the old house, and truth be told, the new house was much nicer. But it still felt like I had lost a big part of my childhood. I could no longer lie on the bed in the room I'd slept in as a child or study at the desk where I'd learned to read. I couldn't look out my window and see the backyard swing set where my sister and I had pretended to be Mary Lou Retton. I couldn't go "home" anymore. I still went to visit my parents, and I still enjoyed the time with them. It just wasn't the same.

Four years later, my mom and dad split up after thirty years of marriage. It was devastating for all of us. My first child was just six days old when they told me they were getting a divorce. And that's when the real loss hit me. My newborn son would never know my mom and dad as I had known them. He would never go to Grandma and Grandpa's house for Christmas, but instead, he would visit one of them and then the other. I cried for what he would never have and for what the rest of us had lost.

We'd lost our sense of family and I felt I'd lost my center—the last remnants of my home.

Just a few years later, my mom got remarried to a great guy named Doug. He was sweet to Mom and great with my kids. I liked him a lot, but he wasn't my dad. "Going home" now meant visiting Mom and her husband. That's how I thought of him. As my mother's husband.

That all changed the day that my own marriage fell apart. My husband called me on the phone and said those three little words no wife ever wants to hear.

"There's someone else."

I dialed Mom's number with shaking hands. How could this have happened? I thought over and over as I listened to the ring of the phone. Finally, someone picked up. But it wasn't Mom; it was her husband. The whole story tumbled out and Doug listened with patience and compassion. He promised to do whatever he could to help me in the coming months.

At that time, neither of us knew to what extent his promise would be tested. Within a few months, I could no longer afford the mortgage payment on my house, and my two children and I had no choice but to move in with my mom and Doug. As he unloaded box after box of stuffed animals, toys, and clothes, Doug just smiled and said, "My grandkids are moving in."

At first, it was strange living there. Before moving into their home, I had never spent more than a few hours at a time there—or with Doug. Their house didn't feel like "home" for me. It was simply a roof over my children's heads.

But gradually, Doug's kindness made me feel comfortable. When he and Mom had dinner plans, he almost always invited the kids and me to join them. He never made me feel like I was intruding on their time or their space. He seemed to enjoy having us there. He called me "kiddo," like I was really his daughter. And more than once, he said he wished I were.

My children and I lived with my mom and Doug for almost five months. Although I hadn't grown up in their house, I grew tremendously during my time there. I cried a lot, but I had a big, strong shoulder to do it on. I struggled, but I didn't do it alone. And because of some wonderful listening ears and caring hearts, I began to heal.

During that time, I discovered that when you're deciding who your family is, biology is the last thing you should consider. Doug was no longer just my mother's husband. He'd become my second dad, and because of his kindness, their house became my second home.

You might not be able to go home again. But sometimes, if you're really lucky, you can find a new one.

~Diane Stark

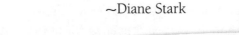

First Place

Act as if what you do makes a difference. It does.
~William James

My stepfather missed what some consider the most important firsts in their children's lives. He wasn't there for my first smile, first word, first tooth, first step, or first birthday.

He didn't come into my life until I was four. However, the poor guy more than made up for the firsts he missed in my baby years.

He bought me my first bike and taught me how to ride it. I can still hear his feet pounding the grass in our backyard as he ran behind me, holding me steady. I could ride that bike as long as I knew he was there. But once I missed the sound of his steps, I would fall. Dad would be a few yards back, hunched over and bracing his hands on his knees, trying to catch his breath. He'd smile, his face red and glistening with sweat, and say, "You did good, Sis. Let's try again."

In my first year of school, Dad listened to me read my first book. Mom loves to tell the story of how I'd pause and stumble while reading for her, but when I read for Dad, I wouldn't miss a beat. What she didn't know was that Dad had promised me that I could stay up late and watch television with him if I did a good job.

He bought me my first car and taught me how to drive it. And while it didn't physically wear him out, I'm sure his heart pounded as hard as his feet had years before when he'd run behind me on my bike.

He was there for my first date. Before my date arrived, Dad

pulled me aside, pushed a coin in my palm and whispered, "Sis, put this in your shoe. If that boy gets out of line, you call me and I'll come get you." That coin in my shoe reminded me all evening that I had a champion at home and I was safe.

On the day of my wedding he walked me down the aisle, patting my hand to reassure both him and me that we'd be okay.

He held my first child, and a few months later held me when my husband left us. He helped me walk through that dark valley and rejoiced with me when I married my husband, Neal. Years later he held my first grandchild.

My dad may have missed the important firsts that new fathers experience. But I don't care about that. He was there for the "firsts" that I remember and I will treasure those memories as long as I live.

Thanks, Dad. You were there for what really matters.

~Linda Apple

65

A Real Father

It is not flesh and blood but the heart which makes us fathers and sons.
~Johann Schiller

Having decided to leave my marriage of seven years, I was fully prepared to take on the new role of single mother, but not necessarily inclined to take advantage of my newly single status. For so long my social circle had consisted of my husband's coworkers, their wives, and other young mothers in the neighborhood. After the divorce, I moved out of the neighborhood and my ex-husband kept the friends and their wives, while I kept the kids. That was fine with me. I wasn't looking for a relationship or even someone to hold my hand in a way that might suggest even the most casual involvement. But just a few short months later I met the man who would become my second husband.

Something in my gut kept telling me not to blow him off, and this time I was going to go with my gut feeling. Kim had never been married and had no children of his own, and as the mother of two young boys, I felt an enormous responsibility to ensure that anyone I introduced into their lives would respect and support my commitment to them.

Exactly two years later we were married. The boys' father, who self-admittedly was more of a part-time "buddy" to the boys than a father figure, readily relinquished the job of parent to my new husband. Kim stepped into the position without hesitation, and with a sincere enthusiasm. His buddies and coworkers were stunned that the man they had seen as the proverbial bachelor was not only a devoted husband, but also a shining example of a committed father.

Suddenly, he was the dad who spent sleepless nights fretting and tossing if he felt that someone had wronged one of the boys. He was a homework cheerleader, even though he had no clue what a linear equation was. He frequently called on his artistic skills to assist in designing Cub Scout derby cars and posters for biology. When the boys were ill, he called from work every hour for an update. When they expressed an interest in sports, he was the one sitting in a lawn chair at every pee-wee football practice and arriving half an hour before game time to watch them warm up. When they didn't get the playing time they had hoped for the first year, he put both boys on a weight lifting program to increase their strength and speed. He surprised the boys with go-carts when they were younger, and dirt bikes and cars as they got older.

Both of our sons are now young men. Both have held national athletic records. The older one, Tom, is currently in college on a full athletic scholarship and his younger brother, Dan, is a senior in high school with the same potential. As they were growing up, I often wondered if they truly understood how fortunate they were to have such a loving father. But looking back, there were moments where the connection was impossible to ignore.

One such moment was Tom's "Senior Night." Senior Night is a common high school tradition recognized at the last game the senior players will play on their home field before graduating. During the game halftime, the field was teeming with parents, siblings and players waiting to line up and be introduced. As tradition requires, I was wearing my son's jersey. The player's father carries his son's helmet. The announcer instructed the players to line up with their families. As I watched, Tom turned toward Kim, silently offering him his helmet. Kim grasped the helmet by the facemask. I waited for one of them to say something, but not a word was spoken. I realized at that moment that there was nothing that needed to be said. There were mutual nods as Tom handed over the helmet and the two men turned and stood shoulder to shoulder, a proud father and his son.

~Barbara Edwards

66

The Stepfather

You will find that if you really try to be a father,
your child will meet you halfway.
~*Robert Brault,* www.robertbrault.com

I was enraged. Furious.

My widowed mother was "dating." At sixty-one, she was, in her own words, "Seeing someone."

That someone was named Irv, and before I ever met him, I was predisposed to hate him. I was, you see, a daddy's girl, though a troubled one. Even by young adulthood, I had not quite unraveled my complicated, intense relationship with the man I had loved so much—and so imperfectly.

So this Irv was a usurper, an intruder, and someone who clearly already had a place in my mother's life just a year and a half after my father's death.

"What is she thinking?" I asked my sister, who had none of my rage. Ruthie had made her peace with our father before he left so suddenly one April day, felled by a massive heart attack. Her conscience was clear. Mine was cluttered with the might-have-beens that could never be.

The loss of my father was still so raw for me that despite my being a thirty-one-year-old woman, I was locked in a battle with myself. The emotions didn't go to college, after all, and the loss of a parent knows no timetable, especially when guilt is the handmaiden of grieving.

So I held off meeting this Irv, and settled for hearing snippets about him from my mother, who was undeniably showing signs of renewed spirit and—dare I admit it?—happiness.

It wasn't my imagination that her green eyes actually sparkled at the mere mention of his name. And that hurt even more.

What about loyalty to my father, her husband of thirty-eight years? What about honoring and cherishing his memory?

It took a good friend to set me straight over a long, painful and honest lunch. She had picked up on my anger, my guilt, my confusion, and made one simple statement that cut through the fog. "This isn't about you," she said. And how right she was.

I wish I could say that it was smooth sailing from there.

I wish I could report that I welcomed Irv with an open heart when we finally met several months into the courtship. But that would be fudging.

It took more visits with Irv for me to begin to acknowledge his humor, his spunk and his obvious affection for my mother. I was not a pushover, and Irv knew it. He had the wisdom to bide his time and let a relentlessly critical daughter make her way to him in her own time.

There was actually no pivotal moment, no dramatic breakthrough. There was just a slow, steady and growing comfort with the man and the relationship he'd forged with my mother. There was a lessening of that early rage, and the sobering realization that I was being a brat about something far too important for self-indulgence.

Irv married my mother in our living room two years after their meeting through a mutual friend. My sister and I were their attendants. My three daughters, still too young to fully understand what was happening, were the excited flower girls in organdy dresses.

It was those little girls who also ultimately got me to the place I needed to be. Irv became their buddy, their "stand-in" grandfather at milestone events. Only the older two even remembered my father, and Nancy, who was a baby when he died, made the purest connection to Irv.

As he shared school plays, the angst of three adolescences, graduations, birthdays and holidays, Irv became a fixture in our lives. I no longer bristled at the notion that it was his face in family photos, and it was his hug at those occasions of state.

Somewhere along the way, I stopped thinking of this gray-haired man with the playful spirit as a wan substitute for my father.

His son and daughter and grandchildren were woven into our tapestry. We were that sociological phenomenon, a blended family, in our middle years.

Irv and Mom were married for nineteen years. They had plans for a twentieth anniversary celebration, but Irv's raging prostate cancer aborted that plan.

It was my final hospital visits with Irv that wordlessly sealed our relationship.

During his last days, I would tiptoe into his hospital room, shooing my mother away from her vigil, and sit beside him. I was never sure whether he was aware of my presence as he slipped in and out of consciousness.

But each time, I held his hand in mine.

Each time, I like to believe, he felt not just my presence, but my total, uncompromising acceptance.

It was time.

A man named Irv was no longer the enemy.

And as he slipped away one fine spring day, I mourned—and also rejoiced—that a foolish stepdaughter and her patient stepfather had finally found their way to peace.

~Sally Schwartz Friedman

As Time Goes By

Most of us, swimming against the tides of trouble the world knows nothing about, need only a bit of praise or encouragement—and we will make the goal.
~Jerome Fleishman

I awoke with a yawn as one of my bridesmaids entered my bedroom, a large smile across her face.

"Time to get up! You're getting married today!" She giggled happily.

I couldn't help but smile to myself as I watched her bounce energetically out of the room. I slowly made my way out of bed, my nervousness beginning to take hold. Today was the day that I would marry the man with whom I had shared the last six years of my life. I would marry my best friend, the man who held my heart, my trust, my love.

As a foster child with a history of alcohol, abuse and disappointments, I did not understand what a father should be. At the age of eight, I was placed in my first foster home. I spent many long, tormented hours wishing and praying that I could belong to someone. I was secretly envious of my friends who were "Daddy's little girl." How I yearned to have what they had. Unfortunately, I didn't find what I was looking for in my first foster home, and five years later, I was placed with a new family. This new foster home proved to be challenging, but I soon "adopted" the family as my own, as they did me. I eventually became comfortable enough to call them "Mom" and "Dad."

As my bridesmaids were helping me place the finishing touches on my make-up and gown, my dad walked in the door holding a package in his arms.

"Hi, Dad." I smiled as he walked over to me and handed me the box. "What is it?" I asked.

"Just a little something from Mom and me."

I took a slow breath as I opened the box and pulled out the gift. It was a beautiful glass vase with a picture frame on one side and a small golden clock on the other. The inscription engraved on the clock read:

> Cindy, As Time Goes By
> We're Always Near,
> Mom and Dad

I smiled at my dad, fighting hard to hide my tears, "I love it!" And with that, we left the house so I could be given away by my dad to start a life with my new husband.

In November of 2006 (two and a half years after my marriage), I called my dad in tears.

"Dad, he wants a separation."

"What?" he asked in shock. "I m sure it's just a fork in the road." I cried harder as I explained to him that this was different. He came over immediately and did everything in his power to try to save my marriage. Sadly, the separation was inevitable and within a week I moved back home with my parents. I was left jobless, penniless, and without the life I had known for so long. I was inconsolable. The pain, the tears, and the feeling of utter devastation were more than I could bear. I truly believed that I would die of a broken heart.

But with the strength, support and love from my family (especially my dad), and the inner strength that I found within myself, I slowly began to heal.

The following Christmas (a year into my separation), I didn't have much money to my name as I was still struggling to get myself back on my own two feet. I felt guilty because I wanted to repay my parents for all they had done for me in the past year, but all I could afford was a Christmas card. Inside the card I wrote the following words:

> Mom and Dad,
> *As Time Goes By*
> *I'm Always Near,*
> Cindy

My dad got up from his chair when he finished reading the card, handed it to my mom and quickly left the room. My mom removed herself from her chair and whispered quietly in my ear, "Your dad is crying."

I took in a deep breath and let it out as my own tears began to form. It was not my intention to make my father cry. I had only seen him show emotion like that twice since I had been with them, both times in relation to me and what I had been going through.

As I look back on the loss of my marriage, on all the tears and the pain that I was certain would never end, I can't imagine not having had my father there for me. Without him I would not have made it through as well as I did. I would not have been able to pick myself up and start my life again. Without him I would not have the beautiful little house that I now own. Without my dad, I would not be the person that I am today.

My father and I have always been close and I know we always will be. There is a bond between us that cannot be broken, a bond that cannot be changed. And I finally realize that it is not blood that binds. It is love.

~Cynthia Blatchford

Chapter 7

Thanks Dad

Making the Ties that Bind

The Cheslatta River Race

Don't wait to make your son a great man—make him a great boy.
~Author Unknown

There is something about shared pain that can bring two people closer together. In this case the two people were my dad and me, and the pain was a canoe race.

My parents split up when I was young. I ended up moving to the city with my mom and my sister, so I didn't get to see my dad nearly as often as I would have liked. Summer was great because my sister and I spent several weeks visiting him out in the middle of nowhere in central British Columbia where we would go fishing, horseback riding, hiking, camping and canoeing. The quantity of time we spent together may have been low, but the quality was always high.

Sometimes I question if the river race was one of those high-quality moments. My arms hurt just thinking about it.

I was fifteen and not an athlete, so actually using my muscles to engage in competition was a new experience. My dad and I had spent many an hour in the canoe, but not in fast-flowing water and never in a hurry. Entering the Cheslatta River Race was my idea, and an impromptu affair that was more of an excuse for a bunch of people to have a party than a real competition. The event was mostly populated by people in tubes and rafts, only some of whom bothered to use paddles. My dad and I, however, opted to be one of the four teams who wanted to go fast.

I sized up the other canoe racers. There was little doubt that first would be taken by the two men with the high-tech canoe that looked fast just sitting there on the beach. I was also certain that second belonged to my dad's German friends, Klaus and Dieter, who were big, strong forestry workers. Granted, their boat looked to be older than dirt, and held together with duct tape, but I figured their logging-sculpted muscles could power a Buick down the river at a good pace.

The last of our competitors was another father-son team, and we seemed to be evenly matched in physical size and quality of watercraft.

"Looks like we're battling for third," Dad gave voice to my thoughts.

Soon after, the race got underway and I blew it.

I'm not sure what I did wrong, but my coordinative abilities reverted to that of a six-week-old puppy. We launched ourselves toward the first turn and I nearly capsized us. The canoe dipped perilously close to the waterline and we ended up with eight inches of water in the bottom of our boat.

"Beach it!" my dad called out from the rear. "Starboard side!"

We ran the canoe aground and leapt out to dump the water. "Sorry, Dad," I said as we climbed back in. The other teams were all rapidly disappearing from view down the river.

"Don't sweat it. We'll catch them."

I wasn't feeling so optimistic, but I dug in with all my strength in the hopes that we wouldn't be the last ones across the finish line. Fortunately, we had a long straight stretch after our near swim, and I was able to get a feel for how to handle the canoe in rough water before we came to the next turn. My dad called out instructions and encouragement from the rear. "Hard right! That's it, dig in! We're gaining on them."

And we were. The other father-son team looked a lot closer.

The dwindling gap and my dad's exhortations motivated me to paddle harder. My shoulders ached already, but after a while they went numb and operated more on autopilot. About halfway into the race, we caught up to third place, coming around a sharp turn where I almost blew it again.

I was anxious to pass these guys, but my dad stopped me before I could cause another catastrophe. "Hang back," he said. "We'll pass them in the straight stretch."

And so we did.

They didn't let us pass without a fight, but my dad and I poured on the gas and we took over third place. I was determined to not lose it; we'd fought hard to make it that far and I had the sense that my arms could last the rest of the race. There was no question in my mind that my dad's would.

I was happy.

Then I saw Klaus and Dieter not far beyond, and I felt another competitive surge of adrenaline. "Let's catch them."

My dad laughed in that way of his that couldn't help but shake the canoe. "I'm game if you are."

Klaus and Dieter may have been tough as nails, but so is my dad. It was a brutal battle of screaming shoulders and creaking vertebrae. We paddled hard to catch them, but when they saw us pull up along-side, their pride would not let us beat them. They had looks of hard determination, refusing to lose to a team that included a teenage city boy. For a few seconds we inched ahead and were in second place, but they renewed their efforts and matched us again.

We hit shore simultaneously to a cheering crowd, and the final torture began. To complete the race we had to carry the canoe over 200 feet off beach and cross the finish line. I jumped out, grabbed the front handle and started to run, but my dad knew better. We may have been able to match them in the water because of our better boat, but he realized we didn't have a hope against them carrying it across land. "It's okay," he said. "We got third. We gave them a good run."

Klaus and Dieter had taken off like two kids who had just heard the school bell ring on a Friday afternoon, and I could see that he was right. Still, I felt victorious because I never knew we could make it so close.

We jogged across the finish line and my dad and I shared a bear hug. Then he gave me a mischievous grin and said, "That was fun."

And he was right. It was fun.

An hour later I was feeling sore and exhausted and working my way through my third hot dog when my dad came up to me. "You've got a big glob of mustard on your face," he said.

I was about to tell him that I was too tired to care, when his eyes flicked off to my left. I took the hint and looked to see Mariah, my teenage crush, walking toward us.

Unlike a mother who would have grabbed my chin and meticulously cleaned my face with a spit-moistened tissue, my dad was discreet. He cupped a handkerchief, did a quick wipe of the mustard then turned the movement into a shoulder clasp.

He spun me toward Mariah, still gripping my aching shoulder, and said, "This boy paddled his heart out today." Then he walked away.

Mariah gave me a smile. "I saw you finish. You almost beat Klaus and Dieter."

I could have said many different things at that point, or I could have suffered from a tongue-tied teenager attack, but I opted to give credit where it was due.

"My dad did most of the work."

~James S. Fell

The Man
Who Learned to Unravel

Memories are stitched with love.
~Author Unknown

Growing up in my family, fiber arts was always the exclusive property of the women. I'm still not sure exactly why. My dad was a feminist who never denigrated knitting as "women's work" in any way; I know he actively cheered when my mother put knitting needles into the hands of all the boys in my brother's Boy Scout troop. But for all of his support, he consistently turned down any opportunity to learn how to knit himself. And so whenever Saturday afternoon rolled around and it was time for a family "fun" trip, it was always just my mother and I who ended up at the yarn store. My dad and my brothers would go off to do something else.

Now, from a daughter's point of view, this was wonderful. It meant that my mother and I had something that was exclusively ours to share, and many of the inevitable bumps and bruises of my adolescence got talked over during those weekly yarn shopping trips. Still, it meant that my dad was somewhat left out—a problem that really didn't become apparent until I moved back home after college, the only child to return to the family nest. The moment my boxes were unpacked, my mom and I picked up our old Saturday yarn shopping tradition right where we'd left off, and this time we added a twist—we'd rent a comedy or mystery movie that we'd watch while we worked on our various knitting projects.

At first, my dad claimed he was only joining us to watch the movie. However, as the weeks went by I noticed him looking less and less at the screen and more and more at whatever projects were growing in our laps. He started listening to our quiet discussions about colors and fiber contents with a curiously wistful look on his face, a wistfulness that only grew as he learned just how much knitting gave my mom and me to talk about, and how close those conversations drew us together. Then came the day when I started loading the coffee table with an entire stack of newly purchased skeins, the beginnings of a sweater I was planning. "Don't those need to be wound into balls or something?" my dad asked. "I used to do that for your mom sometimes, before you kids were born."

In truth, the yarn didn't need to be rewound at all. All the skeins were factory-created pull skeins, not the loose hanks my dad was remembering from the late 1960s. But that wistful look on his face was back, and I nodded—after all, what could it hurt? I gave him a skein and a quick lesson in winding. He waved me away, claiming that my mother had taught him the basics long before I'd been born. And we all settled into our projects, I knitting, Dad winding, and Mom crocheting in the corner.

I must admit I had some doubts about what the yarn my father wound was going to look like. Nevertheless, when the movie ended, he presented me with a tight, perfectly formed little ball that took up half the space of the original skein. When Mom and I complimented him, my dad shrugged awkwardly. "It's better than sitting here doing nothing," he said gruffly. Then he eyed the rest of my skeins with sudden hope. "Want me to do the rest?"

And so a new tradition was born. For the next few months, whenever movie time came, my dad would patiently rewind skeins while Mom and I knitted. Unfortunately, it's possible for a determined man to wind more balls of yarns than even the world's most devoted knitter can work through in the same amount of time, and eventually my dad had worked through all the yarn in our collection, including all the leftover odds and ends in my mom's forty-year-old stash. The whole family was left with a serious problem. What else could a non-knitter do to keep his hands in what had become the family hobby?

The problem was solved the day that I discovered I'd made a terrible mistake in my sweater. I'm afraid I was rather noisy about my frustration; my mom ended up pausing the movie so she could see if she could help. Unfortunately, there was no way to salvage the mistake, and several inches of knitting had to be unraveled. "But I hate unraveling," I complained. "It's one thing in crochet, where you can just rip a row out without worrying about dropping any stitches. But knitting's different."

My mom just gave me the smile of a woman who'd had to unravel a million stitches in her time and went back to work, leaving me to stop complaining and get on with my task. But Dad, who had been listening to the whole exchange, suddenly straightened. "Could you teach me how to do it?" he asked. "That way you could move on to something more fun."

Both my mom and I blinked at him in disbelief. Then I realized just what a gift I was being handed. "Absolutely," I said. After a quick tutorial in the art of the "frog" stitch, my dad got started. And this time, when the movie ended, I received a perfectly unraveled sweater, not so much as a single stitch dropped. Not only that, but the unraveled yarn was neatly wound into its very own ball. "I already knew how to do that part," my dad said with a twinkle. He was rewarded with a huge hug from his grateful daughter.

My dad now considers himself the official "support staff" for all of our craft endeavors. Thus far, he's resisted our efforts to teach him how to crochet or knit for himself, but the last time we went to a craft fair, he spent a lot of time looking at the spinning wheel displays. "At the rate you and your mom go through yarn, it would really be helpful if someone in the family knew how to spin, wouldn't it?" he said.

It would indeed.

~Kerrie R. Barney

Love in a T-Square

Put your heart, mind, intellect and soul even to your smallest acts.
This is the secret of success.
~Swami Sivananda

"**Y**ou know what they say, Sheila?" asked Dad as he neatly set out his lumber, workhorses and assorted tools. "Plan your work and work your plan."

He grabbed a piece of paper and a pencil and proceeded to sketch the stairs we were building for the hill behind my parents' lakefront home. I caught the tail end of a "gotcha" grin on his face.

It was a cool, overcast day in early October, the peak of autumn in northern Michigan, when Dad invited me to assist on this project. I was an independent adult, home for a weekend visit, and I welcomed the opportunity to learn from the master craftsman. But I understood this rare invitation meant I was to stand quietly at attention and follow orders.

We started after breakfast. He wore his charcoal-gray overalls, the ones he donned for serious work like pulling in the dock or hauling brush. A hawk soared above and squirrels scurried about. After we set the posts, he proceeded to notch the stringers.

"Hold this," he said, offering me a two-by-eight.

He lowered his safety glasses. I flinched, waiting for the piercing buzz of the saw, but instead, Dad put down the saw and grabbed the tape measure.

"Measure twice, cut once," he said.

As he pushed the saw through the board, I breathed in the sweet smell of freshly cut lumber and watched sawdust pile on the ground.

My dad was a veterinarian but his hobby was woodworking and he conducted his life with the precision and forethought of a master carpenter. Reticent and highly disciplined, he liked things neat and orderly. His patience was often tested in a family of six children. I remember watching him at his workbench in the garage, his lips pursed in deep concentration. If I stood quietly, without interrupting, he would let me tighten the vise, or try my hand at wielding a hammer.

Though his stern demeanor intimidated me, I respected his skill and talent. When he assigned me a chore, it meant I would have to perform it to his high standards. I paid close attention to his specific instructions for everything from holding a screwdriver to painting (he taught me to punch evenly spaced holes along the gutter of a paint can to catch the overrun).

I paid attention that day when we built the stairs. Like a nurse assisting a surgeon, I obediently handed him tools as he called for them. He cut the treads and showed me how to toenail them to the stringers by pounding the nails at an angle. We spent all day working quietly together except for Dad's periodic instructions. Our task completed, we carefully returned the tools to their assigned spots.

"Put your tools away and leave your workspace clean," he reminded me.

I followed him down the new set of stairs and into the house where we sat at the kitchen table eating butter pecan ice cream and taking pride in a job well done.

He studied a spoonful of ice cream before putting it in his mouth and, without looking at me, uttered the words that contributed to a solid sense of self-esteem that has steadied me through many a trying time.

"Good job."

Dad didn't dole out those words frivolously. When he said, "Good job," he meant it, and his approval comforted me more than a hug. When he praised my work, I felt an intoxicating sense of confidence.

Those occasions when I had the good fortune to work with Dad offered much more than carpentry lessons, more than practical advice on life—plan ahead, double check your work and clean up your messes.

Working side-by-side with Dad allowed me to watch him bask in the sheer joy of work, to catch the twinkle in his eye, to share his sense of pride, to see him as the incredibly smart and talented man that he was. I felt closest to Dad when he let me into his world of tools and do-it-yourself projects.

Those moments were a gift, and they will remain in my memory the way a goodbye kiss lingers in the heart.

~Sheila M. Myers

71

The Best Gift of All

Kids spell love T-I-M-E.
~John Crudele

"**L**ook! There's Dave Righetti!" My dad pointed at the taller of the two men leaving Cleveland Municipal Stadium. It was dusk and shadows had started to creep up the pavement, leaving us in cool summer shade.

"Really?" I stared at the Yankees pitcher. We'd been waiting for a half hour for the players to shower, change and head out so that I could nab some autographs.

"Go!" my dad said, but I was already scooting towards Rags, my ball and pen in hand. When I returned to my dad, triumphantly holding the signed baseball in the air, my dad leaned down and said, "Did you know that was Steve Sax with him?"

The second baseman? I gasped, spinning around, but the Yankees had already disappeared. "Darn." My dad laughed and clapped a hand on my shoulder. Maybe next time.

At twelve years old, this was the first of many annual weekends my dad and I took to Cleveland to watch the Yankees play—and try to get autographs. It became our father-daughter thing. Sometime in March, my dad and I would examine the Major League baseball schedule and see when our Yanks were going to be in Cleveland, only four hours from home. In the meantime, we'd check box scores in the paper together and stay up to watch games on TV.

And once the warm weather came around, we'd take the long

drive to Cleveland, talking about baseball, school, and my softball season. My dad, baseball guru that he was, was also my coach.

"Line up the knuckles on your left hand with those on the right. Choke up about an inch on the bat. There." Dad adjusted my hands as we stood together in the empty ballfield, the summer sun blazing on our backs. He'd just returned from a weekend coaches' camp and had acquired some new tips for improving my batting average. Somehow, those tips were magic. Dad jogged to the mound and lobbed me a pitch. I swung, the crack of the bat a sweet, satisfying sound. The ball flew over the dirt and landed—plunk—in the grass of right-center. Dad nodded, smiling.

"Again," I said, checking my grip on the bat, making sure the knuckles were still exactly right. "Throw me another."

Later that summer, I hit my first home run and my dad caught me as I leapt into his arms after crossing home plate.

"That hit felt good," I said, hugging him hard.

"It sure looked good." Dad grinned as widely as I did and I think he probably was just as happy.

Over the next six years, my dad watched me hit dozens more home runs and take All-Star and MVP status in various tournaments on various teams. He attended every game either as coach or spectator and helped me fine-tune my stance as well as my confidence over the years.

We continued our trips to Cleveland as well as other places. "Do you want to fly out to Kansas to see K-State?" he asked one spring Saturday when I was fifteen.

In the kitchen, my mom raised her eyebrows, glancing at my dad.

"I'll take her," he continued. "I wouldn't mind going back to see my Alma Mater. We can check flights this afternoon."

"Sure!" I agreed. Why not? I'd never been that far west and I'd wanted to see where my parents attended college. And who knew—maybe I'd like the school enough to apply.

And so we went. My dad and I. We sat side-by-side in the airplane, chatting mostly about my life as a sophomore in high school:

teachers I liked, the economics class that made me want to cry, friends, sports, and the future. We were comrades in the rental car, on the campus, getting lost and finding our way again. When I needed an emergency trip to the eye doctor because a fleck of metal had gotten caught in my eye, my dad inquired about where to go and took us there. He took care of me.

After that weekend, I knew I couldn't go to college that far from home.

My dad isn't known for wrapping Christmas or birthday presents, let alone picking them out. That's my mom's job and she does it quite well. But the gifts my dad gave me growing up—college visits, baseball games, a better batting stance, advice, laughter, confidence—created memories that are more valuable than any bracelet or pair of socks.

Now when my dad comes to visit my family, he spends hours rolling around on the floor with my son, making him laugh, pushing him on the swing in the park, or reading to him on the couch. On his most recent visit to Boston—over six hours from his home where I grew up—my dad said, "I'd love to coach Aidan in Little League. I wish we lived closer." To our home, he brought books and new footie pajamas that my mom had picked out, but from him—well, he brought himself. And that was good enough.

For almost thirty-three years, my dad has given me more than any father could. He gave me what a child ultimately finds most precious from her parents. It's the stuff memories are made of, of which photographs are taken and cataloged over the years. What I wouldn't trade for anything is exactly what my dad gave me and what is sometimes, for some people, the hardest thing to give. But he gave it freely, happily, and as often as possible.

My dad gave me—and continues to give me—his time. And for that, I am most thankful.

~Mary Jo Marcellus Wyse

72

Breakfast

Old as she was, she still missed her daddy sometimes.
~Gloria Naylor

"**W**ell, hello!"

"Morning."

My father reaches into the top pocket of his shirt and pulls out a five-dollar bill before I can even consider reaching into my purse for my wallet. Every day that he has been in town since the day after Christmas, I have stopped by the McDonald's on De Renne Avenue, which he frequents whenever he is in Savannah visiting me. It is a simple affair: he is always there first, finished with his sausage biscuit and coffee, his eyes focused on the newspaper in front of him, pen in hand, reading glasses balanced on his nose, looking unassuming when I walk in. I am no surprise at this point—he has been in town for a week, leaving my house early each day to "get out of the way" as I prepare my daughter for school—and I am tickled that each morning he raises his head from his crossword puzzle to watch me as I approach his table, his whole countenance lighting up as if my coming were a surprise.

"Thank you," I say as I take the five-dollar bill. Our faces wear expressions of mutual pleasure, and I enjoy being surprised with every visit that he is Daddy again, reveling in the fact that this means that I get to be a daughter again. Not wife, or mother or teacher. Not dishwashing machine expert. Just daughter. For this morning, I get to just be a girl.

As I approach the counter where the menu glows above me,

seeming more to me like a five-star restaurant than a fast-food joint, the scents of sizzling buttered things tickle my nose and I feel comforted by the robotic buzzing of soda machine beverages trickling into plastic cups. Since I no longer have a childhood home, or kitchen, to meet my father in for breakfast, this has become a surrogate home, and it is really fine by me.

Here, there are no memories of family arguments or reminders that the room is too light or too dark or needs updating. There is only us, the gentle chorus of laughter from the post-holiday retirees who also frequent this popular spot at their usual tables, and my father's five-dollar bill between us, which I use each morning to buy the same favorites: a breakfast combo #1: one egg McMuffin, a hash brown, and a sugary-brown Coke that bubbles through the straw into my mouth and wakes up my still-sleepy eyes.

Over these meals, my father and I talk. We debate politics and finances, share a newspaper, and review the past. We are interrupted only by the casual comment my father makes to a person passing by: "Need any help with that?" he says to the woman with a walker who is struggling to squeeze by the Christmas tree, or "How 'bout today's crowd? Pretty good today, eh?" to the mustached-manager of the McDonald's with whom he has become friends.

But my favorite topic of conversation over our meal is my father's memories.

"I was the fastest thing in Darlington County," he says, and his eyes light up like they have fire in them as he reminisces about playing football, about how playing for St. John's High School in South Carolina was the closest thing to pure glory he had ever known. He reminds me of just how fast he was as he trades his crooked smile for a grimace, shifting in his seat since "that bad shoulder has taken to aching again."

We sit at a small square table as close to the direct sunlight as we can get. My father positions himself in a way that the sun's rays scissor straight down upon his bad shoulder and hip through the restaurant glass, this portrait of him sitting there reminding me of a cat. My father the cat, who could once sprint across a football field like one, like a mean cougar, and who now stretches his limbs under the small restaurant table so that the sun can massage away the aches of too many years of work and sacrifice and miles of football fields.

The morning hours pass into the afternoon. How long since I first strolled in to see him sitting here? The egg McMuffin and sausage biscuits have long been eaten, coffees and Cokes filled and re-filled, and my father's ritual of pulling out the breakfast "dessert" before I get up to leave has now come: homemade ice-lemon cake from an old neighbor who lived across the street from my childhood home.

"Just one slice," he requests before I go, pulling out the plastic knife to make the incision.

I have one small slice, and it is delicious. But I certainly don't need it. I just want to enjoy the taste. But not the taste of the ice-lemon. I want one last tangible experience of my father. One for the road. Tomorrow he leaves.

With the final serving of the lemon cake come a few more stories about him as a boy, and I can't resist. I chew my cake. I close my eyes and listen to his laugh—the mix of a rumbling clearing of his throat and a wise-cracking guffaw. I memorize this laugh, soaking it in like the warmth of the sun flowing in through the restaurant glass that is covered up by decorative holiday paintings of snowmen and candy canes. As I rise from my seat to return to the rigors of life, I am filled with gladness and comfort. Whether I am age five or thirty-five, my father still rescues me sometimes from life's responsibilities and feeds me breakfast, and in the process, nourishes both my appetite and my spirit.

~Donna Buie Beall

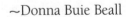

73

Coach

When you teach your son, you teach your son's son.
~The Talmud

"**G**o Steffie!" The cheer, followed by a deep, throaty cough, buoyed me somehow. Skating around the rink in my sassy red rhinestone-embellished competition dress, I tried to stay focused on my warm-up routine. *Forget the other skaters. It's just me out here. Do a toe loop and get the feel of the ice.*

Cool air rushed through my lungs as I stepped into a simple scratch spin.

Dizzy but exhilarated, I barely remembered to hold my pose. Skating judges were known to get an early glimpse of the competition by viewing practice sessions. *Could that smiling gentleman with the clipboard be making a few notations already?*

"Welcome to the Tri-State Figure Skating Championship," the announcer boomed. "Skaters in Juvenile Ladies have three minutes remaining in the warm-up."

Twelve-year-old skating pixies twirled, their perfectly French-braided hair flying as they tried to fulfill the demands of overbearing coaches.

"Do the Lutz again," a bejeweled lady in a full-length mink barked over the hockey boards at her protégé. "And this time, don't forget to breathe."

"Of course you can skate first and still get the gold," another instructor assured her medal-hungry student.

Gliding over to the boards, I looked up at my coach for this event: my father. Standing at the boards, Dad wore his best brown tweed sport coat—the one with a coordinated rust-colored silk hankie peeking from the outer pocket. Dad smelled of his ever-present warm cherry wood tobacco and a dab or two of the Old Spice cologne I had bought him for Christmas. This dapper gentleman could easily have passed as a revered skating coach. Little did the other skaters know that Dad was a regular guy with a steady job at a chemical plant, a wife and two daughters, and a simple home in suburban Cleveland.

Sure, he had skated a time or two with my older sister, but Dad's real passion was Cleveland Browns football, not figure skating. So why was he here, in Michigan, acting as my coach at Tri-States? And why did I feel so at home and comfortable, without my usual racing heart and head full of negative thoughts?

Quickly, I ran through my two-minute routine, getting a feel for the slick, freshly Zamboni-clean ice.

"Go Stef!" I heard my mom and sister shout from their seats high atop the metal bleachers. But it was Dad who stood nearest, a solid rock of support, his very presence somehow softening my usually stiff, jittery leg muscles. Axel, Axel, Axel. I repeated the jump, amazed at how effortless the landings seemed. Even my usually nauseous, queasy stomach was under control. When the announcer called, "Skaters, please leave the ice," I knew I was ready.

"You'll skate third," Dad said, handing me my pink skate guards. "You looked good out there!"

With a pile of fifth and sixth place consolation ribbons sitting at home, I knew I was no Dorothy Hamill. My jumps were often "cheated" or two-footed, which didn't bode well with figure skating judges. But I still loved to skate. Nothing compared to the soaring feeling of stroking around the ice, cool air flying in my face. Nothing compared to my program music—"Ave Maria"—a spiritual piece that filled my heart to bursting. And I knew that no coach in the world compared to Dad. He would love me no matter what—win or lose. Unlike my "real" coach, who couldn't rearrange her travel plans to accommodate a Juvenile skater, Dad stood by me. Despite the chilly arena air, I felt oddly warm inside.

"The next skater, representing the Euclid Blade and Edge Club — Stefanie Sper!"

"Go get 'em," Dad called out, giving me a quick kiss on the cheek.

On the ice, a magical feeling took over. Joy flew through my veins as I stepped into a sit spin. Smiling widely, I picked up speed for my first jump, a backward-entrance Lutz. After picking my toe into the ice, my body was supposed to whirl one revolution in the air before landing again on the same thin steel blade. To my surprise, my toe went into the ice, but my body refused to lift.

"Oops." Though he stood at the opposite end of the arena, I could almost hear Dad's voice pulling me forward: "You can do it. Just turn around and keep going." I knew I had to nail my next move, a spread eagle, followed by an Axel-loop combination.

"Yeah, Stef!" Dad's voice called out as I whirled past the hockey boards, preparing for my most difficult jump. Adrenaline, a father's support, and sheer determination worked together as I jumped, this time lifting into the air and returning for a clean landing.

A flip jump, some footwork, and soon it was time for my final scratch spin. Though my program had been far from perfect, I lifted my arms in victory, feeling like an Olympian. On a high from the inspiring music, the invigorating arena air, and freedom from my coach's scrutiny, I hurried into Dad's waiting arms.

"Great job, honey," he reassured me.

"Yeah, but I messed up the Lutz."

"You'll always be number one in my book," he smiled.

A half hour later, as the final competition results were thumb-tacked to the hallway bulletin board, Dad quickly lifted two big fingers in the air. Second place! I was a silver medalist! Jumping up and down, I gestured wildly into the stands at my mother and sister, holding up two fingers on each hand.

"Wow, fourth place! Good job," Mom exclaimed as she made her way down from the bleachers.

"No! I got second! I got second!" I screamed. "The silver!"

As I stood on the podium and bent forward to receive my glistening silver medal, I tried to take it all in: my sister proudly taking flash photos, Mom quietly smiling, and Dad beaming in the wonder of the moment.

It was, in fact, a small miracle. I was no athlete, and never again would earn a medal in ladies figure skating. Perhaps my success that day was a fluke. But my heart tells me that something else was at play—a father's steadying presence, a comforting calm in the often slippery world of figure skating.

My favorite coach is no longer by my side. Cherry tobacco aromas, once warm and nurturing, now seem bittersweet. Emphysema, a steady, silent criminal, robbed Dad of breath, life, and the chance to know my own daughters. But as my two little girls skate around our neighborhood ice rink, I can still hear Dad's voice echoed in my own words:

"That's the way! Good job! Keep your arms out for balance!"

As my daughters tumble onto the hard, unforgiving surface, I hurry to their side.

"It's okay," I say, dusting ice shavings off their knees. "Let's take a break and try again later."

Skating glory, after all, is short-lived. But a parent's love and support? That legacy can last forever.

~Stefanie Wass

74

The Garage

*Some of the most important conversations I've ever had
occurred at my family's dinner table.*

~Bob Ehrlich

As we sat and ate dinner in the garage, it occurred to me that we were not like most families. Surrounding this dinner table were baseball hats, war memorabilia and beer steins. We sat in a garage heated by an old woodstove, and cooled by a sliding window above the countertop where my father sat in his favorite barstool. This was the kind of place that was warm, inviting and where every stray dog, cat and person could easily find a warm place to sit and a cold beer to drink.

Dinners here were special. They often, but not always, had a purpose. A big promotion, new job, new house or new friend would be reason enough to put out a big spread of cheese and crackers, coleslaw and meat of some kind on the handmade table. Tonight, we would gather to remind each other that we were family. Tonight, we would talk and laugh, all to avoid a more serious issue that was looming over us. As a family, we were facing Dad's cancer surgery, and as a family, we gathered in our meeting place to enjoy each other's company.

The garage was special. If walls could talk, I wondered what secrets they would share. They had definitely heard of hard times, worries and shortcomings. They had had their share of good news as well. All sorts of events were celebrated in the garage, and even a perfect summer day or magnificent snowstorm would be cause for celebration. On one night, an unexpected blizzard blew through town and we laughed, telling stories until the snow piled up so high outside we were all stranded at Mom and Dad's house. The wood-stove popped, the window frosted up and we enjoyed the magic of family and the solace of the garage.

Part of its magic was that it did not discriminate. The garage had held us together during the most trying of times. Together, we sat in silence at the loss of those closest to us, and wonderment as to the reasons that must exist for sudden passing. We watched the Red Sox do the unthinkable, and then only days later we gathered to deal with a personal crisis. We watched in silence as our nation was attacked, and prayed even when praying was not what we were best at. What most people did individually, we did as a family, in the garage.

By looking at it, it was certainly nothing special. No fancy deco-rations adorned its walls and the furniture was either handmade or handed down. It was special, though. The garage was a safe place. It was a place to share secrets, problems and great stories. It was in the garage that I learned how to heal from a broken heart, how to ask for help, and how to listen with both ears. It was there that I learned the secret of life.

As we sat around, laughing and sharing stories of long ago moments, I caught my father's eye. I saw something I had never seen before. He was sitting back in his tall bar chair admiring his family. (My father's family extended well beyond blood relations. He wel-comed friends and neighbors into his family and never let anyone forget how lucky he felt to have such wonderful people in his life.) As he sat quietly, listening to us jokingly discuss what it was like to grow up in a Polish, English and Irish household, his eyes glistened. It was then that I knew that he, too, had learned the secret of life.

The garage had given us a place to grow up, grow old and grow together. Although an outsider may think it odd that we ate in the garage, anyone who knew us would see something different. It was in that garage that we were most ourselves. We were family.

~Christine A. Brooks

75

Dad's Tomatoes

Many things grow in the garden that were never sown there.
~Thomas Fuller

My father was always an avid gardener. I think his Irish blood called to the earth in much the same way his own grandfather's had. One of my earliest memories is standing barefoot in the freshly tilled soil, my hands blackened from digging in the ground, still a bit cold from the turning. As a small child, the garden was an amazing fairyland, full of possibility. As a teenager, though, it was often a source of contention between the old man and me.

As a child, I loved following Dad around in the garden. I remember Daddy pushing the tiller ahead in perfectly straight lines. His gardening gloves, banana yellow, would grip the handles of the old tiller; the roar of the machine was pleasantly deafening. After a while, he would stop and pull the gloves off to wipe his brow. Daddy loved growing all sorts of things: yellow and green onions, watermelons almost as big as me, rows and rows of yellow corn, and our favorite—ruby red tomatoes.

As I grew into a cantankerous teenager, I didn't get so excited about gardening with Daddy. Instead of the magical land of possibility, it had turned into some kind of medieval prison. It was one extra chore, one more thing to keep me busy and out of trouble. One more thing on a list of demands that I imagined no one else in the world had to deal with.

Dad would say, "Tina, come help me plant the garden today. It's a beautiful morning to be outdoors."

"Aww, Dad, I was going to the movies with my friends," I would whine.

"Tina, I could sure use a hand weeding the garden today," he would remark.

"Today? Sorry, Dad, I already made plans," I would stubbornly say, digging in my heels. "Why do we have to have a garden, anyway? It's stupid. You can buy carrots for a quarter at the grocery store," I would point out. He would just smile knowingly. I usually got my way, and didn't have to help out if I really didn't want to. After all, I had better things to do with my time.

As Dad grew older, his passion for gardening never waned. After all the kids were grown and had started families of their own, Dad turned to gardening like never before. His garden took up most of his backyard, which was quite a stretch. Even when he was diagnosed with stage four kidney cancer, he still put out his garden. Still, he planted the zucchini and yellow squash, the juicy cucumbers, the spicy jalapenos, and of course, the tender tomato plants. Sometimes, I would come over to visit, and we would enjoy a glass of iced tea or a cold soda on the patio while he lovingly watered his garden in the evenings. The sunlight reflected off the spraying water and created shimmering rainbows that played hide and seek on the grass. He would share the bounty of his garden with me, as we would walk together through the carefully weeded rows.

But then, something changed. Like the weeds he so carefully kept from his little patch of heaven, the cancer, bit by bit, invaded his body. Like the weeds, it stole his livelihood, his independence, his humor. Like the weeds that took over his garden, the cancer grew rampant in Dad, and the oncologist had run out of treatments.

Hospice is a whole other ballgame. Somebody has to be with the family member twenty-four hours a day. I found myself in all kinds of uncomfortable situations with Dad, and more than once I felt the brunt of his anger at his helplessness. Little by little, I had to do the things he used to do. Soon I was cutting his grass, paying his bills, putting his pills in a cup, and adjusting his oxygen. These things he resisted, but I knew things were definitely changing when I began caring for the garden.

Though I had heard the words of the oncologist as well, what really convinced me that Dad was dying was the state of his garden that year. That year, the rows and rows of multicolored vegetables were gone. That year, he only planted tomatoes. Too tired to weed them, he simply tied them with twine to the fence and let them be. It made me sad to see them neglected, so I would come over and water them occasionally, and pluck out the weeds. I still remember the day I picked the last tomato from the vine. That day was one of the saddest I had ever experienced.

Five years ago, Dad planted his last little patch of tomatoes. For the first few years after he died, I couldn't even bear to look at anyone's garden without having strong memories pour over me like cold water from a bucket. Three years ago, though, something changed, and I decided to plant my own garden. I decided I would start out with just a few tomatoes.

That morning, I got out the old tiller and it roared to life, almost as if it had been waiting. After breaking up a fair amount of soil, something caught the corner of my eye and I had to smile. It was my eight-year-old son Nathan, standing barefoot in the freshly tilled soil, his hands blackened from digging in the earth. He was happily playing in the freshly tilled soil, still a bit cold from the turning.

~Tina Bausinger

76

Alaskan Adventure

An adventure is only an inconvenience rightly considered. An inconvenience is only an adventure wrongly considered.
~G.K. Chesterton

He wanted to go to Alaska, and he couldn't go alone. My father had been stationed there while in the Army, and now, so many years later, he wanted to go back, this time for pleasure. But an illness in that same Army led to the eventual loss of his hearing, and now his near deafness made traveling alone virtually impossible.

Naturally he turned to his family for company on the trip. My brother and sister had summer obligations already that year that caused them to decline. My mother didn't like to camp and preferred desert heat to glacier ice. So he turned to me and I enthusiastically signed on. A lover of the outdoors, I looked forward to the adventure—three weeks of driving and camping up the western edge of North America, this back in the days when most of the highway to Alaska was still just a gravel road. We planned to leave immediately following my college graduation that June.

There was just one problem. I got a job. Not just temporary summer employment—I was hired by a privately-owned paper company for a position from which I could travel the career path I'd mapped out in college. My new employer wanted me to report to work immediately and I promised to show up on time, mentally canceling the trip to Alaska.

Taking the job was the logical thing to do. It didn't make sense to go to college for four years, endure the strain of countless job interviews and then turn down the very career opportunity I'd been looking for. There would be other vacation invitations from my dad. Accepting the position was the right course of action for this time in my life. At least it seemed to be so... until I saw the look on my father's face when I gave him the news. All of a sudden the decision was settled in my heart rather than in my head. I simply loved my dad too much to put my choice over his.

Without another word, I called my new boss and explained the situation. If he couldn't hold the position for me for the three weeks I'd be traveling, then he'd simply have to give it to somebody else. I knew he wouldn't have any difficulty with the latter choice—career opportunities in the field of forestry at that time were few and far between, and there were many more job applicants than positions available to them.

It turned out to be the right decision. That trip to Alaska was absolutely incredible. The scenery seemed to get more beautiful with every passing mile. We ate meals at the side of beautiful lakes or in little diners we found scattered along the side of the road. Camping was a constantly challenging but enjoyable adventure as we learned how to set up our tent in record time during thunderstorms and dressed like space aliens in the mosquito net hoods we wore to protect us from the swarms of pesky insects.

We conquered the worst the Alaskan Highway could (quite literally) throw at us—the stones that cracked our windshield and popped our tires, the bugs that were soon plastered over our windows, lights and radiator grill. We even learned to sleep when the sun was still bright in the nighttime sky. And our excitement mounted as we drew ever closer to our destination, until we were cheering wildly as we crossed the Canadian border into Alaska.

But the best part of the trip wasn't the incredible scenery or our activities along the way. It was what happened between my dad and me. We bonded in a way that I doubt we ever could have had we not traveled the Alaskan Highway together. Not that everything between us went smoothly from the start. I was a difficult traveling companion at first. I was terribly homesick for college life and the friends and good times I'd left behind. I'm also sure I felt at least a little bit of resentment over having to put my own plans aside to accommodate my father's. I freely admit I wasn't much fun in the early days of the vacation, but my dad waited me out. Thankfully my moodiness didn't last long. It was impossible to resist the beauty surrounding me, the adventures awaiting me, and the father's love enveloping me. Soon those long periods of moody silence in the car were replaced by jokes and laughter, stories and tall tales galore, hours spent studying maps, taking naps or stopping for snacks. I loved it all.

I look back on that trip now, and rejoice again at the wonderful time we had together. I shudder to think of what I'd have missed had I insisted on keeping my own plans for that summer. As it turned out, my employer did hold my position open for me, and I worked for that company for eight wonderful years in various capacities before moving on to other opportunities.

When I chose to honor my father's wishes above my own, I truly got the best of both worlds.

~Elaine L. Bridge

77

Dodging Failure

Love is the most important thing in the world,
but baseball is pretty good too.
~Greg, age 8

We lived in Brooklyn, five blocks from Ebbets Field, and I was a rabid Dodgers fan. To paraphrase a future Dodgers manager, when I cut myself, I bled Dodgers blue. I was ten years old in 1947. I could quote the statistics of all the players, including their batting averages, fielding percentages and ERAs. I even knew how the prospects in the Dodgers farm system were doing. My father wished that I knew as much about my schoolwork.

During the season, I'd see the end of most home games because they let the kids in free after the seventh inning. I even managed to sneak into a few games after the first inning, when the ticket takers weren't looking. I saw other children scream in their fathers' ears as they watched the game. But I had never gone to a game with my father. When the Dodgers were on the road, I'd be out in the street, practicing my swing with a broomstick and a Spalding ball.

That year, I had high hopes for my Dodgers bringing their first world championship back to Brooklyn. I was devastated when they lost again to the hated Yankees. My father was unsympathetic. "Why do you spend all your time on this foolishness? You'd be better off studying hard and make something of yourself—be a doctor."

"I want to be a baseball player and play for the Dodgers," I said.

The look of disappointment on my father's face became ingrained in my memory. Why couldn't he understand my love for baseball?

Later, I learned that my father had immigrated to this country at the age of eighteen, leaving his parents behind in Russia. He couldn't speak English and he had no high school diploma. In seven years, going to school mostly at night and working during the day, he obtained a high school equivalency certificate, completed college and received a master's degree in chemical engineering. That's why he had no tolerance for wasting hours in nonacademic pursuits. At the time, though, I didn't understand and was deeply hurt by his actions. I wished that I could share my passion for baseball with him.

When the 1948 season started, I continued badgering my father to take me to a baseball game. His response remained constant. "I don't have time for that foolishness." My reaction also remained constant. I pouted but didn't let that stop me from sneaking into games or honing my baseball skills with my trusty broom handle.

When my teacher handed me the next to last report card for the year, it was pretty much the same as all the rest. On the academic side, I received outstanding for math, science and geography, and "satisfactory" for history, art, and English. On the deportment side, I had a number of "unsatisfactories," including one for conduct. In the comment section, the teacher wrote, "Runs with scissors, interrupts other children, chatters incessantly, particularly about baseball."

When I showed the report card to my father, his disapproval bore into me again. I expected him to yell. Instead, he said, "I'll tell you what I'll do, young man. On your next report card, if you get all 'outstandings' in the academic subjects and at least 'satisfactory' in the deportment categories, I'll take you to a baseball game."

"I will, Pop. I will."

I sneaked into fewer games and left my broom handle in the closet. I memorized dates, times, places and vocabulary words. I tried to keep my mouth shut in class, which was difficult for me. I held my breath when the teacher handed out the report cards. My hands trembled as I looked at mine. I had done it—all outstanding grades in academics and satisfactory in all aspects of deportment. The teacher wrote in the comment section, "Much improved!"

I glowed as I handed my father the report card. He did too. "You pick out the game and I'll buy the tickets," he said.

I think I picked out a Saturday afternoon game with the Dodgers' cross-town rivals, the New York Giants. I dragged my father there early on the day of the game so that we could watch batting practice. He bought me popcorn and a Coke. I had already come fortified with a box of Good & Plenty and a Baby Ruth bar. I hoped that I'd be able to get my father to show an interest in baseball.

We had great seats along the first base line. I had never been so close to the players. I saw Jackie Robinson, the first black player in the major leagues, and was excited because he had been the most valuable rookie the year before. The game started and the Giants quickly jumped into the lead. My father yawned.

"Don't worry, Pop. The Dodgers will come back."

By the fifth inning, the rout was on, and my father was fast asleep. Thank goodness there was enough noise to drown out his snoring. After the seventh inning stretch, only dyed-in-the-wool fans like me remained. I guess I had mixed feelings about my father still being asleep. On the one hand, I'd get to see the whole game. He wouldn't push to leave early. On the other hand, we weren't screaming together. I wasn't sharing my love for baseball. The game was about as interesting for him as watching test patterns on our new television set.

The Dodgers batted in the ninth inning, trailing 11-2. My father continued to doze. The first batter singled up the middle, but was erased by a double play. The remaining fans edged toward the exits. Then the floodgates opened and the Dodgers bats came to life. Hit followed hit. Soon the score was 11-6 and the Dodgers had the bases loaded. The crowd was shrieking, which woke my father up. "What's happening?" he asked.

"I told you they'd come back."

Another single, then a walk, brought the score to 11-8, and the bases were still loaded. I got up on my chair and screamed. My father stood. Another single and the score was 11-10. I howled, and to, my surprise, my father said, "This is terrific."

The next batter hit a grounder to short. I thought it was all over, but the shortstop booted the ball, loading the bases. I grabbed my father's sleeve. "We got lucky, Pop."

"We sure did." Then he screamed at the next batter, "Get a hit!"

The next hitter smashed a screeching line drive down the third base line. It looked like the Dodgers were about to win the game when the Giants' third baseman made a leaping catch. I felt my heart sink. The Dodgers rally had fallen short.

I turned to my father and saw the look of disappointment on his face, and he saw mine. He put his arm around me and hugged. "I love you," he said.

I reached up and put a bear hug around his neck. "I love you, too, Pop."

We walked out of the game holding hands and I waved the Dodgers pennant that he had bought me. He gently squeezed and I squeezed back.

~Paul Winick

Building 101

Eighty percent of success is showing up.
~Woody Allen

"I t's every little girl's dream," he said, rubbing his scratchy chin. "I'm sorry it's taken me so long to build." Dad and I walked around my yard. "Location is everything," he said grinning, "especially for a dollhouse."

The corner yard beside the pear tree was ideal. I frequently glanced through the kitchen window at it. A playhouse there would give my daughters a safe place to play.

At seventy-three, my heavy-set father convinced me we could build it. "It'll be a piece of cake," he said, "and we'll enjoy working together."

Dad brought his engineering experience to the project. After I reviewed his plans, I doubted we could build a miniature house. We were both out of shape and Dad was a cancer survivor. I didn't own a hammer, but Dad came with old tools from his father's workbench.

Dad had the vision, plans, and the means to make it happen. I had determination. I was a rookie embarking on Building 101. Class was outdoors. My retired father was the teacher. And this project turned out to be the turning point in our father-daughter relationship.

The foundation wasn't a piece of cake. It was the hardest job I'd ever done. Dad taught me how to mix cement, lay cinder blocks, and attach the floor frame. It got done, but I couldn't do it again in my wildest dreams. Three days later the floor joists were completed. It had to be perfect.

"The floor must be level," Dad said.

After days of precise measurements, calculations, justifications and modifications, I didn't want a perfect floor. I had been hunched over all day in the blistering hot sun. I was tired and wanted to settle for a second-best type of floor. I felt like a crooked woman, walking a crooked mile, and longing to live in a crooked house. Dad wouldn't hear of it. But he was right. I felt proud when it was finally level.

He taught me how to hold a hammer and drive in a nail with three good whacks. I learned the importance of a good hammer. Dad gave it to me for my birthday. It was a beauty. It was the first time I owned a tool and referred to it with affection. I got ten years of frustrations out in one afternoon by nailing the floorboards down and assembling the sidewall studs with my very own hammer.

Holding up an entire sidewall stud was nothing compared to attaching it to the other four-sidewall studs and hoping it was level. Dad said "hoping" wasn't a part of the assembly equation. It had to be level.

With the sidewall studs attached to the floor, we spent the remainder of the week putting the roof on. We painstakingly erected a center ridge post, attaching triangular roof rafters to it. I wasn't sure of the difference between the truss and the struts, but it's possible we had both. We fit sheets of plywood on top of the rafters, holding it securely in place with a million nails. A drain spout was fashioned around the sides and black shingles were tacked on.

I saw shingles every time I looked at a house, but I had never really seen a shingle before I held one in my hand and had to figure out what to do with it. My shingles had a thin layer of tar with ground up stone in it. They were also hotter than Hades when sitting on a rooftop under the blazing sun as I struggled to nail them down. They smelled disgusting and felt like rough sandpaper.

"The walls will be a piece of cake," Dad said, hoping to make me feel better.

I wondered what kind of cake he was talking about. We calculated, measured, and cut sheets of plywood with an electric saw. I still can't hear right because of that noise. We made adjustments to fudge it when we miscalculated. For five brutal hours we struggled to erect four walls.

When window day arrived, I appreciated what a cake job was. They popped in effortlessly. The door wasn't so easy. It didn't pop into anything. We bought a beautiful solid pine door. It was heavy and it took a lot more muscle than I had to drill a hole for the doorknob apparatus. Dad thought we should do it the "old fashioned" way with tools from his father.

Sheetrock day was puzzling. I felt like I was trying to fit a square peg in a round hole. Lugging it, holding it upright, and nailing it was another challenge. At the end of the day my body cried for a massage, but all I got was a hot shower and a good night's rest. It was enough to rejuvenate me for the next day's work—taping seams.

It was like taping packages on birthday presents. Spackling the seams reminded me of opening a giant can of ready-to-spread frosting and slopping the interior of the house with it. Everything was coated. It was fun and I didn't mind the mess. I felt like a baker frosting the inside of a cake house. I wanted to decorate the walls with gumdrops and candy canes like a gingerbread house for Hansel and Gretel. It must've been the cake job my father had been talking about.

I didn't realize once the putty dried, the walls had to be sanded smooth. It only sounded easy. I was covered from head to toe with a film of white dust. I looked like the Pillsbury Doughboy saturated in flour. The floor needed a thorough sweeping once the walls were smooth. White dust billowed from the windows like smoke dissipating from a fire. There was no fire, but there was a burn in my muscles from overexertion.

For months we had been working on the project, wondering if it would ever take shape. Finally the form of a real house towered over us. Paint brought it to life. Slapping on a coat of paint didn't sound hard until I had to do it with arms of rubber. Mine felt useless. They were tired from all of the other things I had been doing. I was beginning to make mistakes. Paint dripped everywhere.

It took three months to build. It was the most incredibly prolific thing I'd ever done with my bare hands and a few meager tools. It was backbreaking work for a greenhorn, but I loved every minute of it. It went way beyond providing a safe place for my children to play.

Still, it wasn't completely about building a playhouse. It was about carving out a portion of my life and building a relationship with my father, overcoming obstacles, and using creativity that I didn't know I had. While the nails and glue held the wood structure together, our time together bonded us closer than any tool imaginable. When I gaze through the kitchen window, I don't even notice the pear tree anymore. My eyes go directly to the structure that I built with Dad. He taught me many incredible things that summer, most of which revolved around building a relationship meant to last a lifetime.

~Barbara Canale

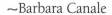

Waterskiing with Dad Is Okay

Your children need your presence more than your presents.
~Jesse Jackson

Most water skiers yell "hit it!" But when my dad is driving the boat, he knows my "okay" is the cue to push the throttle as far as it will go and pull me out of the water.

Dad has been pulling me out of the water for twenty-seven years, since the summer he taught me to ski. I was ten and we had rented a lakefront cabin for the week. Every morning, afternoon and evening that week, he climbed into the boat and, with my mom or brother or uncle spotting, he threw me the rope. My face tense with concentration, I'd grip the bar until my knuckles turned white, watching the boat slowly move away until the slack in the rope disappeared.

Then I held my breath and struggled to keep the ski tips above the water until I thought maybe I had the balance to holler "okay." I didn't like the command "hit it." I'm not sure why, but it didn't matter, Dad knew what I meant. His response was quick and the boat lunged forward. But my untrained muscles and mind didn't respond so well.

Sometimes the skis went under immediately, like they were diving for lost treasure, and I'd get a face full of water while my body flopped forward and my skis flipped free. While I coughed and snorted, my dad pulled the boat around so the rope came right to me. He'd offer several encouragements and a suggestion; then we'd try again.

Sometimes just one ski went under and I fell to the side. Other times, both skis surfaced while my bottom stayed in the water and I fell backward with a splash. And then there were the times I got up for a moment, but then couldn't control my unruly skis, which seemed to go in every direction at once. Those were the hardest falls. Water went in every orifice and my body performed unnatural contortions as I crashed. Each time my dad circled the boat back around, offering encouragement and gentle tips. Sometimes it really hurt and I gave up for a while.

But a few hours later, when I asked Dad, "Can you take me skiing again?" he'd put down his soda, his card game or his book and back to the water we went. I don't remember him ever telling me no. If he was tired of spending his vacation driving in watery circles, he didn't show it. Over the course of that week he responded to my "okay" at least a hundred unsuccessful times.

On the last day, we had victory. I got up and skied around our bay. It was like flying, the wind whipping my wet hair as my skittish skis skimmed the water. The joy was worth suffering through a week of failure and I've skied every summer since.

Since then, my dad has taken me skiing countless times, often rising at 6 AM with me so I could ski the glassy water of early morning. It is always exhilarating—gliding across the water's surface, whipping around the outside curve on a tight turn, jumping the wake and waves. Skiing is my happy place, but I think it's more than the sport. While fun, skiing isn't quite the same behind another boat or driver, where I yell "hit it" like everyone else. It's best when Dad drives.

My dad has since taught my three kids to ski and with each one I saw again the same patient encouragement he had for me. He's proud of them, joyful at their accomplishments and happy to teach something that provides pleasure. And he's shown them, like he showed me, that success can come after failure, and a word of encouragement can literally pull you up.

My kids are light and pop out of the water like corks while I now have to hold my breath and hold on, praying the boat has enough power to heave me to the surface. But when I'm done flying across the water and the boat circles back around, I love that my dad still says "nice run" or "good job." It makes me feel like I can do anything.

I still say "okay" when I ski with my dad. I think it fits my mood about my favorite sport. It's also an understatement for how I feel about my dad. He's a lot more than okay.

~Jill Barville

The Saturday Treat

Perhaps the most important thing we ever give each other
is our attention.
~Rachel Naomi Remen

Lollipops fanned out in a rainbow of colors. Gum so chock full of sugar that the crystals actually sparkled on the surface. Chocolate bars wrapped in shiny paper, reflecting the store's fluorescent lights.

And most important of all: my dad.

This is how I remember the Saturdays of my childhood. On that glorious day of the week, Dad took me out for our "Saturday treat." I could buy whatever I wanted, as long as it didn't cost more than a candy bar.

Though I had three siblings, my early "Saturday treat" memories feature just my dad and me. My older siblings had outgrown the tradition, and my younger brother was too little.

On our special day, Dad and I sometimes drove to the store. But in good weather, we would walk to our town's shopping district and chat along the way. Dad would point out interesting sights, like the ants on the sidewalk or a fallen tree branch. We'd stop at our halfway resting spot—a short wall of cinderblocks, just the right size for a kindergartner to perch and dangle her legs.

Soon my younger brother was old enough for candy and began to join us on our trips.

And Saturdays changed.

My brother and I thrived on pestering one another. Dad became part referee, part chauffeur. My brother's predictable purchase — a grape Charms lollipop — made me roll my eyes. My goal became locating a more delectable item than his.

Time passed and I entered junior high. One Saturday afternoon, my younger brother and I sat under the television's spell. My dad popped into the room. "I'm going to run some errands," he said. "Anyone want a Saturday treat?"

We pulled our gazes from the flickering screen. "Yeah. Can you get me a grape Charms?" asked my brother.

"I'll take a Three Musketeers bar."

Dad waited. Neither of us budged. The features on his face shifted. Then he turned and left.

Soon after, the Saturday treat tradition ended.

In the rush of junior high, and then high school, I didn't mourn my lost candy bars. I had better things to do. Or so I thought.

Several years later, I teetered on the edge of adulthood. College loomed, only months away. My nerves jangled. Nostalgia washed over me at the slightest provocation. I'd catch sight of the green living room couch and feel compelled to appreciate it. All those stripes of different shades! How had I never noticed that before? I fell in love with every square inch of my house.

I tried not to think about leaving the people who dwelled inside.

On a spring Saturday, I found myself in the dining room with my dad. Just the two of us. I watched him as he read the paper.

How odd it felt, in the quiet stillness, just he and I.

Growing up in a house packed with people, I rarely had Dad to myself. In addition, Dad had a long commute to work, so he left bright and early. He arrived home for dinner, but shortly thereafter the younger children would be in bed, the older ones deep into their homework.

When did we ever have time to be with our dad?

And then it hit me: Saturday treats.

I sat up straight in my chair. "Hey Dad," I said. He looked up from the newspaper. "Want to go get a Saturday treat?"

He grinned. We headed out to the garage and grabbed our bicycles. Now that I was no longer a kindergartner with little stamina, we could hit the bike trail and head into the neighboring town for a yummy confection.

As we pedaled, we chatted. Well, actually, I did most of the chatting. Instead of anthills and fallen tree branches, I spoke of friends and school, hopes and fears.

Our tires whirred, our pedals clicked. Dad said little. But his silence was not passive. It hummed with energy. This, I realized, was how he had nurtured me for years. He was listening to every word I said.

One thought crystallized in my head that afternoon. I mattered. To my dad, I would always be someone worth listening to.

I don't remember getting to the store. I don't remember what I bought. But I do remember the peace and security I felt knowing that my dad would always be there for me—whether next to me on his bicycle, cheering me on through college from across the country, or tucked safely inside my heart.

He cared. He loved me. Unconditionally.

What sweeter confection could there ever be?

~Sara F. Shacter

Thanks Dad

Everyday Heroes

81

Hero to Many, Father to Me

All men are created equal, then a few become firemen.
~Author Unknown

When my mom didn't pick me up at the bus stop I knew something was wrong. Our neighbor, Dolores, was there and she motioned for her daughter, Michelle, and me to go with her. As we walked down the block, her face looked stiff. Her mouth was tight and there were little wrinkles between her eyebrows. The silence was intense as she placed her hand on my shoulder and pushed me along.

After what seemed like an eternity, we finally reached my neighbors' home. I tried thinking of anything my mom might have had to do that day. A doctor's appointment, a meeting—nothing came to mind. Dolores opened the front door so slowly that the hinges creaked. As we walked into the house, she motioned for Michelle and me to go to the living room where the rest of her family was watching television.

The image I saw was indescribable. It looked like the factory steam stack I always passed on the way to my grandma's. I used to believe that steam stack was a cloud maker. A beautiful, white, puffy cloud maker. But the cloud maker I was watching on the TV was making big, black, evil rainclouds. I sat there in confusion until Dolores finally explained to me that this building was burning. The famous, big Twin Towers were burning down right before my very eyes.

I was nine years old on September 11th. It took hours for Dolores to explain to me what, how, and why. I had never heard of something so cruel and tragic. When my mom finally picked me up from Dolores's she was crying. I asked her why, but all she could do was tell me everything would be all right. The phone calls to my house were endless. My mom would hang up and the phone would ring again immediately.

As the phone calls slowed, my mom sat me down and told me that Daddy wouldn't be home for a little while, but that he would come home. When I asked where he was, my mom replied, "Saving lives." My dad? Saving lives? In THAT building? Each day that my dad didn't come home got harder, but I knew he would come home. He always did. One morning, on the front page of the newspaper, I saw my dad. He was with three other men and they were all in their fire gear. They were pulling a man out from beneath rubble and debris. The man had lost his hair, and many of his teeth, and his eyes were caked with dirt. My dad had rescued someone, and I was so proud.

I wore red, white and blue to school every single day until my dad came home. When he walked through the front door, he looked disheveled, his hair a mess, his clothes dirty, but I didn't care. I ran to him and wrapped my arms around him so tightly they hurt. He reciprocated the hug and began to cry. I looked into his eyes and I asked, "Daddy, why are you crying? You're home with us now."

He smiled at me and said, "The whole time I was trying to be a hero to all those people, all I could think about was how scared I was. Scared because I was thinking that I wasn't going to get home to be a hero to you."

Hundreds of firemen and policemen died in the World Trade Center that day. I ask myself every day how I got so lucky. I also think about how unfair it is that I got to keep my daddy, and some other kid out there just like me didn't get to keep hers. Thank you Dad for saving lives, for fighting and for coming home. I love you.

~Danielle

82

A Quiet Hero

There are times when silence has the loudest voice.
~Leroy Brownlow

One of the most important lessons I learned from my stepfather is that true heroism is silent and sober. Heroes take journeys, fight wars, and battle incredible odds, but they never seek praise.

My stepfather used to keep a large wooden locker in the tool shed behind our garage. The locker, a big, heavy chest with an iron handle on each end, was painted battleship gray. His name, Ernest McKenzie, was stenciled on the lid. The locker was old and splintered in places, and padlocked with a tarnished brass lock, the key to which was kept on a ring in the house. I saw him open the box only once when a friend came to visit. He lifted the lid of the chest and pulled out a dusty photo album filled with pictures from the war.

Ernie had fought in World War II. His visitor was an old Navy buddy. They had served on the same ship together. They laughed over photographs and drank beer as I stood outside and listened. I don't recall much of what was said, but I do remember the man calling my stepfather "Duck" and commenting on what a strong swimmer he was.

"You're the one who saved us, Duck," the man kept saying over and over. "You kept us alive out there." And I think they cried together, or maybe it was just drunken giggles. I'm not sure. That was the only time I ever saw my stepfather open the footlocker. That was 1961 and I was twelve years old.

Ernie had served four years in the United States Navy during the war. Despite his years of service, our house was entirely devoid of memorabilia. A visitor would have no idea about my stepfather's military career were it not evident in his walk and demeanor. Civilians might miss even these clues. I knew that my stepfather had served in the Navy, but I did not find out what a highly decorated sailor he was until several months after his death.

I was cleaning up the yard and stepped into the tool shed for a rake. That's when I spotted the footlocker. I went back into the house, found the key, and took it out to the shed. Quietly, and with an archaeologist's caution, I unlatched the lock and lifted the lid of the locker. An amazing smell rushed out, deeply sweet, of mothballs and cedar. The smell also belonged to the contents of the chest, to the history inside.

The first thing I saw was a tray full of medals and wooden plaques commemorating different things my stepfather had done during the war. There was a Purple Heart, a Bronze Star and a Silver Star. There was a plaque for being on the commissioning crew of a ship, and another one for serving on a ship that was sunk by a Japanese submarine.

Underneath the top tray I found uniforms—dress blues neatly pressed and folded. I found a shoeshine kit and a white sailor hat with my stepfather's name stenciled on the inside brim. There were newspaper clippings and a book in the trunk as well. The book was a thin *U.S.S. Indianapolis* cruise book, dated 1943. I flipped through the black-and-white photos, looking for pictures of Ernie. The photos were mostly headshots of similar-looking young men in dress blues and white hats. I found pictures of my stepfather standing in front of an anti-aircraft gun, on the mess deck with his buddies, and sitting on his bunk. He was still youthful and very masculine, stern-looking but not weary.

Underneath his uniforms, wrapped in a white handkerchief, were his dog tags. His name was pressed into the thin aluminum. Under the dog tags I found more uniforms. Dungarees this time, work clothes with "McKenzie" stenciled on the pockets. There was also a pair of black work shoes, a blue web belt, and several more sailor hats.

That afternoon I discovered that my stepfather had been a Gunnery Petty Officer in World War II, and had two ships sunk out from under him: A light cruiser, the *U.S.S. Bismarck Sea*, and a heavy cruiser, the *U.S.S. Indianapolis*.

Two Japanese torpedoes sunk the *Indianapolis* shortly after transporting components of the atomic bomb to the island of Tinian. The ship sunk within minutes, along with 300 of its crew. My stepfather was one of the lucky ones who made it into the water. The *Indianapolis* had been observing radio silence during that time. No one other than the crew of the Japanese submarine knew of its location. When they were rescued four days later, only 317 men were still alive. The rest died of exhaustion, exposure, and wounds inflicted when the ship was hit. Many others were victims of shark attacks. The sharks fed nonstop, day and night, darting into the men with speed and fury. The water around the dwindling crew remained a constant crimson.

All during my childhood, my stepfather never talked about that harrowing ordeal. Occasionally, if we were alone, he would speak of some aspect of his years in the Navy, such as how it was to live on board a ship or how a five-inch gun battery was operated, but that was it. Ernie never once bragged about surviving the sinking of the *Indianapolis*, or how he had saved the lives of other sailors. Had it not been for that footlocker, I would have never known.

Through my stepfather I learned that the greatest heroes are those who find the courage to serve others and face overwhelming obstacles, yet expect nothing in return, not even praise.

~Timothy Martin

83

My Dad Is as Nice as a Fish

One night a father overheard his son pray:
Dear God, Make me the kind of man my Daddy is.
Later that night, the Father prayed,
Dear God, Make me the kind of man my son wants me to be.
~Anonymous

I still remember the sounds of my dad beginning his day: the ringing of his alarm clock, the running water as he shaved, the coffee maker, and the rattling of cupboards and dishes in the kitchen. The sounds of leather straps against cowhide told me he was lacing up his work boots while his coffee was cooling. His quick breakfast was followed by the thud of the kitchen door closing, his old pickup coming to life, and the crunch of gravel under tires as his truck left our driveway.

Only then would I tiptoe downstairs, grab his still-warm mug, fill it with milk and add a couple spoonfuls of sugar—just like him. While my pretend coffee was pretend cooling, I would lace up my pretend work boots—Keds high-top sneakers. After consuming the horrible milk and sugar concoction with coffee grinds floating on top, I'd quietly sneak outside and climb on my bicycle—now magically transformed into a truck. As gravel crunched beneath my two wheels, I'd ride off to the pretend house I was building. In the make-believe world of my four-year-old existence, I wanted to be like him. After all, he was more than just my dad; he was my hero.

I suspect the vast majority of young children view their fathers, as I did, in awe—a real life super hero able to do anything. During my early years there was nobody bigger, stronger or more important than Dad. At the end of his workday, when he'd come home, he'd pick me up, rub his day-old whiskers against my giggling face and then launch me into the air above his head. The thrill of momentary flight coupled with the knowledge that his strong arms and calloused hands would always catch me and keep me safe remained a metaphor for all he would become to me.

As I grew older, his hero status began to diminish as my world expanded. I started seeing him as a man with foibles like the rest of us mere mortals. I also began seeing less of him as my life took me in different directions. But on occasion, our paths did cross as he coached my baseball team or volunteered with my Scout troop. Sometimes we'd even see each other across the kitchen table during dinner. I was entering my teenage years and, at the time, I was certain it was my dad who was changing. And losing his ground as my hero.

By the time I reached my twenties, his status had been fully restored. It remained a comfort and blessing to know that no matter where my life took me, his strong arms and calloused hands would always be there to catch me and keep me safe should I fall. By the time I married, his hero status was cemented, but he'd become more than just my dad and my hero—he'd become my friend and would remain so for the rest of his life.

When my own son, Michael, was seven, he completed a classroom handout for Father's Day. His fill-in-the-blank answers to the incomplete questions afforded me a peek into the state of our father/son relationship. To the question, "My dad is special because," he wrote, "he cares for me and listens to me." I was moved. "I like to make him smile by," "doing my best at school." I was pleased. He noted that I looked at the things he did and that I taught him how to catch a baseball, but one answer puzzled me as much then as it does today. To the question, "My dad is as nice as…" he wrote, "a fish."

I was confused. I asked him what that meant and he just smiled—and gave me a hug. He never did explain his answer, but his hug required no explanation.

A few years later he had to compose a short piece about someone who was his hero. Many of his classmates picked sports figures, celebrities, and cartoon characters to write about. Michael picked me. And so it goes—like father, like son. I'll forever remain thankful for having been a fortunate recipient of my dad's love and friendship, and I can only hope that as Michael's teenage years are winding down, he will still feel the same about me. If he does, I'll promise to do my best to live up to that honor. And to remain as nice as a fish, whatever that means.

~Stephen Rusiniak

84

The Shopping Trip

Every action in our lives touches on some chord that will vibrate in eternity.
~Edwin Hubbel Chapin

"Jane, hurry and get your coat. We're going to the store."

I ran to do as my father instructed. A shopping trip with Dad was a rare treat. He traveled a great deal of the time, and I cherished the unexpected opportunity to be alone with him.

Once in the car, I asked, "Where are we going?"

Dad only smiled. "You'll see."

To my surprise, we didn't take the usual turn to the area's one department store. (This was in the pre-mall era.) Instead, we turned down an alley where small row houses lined the road. Dad parked the car, got out, and walked to the front door of the first house on the street. Within a few minutes, he returned with Connor, a boy from our church.

I tried to hide my disappointment. I had wanted my father to myself. Now it looked as though I would have to share him with someone else.

"Hi, Connor," I mumbled, barely able to keep the resentment from my voice.

"Hi," he mumbled back. He looked as uncomfortable as I felt.

Dad drove to the store. Once inside, he steered us to the boys' clothing section. My indignation bubbled over. Not only did I have to share my dad, I had to endure looking at boring clothes for boys.

"Connor is going to receive his confirmation tomorrow," Dad said. "He'll need a suit to wear for the occasion."

Connor looked with wonder at the row of clothes.

Dad must have noticed my stiff posture for he drew me aside.

"We have an opportunity to help someone in need," he said in a quiet voice.

Finally, I understood and was ashamed at my lack of compassion. Connor came from a family of modest means where his single mother worked to provide for her four children. I guessed that Sunday clothes had no place in the budget.

With Dad's help, Connor chose a dark suit. I watched as Dad gently encouraged Connor to add a white shirt, tie, dress shoes, and socks. Connor's eyes grew wide as the purchases mounted.

"Th… thank you," he stuttered when we returned him home.

Dad smiled broadly. "You're welcome. And remember, this is our secret. Only your mother knows."

"Yes, sir."

"Thanks for coming with me," Dad said once Connor had gathered up his bags and run to the front door. "What if we stop and get a chocolate milkshake?"

I nodded, but without my customary eagerness for my favorite treat. I had a lot to think about. Other things began to make sense. I recalled holiday dinners where the table was filled with widows and others who were likely to be alone.

"Why," I had asked Dad at one time, "do we always have to invite those ladies to dinner? They never invite us to their houses."

Dad's answer has remained with me. "It's easy to invite those who can return the favor. Taking care of those who can't do something for us in return is the hallmark of love."

I didn't realize it at the time, but in those few words my father had given me the greatest definition of charity I would ever hear.

~Jane Choate

Laughter

Mirth is God's medicine. Everybody ought to bathe in it.
~Henry Ward Beecher

There's an old adage: "laughter is the best medicine." No, it won't cure a cold or fix a broken bone, but there's something to say about letting go in a moment, no matter how nervous or nauseous or achy you feel, and letting yourself get swept up in anything from a raunchy joke or a witty riddle to something silly in between. I learned that important lesson from my father.

My dad is the king of puns. Actually, let me clarify that a bit by saying he is the king of questionably amusing word play. Whenever the opportunity presents itself for a quick rejoinder or a snappy comeback, you can see a look of fierce concentration on his face as he works out the details to his latest vocabulary concoction. Conversation halts for a moment or two as we all wait for the inevitable, and invariably we groan, as his comebacks are masterpieces of cheese. He always looks so proud of his latest accomplishment, often repeating it more than once to make sure everyone heard him, as we visibly cringe, which makes him chuckle harder than he did at first telling.

I've wracked my brain to list a few, but they're generally so light and fluffy that within moments they've evaporated without a trace. And as if his pun play wasn't enough, Dad always has a relevant joke to toss out. This past Jewish New Year's dinner, he showed up with a folder filled with pages of one-liners he found online, just in case there was a lull in conversation. As he ran down the list, his eyes lit up with delight at eliciting any sort of even slightly amused response.

Of course my dad isn't different from many relatives who use family dinners as their comedic stomping ground. What sets him apart, however, is that he's constantly looking for the humor in things, despite what he does all day. My dad is an oncologist, a cancer specialist. His days are filled with chemotherapy and painkillers, delivering hard-to-hear news to patients, helping them through their last months and days with grace and empathy. And a good laugh or two.

When I was growing up, I remember hearing Dad's car pull into the driveway after I got home from school, and running to the front door to ask how his day was. He would fill me in on patients he'd seen, how they were feeling, if they were getting better. Or worse. He'd tell me if they'd gone into remission or if they'd gone into the hospital. I remember hearing about one patient who asked him to keep her alive until her daughter's wedding, another until her grandson's bar mitzvah. We'd talk about patients who wanted to make it through the holidays so their families wouldn't be plunged into mourning at a usually happy time.

Through weekly visits, lengthy chemotherapy treatments, and hospital stays, my dad became a friend, a confidant, a therapist to his patients. He worked with some for months, some for years. I never could understand how he seemed to handle so well the pain of sharing bad news, and then watching people he cared about deteriorate.

Looking back I realize that perhaps my dad was so well suited to his job because he came from a broken home back when divorce was shameful. I could feel his pain when he told me how he would spend weekends taking two subways, alone, to visit his own father, too embarrassed to tell anyone where he was going. Neither of his parents remarried and he didn't have siblings. He lived with his mother and grandfather, who rarely spoke to each other. His childhood was filled with silence and solitude. In spite of his emotionally bereft family life, or perhaps because of it, he was able to develop empathetic bonds with his patients. Relating to his own family often remained difficult for him, as if by the end of his workday he was completely empty. He would regularly disappear into his study to spend hours alone, listening to classical music and dealing, in his own way, with the sadness that surrounded him from both the past and the present.

What's truly inspirational about my dad is that somehow he found grace in that sadness. He explained to me once that when people have a finite amount of time left they often face the future with a heightened sense of appreciation and gratitude for what they have left. Being able to help them gave him purpose and he often used humor to bring them back into the moment. He taught me that laughter is a remarkable way to be present. What my father was doing was helping his patients find moments of Zen (although he'd adamantly refuse to call it that). Being fully present gave them a little break from the enormity of what they were dealing with.

Years ago, a friend of my husband's was in the hospital with cancer that had been in remission since he was a child. But it was back and his prospects were now bleak. When we got to his room, it was filled to capacity — I think the staff knew time was limited so they let everyone stay. Rich was in bed, barely talking, surrounded by whispering friends and relatives. I started chatting away, as I do in stressful situations, telling him about a book I had recently written: a collection of silly, embarrassing, and laugh-out-loud funny vomit stories. At that point the room was silent when Rich said he had a story for me and shared a hilarious tale of college buddies (many of whom were near his bed), a case of beer, and a car air conditioner that spewed out fetid fumes every time it was turned on after that night.

Rich's eyes were sparkling and the tension in the room evaporated as everyone cracked up. The door opened and his mom walked in, looking worried, having heard all the noise out in the hallway. In that moment though, we had been transformed from anxious well-wishers back to college friends reminiscing about old times. Humor brought us together and made us forget the pain and sadness for a little while.

When I find myself in stressful situations, humor is my default coping mechanism. I find that laughing relieves anxiety, breaks tension, and effectively distracts unhappy children. It takes the edge off the pain of being in a different homeroom than a best friend. A baseball team loss becomes less tragic. An endless wait in an airport goes by faster. While I'm the world's worst joke teller, I specialize in sharing embarrassing personal stories. Recounting how I broke my own finger in a step class, or the time I unwittingly had my hair chopped into a boy cut, can force a grin. Asking for help recounting a silly scene from a movie works. Sometimes I even resort to a quick tickle, knowing that once a smile breaks through, I've got a chance to help someone find a little joy and be in the moment.

Thanks, Dad.

~Elissa Stein

86

Rules of Engagement

*Courage is not the absence of fear, but rather the judgement that
something else is more important than fear.*
~Ambrose Redmoon

Growing up in a small, North Carolina tobacco town
in the 1970s and '80s, I developed a few personal
rules of engagement, by which—yes—I mean rules
for becoming as attractive as possible, so that Mike Watson (whose
Camaro was of that enviable species sporting a painted spread eagle
on the hood) might someday, somehow find me worthy of a two-keg
rehearsal dinner. Rule One: If your perm gets "ruint," get another one
before anyone remembers that your hair was, at one time, pretty darn
straight. Rule Two: If you know someone whose mom runs a beauty
salon in the basement of their home, be friends with her. And Rule
Three: If you plan on winning the Queen of the County Fair pageant,
you are probably going to need a bigger perm.

It was a simple life. People tended not to lock their doors.

Now, my father happened to be the District Attorney of the
region, which spanned three counties including ours. So he saw
some things. There were drug dealers in Kinston. There was a small
arson ring in Goldsboro. Within my own rural school community, a
science teacher was murdered after a domestic dispute. But to me,
these seemed like peculiar events, happening in isolated homes.
Even when I overheard my father talking on the phone, using words
like "assault" and "larceny" and "homicide," I was not afraid. Those
were courtroom terms, used by men in suits to impose order in the

shadows. As far as I could tell, the lawyers shook their papers and the bad people went to jail.

I also came to understand, pretty early in life, that my father was an excellent prosecutor. He was absolutely, unshakably honest, both inside and outside of our home, and he poured himself into every case, no matter how small. His brand of fighting crime was, very plainly, to run at it hard with the truth. He almost always won. In some sense, the more I learned about his cases, the safer I felt.

Until.

In 1976, my dad received a call from an agent with the State Bureau of Investigation, the S.B.I. It seemed that a notorious drug lord in New York City had—for years—been using partners to smuggle his premium "Blue Magic" heroin supply from Thailand into the United States through military airports and post offices, all in our section of eastern North Carolina. Hundreds of kilos of heroin traveling through our little district every year.

Today, we know that kingpin as Denzel Washington's character in the movie *American Gangster*. Back then, he was known as Frank Lucas. His heroin was ultra-cheap and ultra-potent, and many of its users were dying, sometimes right in the street. At the height of his empire, Lucas claims to have made one million dollars per day in sales of Blue Magic. The secret to his success, the particularly "American" aspect of this gangster's operation, was that he had a competitive advantage: sourcing the drugs directly from the fields of Southeast Asia. He had a gushing pipeline of heroin—one that was ultimately crippling whole sections of New York City—and it was being managed by forty of Lucas's North Carolina relatives and associates. My father would be responsible for prosecuting every single one of them. The series of trials would take years.

Now, like I said, my father was an exceptional attorney. Already in his career he had prosecuted more than one hundred people in our three-county district on drug charges, with virtually all of them ending in convictions. But this was one of the largest heroin operations our country had ever seen. Frank Lucas and his associates were the stuff of movies. For them, murder was a business strategy. When the

S.B.I. began taking steps to try to protect my father's life, I knew that everything had changed.

Over the next five years, between *Love Boat* specials and *Happy Days* reruns, I watched my father. He was constantly reading and writing. He was traveling to New York City to interview Frank Lucas, now on Rikers Island, offering evidence. My father also began starting his car from inside our house, to detonate any bombs that might have been planted. He kept a gun in his bedside drawer. Sometimes when I was trying to fall asleep, I would notice an S.B.I. agent parked outside, near my bedroom, in an unmarked car. It didn't make me feel safer. And I will never forget one night, before the opening day of the lead trial, when I saw my dad hunched on our small brown couch, his leg shaking.

During that five-year odyssey, our family did a lot of praying. My father was in the fight of his life, both in the courtroom, against vices that he could articulate, and in our home, late at night, against demons that he could not. Together, my parents prayed for assistance and protection, wisdom and peace. They also prayed for the young men and women in New York who were dying. My own prayers were fairly simple: *Dear God, please stick with my daddy today. And please, please, please, don't let his car blow up.*

In the end, my father emerged safely, with thirty-four convictions to his credit. Suddenly, the world felt inflated again, as if we had finally slipped out from under a wall. We took a trip to Disney World. Just a few years later, I moved out of our farming community to go to college. And if you must know—yes—I still had one of the biggest perms going. But my old rules of engagement were not built for the real world, and I knew it. There were plenty of things around me that could never be fixed in a beauty shop. By the time I left North Carolina for, of all places, New York City, my hair was straight and my values were straightening.

These days, there are plenty of things that I miss about my hometown. I miss my best friend, who taught me how to jump a ditch and shinny up a television antenna on the side of a house. I miss riding my bike to Westover's Store for hot fries and Dr. Pepper and penny candy. I miss the people who worried just as much about adequate rainfall as about excellent SAT preparation. And lastly: I never did marry Mike Watson. Although on that score, thank goodness. I'm pretty sure you can't fit three car seats into the back of a Camaro.

Still, there are plenty of things from North Carolina that I carry with me, wherever I go. In particular, I cherish the new rules of engagement for life that I was learning, however slowly, during those years of watching my father—rules which, on my very best days as an adult, I sometimes come close to following. Rule One: Don't lie, even when you are afraid. Rule Two: Stand up for people who, literally and emotionally, are dying in the streets. And Rule Three: Try to understand the real meaning of the phrase *so help me God*.

For these things, I thank my dad.

~Jill Olson

87

Chicken Soup for the Soul

Living My Father's Dream

There is nothing like a dream to create the future.
~Victor Hugo

I loved my father. Shortly before I was to be married, my father looked at me from across the breakfast table and said in his great Italian accent, "I know a lady who was thirty-five before she got married. And her father didn't mind that she was still living at home."

"But, Dad, I'm twenty-nine," I replied, thinking it was kind of nice that my father cared enough to say that. But I knew where he was going with this. He made the same speech to my sisters before they got married. My father hated to see his children leave the nest, especially his daughters. Thinking back on this father-daughter chat over hot espresso and fresh biscotti often reminds me of the decision my father made to leave his own nest at seventeen and travel across a huge ocean to a faraway land called America. He had dreams for himself, and for the family he wanted. It is in those dreams that I now find myself.

My father's formal education was limited, but he was one of the most brilliant people I have ever known. When he arrived in his new country, he embraced it by frequenting places where he could absorb the rhythm of the land and its culture. He attended night school, learning to speak, read, and write the English language. He wanted to be able to share his children's American heritage, the children he would one day have.

More than anything, he wanted his children to have the education he never had the opportunity to get. He dreamed that his children would one day graduate from college. And America was the country that could help them fulfill that dream. "If you have your education," he would say, "you have the world."

My father worked hard as a bricklayer to put us through school. Some nights he would come home from work with his hands cracked and bleeding from the cold weather and wet cement. He would rub petroleum jelly on his skin, and my sister and I would help him put gloves on before he went to bed. By morning, his hands would be healed enough to go back to work.

But living my father's dream wasn't always easy for me. I had quit in my senior year of college. "When the time is right," my father would say, "you will finish. And," he continued, "I've saved the money for your education."

My father died before I graduated from college thirty years later. After my last class for my Bachelor of Arts degree, I came out of the classroom on a warm spring night and looked up at the stars. "I did it, Dad!" I cried. "I graduated from college!" I was fifty-one years old. I had finally accomplished what he had dreamed for me. I could feel my father with me at that moment. I knew he was proud.

I went on to attain my teaching credential in elementary education and a Master of Arts in English and education. I was in my final quarter of graduate school, however, when I was diagnosed with cancer. I was almost fifty-five, and I would have given anything to have my father there with me — to have his arms around me, giving me words of encouragement.

For the next seven weeks, I finished my studies while undergoing radiation therapy. I graduated with my master's degree and a clean bill of health. "I did it, Dad!" I cried again, my tears rejoicing.

As I entered my classroom of thirty-five fifth-graders, I could feel my father's presence. He believed teachers were to be revered; they held the key to knowledge and freedom. And somewhere along the way I must have passed on my love of learning to my children. My daughter is a teacher and my son, a psychologist. My father would be so pleased to know that his American dream lives on.

"If you have your education," I used to say to my children, "you have the world."

Thirty-five years ago, I typed my father's autobiography for him. He loved to write. Some mornings I would find him sitting in the chair by the living room window with a yellow pad on his lap and a pen in his hand. I would watch his rough hands glide over the page in soft, rhythmic strokes. Seeing him sitting there in the light of a new day awakened the writer in me.

After my father suffered a massive stroke, he could not speak for the last ten years of his life. But he would grab my hand and squeeze it tightly, and I knew exactly what he was saying. It was all there in his handshake.

"I love you, too, Dad," I would answer back, gripping his hand even tighter.

And now, when I sit in the chair by my living room window with a pen in my hand, I think of my father and how I am doing what he loved to do. "Thanks, Dad," I whisper into the light of the morning. Thank you for coming to a land called America where dreams do come true. I am living your dream. And in living your dream, I am living mine.

~Lola Di Giulio De Maci

The Greatest Lesson Never Spoken

Leaders don't create followers, they create more leaders.
~ Tom Peters

Sometimes, the greatest lessons taught by our fathers are those that they never so much as mention.

Growing up, I understood my father only as a man known for his business accomplishments: a leader of convention, an attorney and small business owner whose law firm had earned a respected reputation; and who had worked alongside important state officials, unions, and municipalities for decades.

In my youth, I understood my father, the attorney, to be an indistinguishable part of who my father was as a dad at home. I connected his distinguished, structured style of teaching my siblings and me as no different from the way in which he would formulate an argument in court.

He would often teach us lessons like, "You cannot judge your actions on the basis of what others do or don't do," and "The ways the world works cannot be separated into black and white." I concluded that these parenting lessons were nothing more than results of his years of experience with the complexities of practicing law. In many ways, they were.

But, all the while, my father was teaching me a great lesson that I would not come to realize for decades. Remarkably, this lesson was never so much as spoken. I've only come to understand it now, after having realized that I inherited this quality from him as much as I have any physical characteristic or personality trait. The unspoken lesson that my father taught me was by his quiet example as a constant, selfless giver.

A product of my dad's immigrant family's impoverished history and the family's general "lack" of everything throughout most of his young life, my father became a quiet giver, one who sought to provide beyond his means and at his inconvenience to both family, friends and strangers alike. In his career, giving took the form of upstanding moral integrity and public service as an attorney.

Much of his giving, I've realized, has been often without reason and without purpose. But thankfully, it has also been without limitation.

As if to counterbalance the utter deficit of material and emotional comfort that he had growing up, my father has strived to provide a surplus of both forms of comforts to his family and friends: to always open his home to others without question; to grant the foremost opportunities for his children through the best schooling and college education that he could afford; to provide an unquestionable amount of moral support and encouragement; to provide the means to alleviate any possible financial burden that might fall upon us; and truly, to allow us the means to follow our hearts and pursue our most sincere passions in life.

After years of witnessing his quiet but persistent giving, something dawned upon me: my own will to give beyond my means and at my inconvenience was a trait I inherited from my father, like any other. My father's quiet example was a subtle side to him that I had felt and witnessed all of my life. But because this side to him was never advertised, discussed, or iterated, I emulated his example without so much as ever realizing it. And so it became as much a part of me as any other inherited quality.

My father, I now realize, has not been just a leader of convention as an attorney. He is also — and, perhaps, more importantly — a quiet leader who teaches by loving example. Whether he knew it or not, his quiet leadership was an integral component of his fatherhood and influenced his children perhaps more notably than any spoken lesson that I can recall.

The dualistic nature of his fatherhood is an integral component of teaching by example: on the one hand, to lead by traditional fatherly example, and on the other, by being a living example of an individual who his children naturally want to emulate.

Sons inherit much from their fathers. Physical characteristics, like body type and eye color, are easy to recognize. Personality traits, like one's sense of humor, can be measured in laughter. But a quiet life lesson like the one taught by my father to be a constant giver and to give beyond one's means and at one's inconvenience—a lesson that was never spoken, and taught only by quiet example—can only be measured by the extent that others feel it, and oftentimes, never realize it.

~Dave Ursillo, Jr.

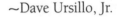

Not Afraid Anymore

Example is not the main thing in influencing others, it's the only thing.
~Albert Schweitzer

Daddy,

Do you understand what you have done? As you receive your token for seven years of sobriety, I hope you realize the impact you have made in my life. The day you decided to turn your life around was the day I began to truly appreciate you. You kept saying you were doing this for you, but you did this for me, too.

I used to be afraid for myself. I knew I had the addictive gene. Just one little sip and my life would be over. Now I know I have a better gene from you — determination. You were determined to never take another drink of alcohol again, and that is what you achieved. When I go to parties it is not hard for me to say no to peer pressure, for you have inspired me to be aware of my potential. You have thanked me many times for helping you through AA, but now, Dad, I thank you.

~Sydney Wain

A Faithful Father

We often take for granted the very things that most deserve our gratitude.
~Cynthia Ozick

As my husband of just four years reached over and kissed me goodbye, baby Aaron began to wiggle and groan. It was breakfast time, and he was not willing to wait. My sweet husband took one last chance to stroke the baby's cheek and then he hustled out the door and into his busy day.

With the briskness of the morning fading, it was time for the baby and me to settle into our little routine. It began with the two of us snuggling into our rocker recliner and me feeding my very hungry small one. Once this feat was done and the burping successful, the baby fell fast asleep. Usually at this point in the day, I would place the baby in the basinet and quickly run through the shower, barely letting the water hit me so that I could be completely ready and have the house somewhat in order before the baby awakened.

However, this morning instead of rushing around trying to get ready and playing catch-up on the housework, I stayed seated in the stillness and quietness of the moment, just thinking. I began my thoughts with the baby in my arms. How sweet and vulnerable this sleeping child seemed, the sheer goodness of life floating out upon each wisp of his little snores. These thoughts ran headlong into memories of the morning with my husband, a father rushing out the door to meet the obligations of life that now were his. It was only a small jump to thoughts of my own father, an ordinary man like my own husband.

There he was before me in my thoughts. I could see him standing in the kitchen as he had every morning, wearing his police officer's uniform and drinking his cup of coffee. "Good morning, Bud." He called everyone Bud. "Morning Dad." It was a small exchange each morning, but it happened like clockwork. My mother passed away when I was ten, and as I looked back, I could see how much of a family man my dad was. Because of his love of home and family, he had remarried rather quickly. He went to work every morning and returned to his family every evening. He provided food, clothing, warmth, and protection. He was a faithful father.

Setting the baby down, I dialed a familiar number with tears in my eyes. My heart had just realized the magnitude of the ordinary — the daily life that goes on around us that we too often take for granted, and it needed to be recognized and celebrated. It needed to be applauded.

"Hello?"

"Hi, Dad," I said, as I fought back tears.

"Hey, Bud. How are you?" Concern was in his voice.

"Fine, I'm just calling to say… thank you." I got it out before my throat tightened too much for me to speak.

"What for?" he asked, trying to remember if he had sent something to me recently.

"For getting up and going to work every morning of my life. Now that I have my own child and I see my husband doing the same, I just wanted to thank you, Dad. Thank you for being faithful."

There was quiet on the other end of the phone for a moment as my dad composed himself, and with a small tremble in his voice he said, "You're welcome, Bud."

I don't remember much of the rest of the call. I am sure we talked about odds and ends, the everyday things that take place, but that moment of revelation about my father, I will never forget.

There are those who are known for their heroic deeds, and there are those who are known for their fortunes and fame, but it is the ordinary everyday fathers who are the true heroes. They are the ones who kiss their wives goodbye and stroke the cheeks of their children before running out the door, day after day, being faithful. My father was one of those ordinary faithful fathers and I am thankful that he was.

~Bonita Y. McCoy

Thanks Dad

Moments that Last Forever

The Cradle

Christmas is a time when you get homesick — even when you're home.
~Carol Nelson

"What's Dad doing?" I asked as I helped myself to a steaming cup of coffee. I sat down across the kitchen table from my mom.

"He's downstairs. In the shop," she said.

I was puzzled. It was December and the basement was cold. I took a sip of my coffee and added another packet of sugar. "What's he doing down there?"

Mom shifted in her chair and then folded her hands around her mug. She looked uneasy and was quiet for too long. "He's making doll cradles. For the little girls' Christmas gifts." Her eyes searched mine.

"Oh," I said with a smile. But my heart twisted in my chest. I ran my finger along the rim of my coffee cup. "It's a wonderful tradition."

"He wants to make sure that all the granddaughters get one. We're not getting any younger."

I didn't like when my mom talked like that, but she was right. They weren't getting any younger.

"The girls will love them. The cradles are keepsakes," I said.

They were.

My dad is the father of four girls. For decades he witnessed little girls taking care of toy babies. He has a gentle and tender heart, and when his own girls had real babies, he began a tradition. He handcrafted a cradle for each family, for the little girls, to hold their beloved dolls.

But there wouldn't be a cradle for my family. My husband and I had five sons.

As I drove home that evening, I addressed the ache in my heart. It was silly. God had blessed me with five boys, and I wouldn't have changed that for the world. I was happy and content and delighted in each son. I loved the boyish qualities of our home and enjoyed being the reigning princess.

Why did I feel so sad?

By the time I'd completed the thirty-mile trip, I'd pinpointed the problem. It wasn't that I didn't have a girl. It was that I wouldn't have a cradle. A treasure. Handmade by my dad. I knew that the boys' rooms were filled with treasures from Papa—shelves that were shaped like trains and coat racks cut to the shape of baseball bats. But trains and bats didn't connect me to my own childhood. Trains and bats didn't remind me of rocking and singing to my own toy babies—often while I snuggled into Dad's arms.

I decided that the best way to diminish the longing of my own heart was to celebrate another person's blessing. I prayed for my dad as he made the cradles. And I prayed for the nieces who would receive them. I thanked God for a father so tender—one who'd poured love into his family and was cherished by my little boys.

And it helped.

One afternoon, Dad and I had a rare chance to talk while their house was quiet. We'd come for a visit, and Mom had taken a few of my boys out to play in the snow. Dad gently rocked my toddler son as the winter sun spliced a bright path across the living room floor.

"How are the cradles coming, Dad?"

He looked surprised. A shadow of emotion flushed across his face. "Just fine. I'm working on staining the spindles. It takes a lot of time."

"Most good things do," I said.

Dad raised my small son to his shoulder and rubbed his back.

My heart twisted only a little when I saw the wood stain on his fingers.

Christmas Day came and our home was filled with joy. My husband and I spent the morning at home with our boys, and when evening came, we ventured to Mom and Dad's for the family celebration.

When each and every person had been stuffed with Mom's good cooking and the children could stand the suspense no longer, we exchanged gifts. A dozen children, at their parents' feet, played with their new treasures. When the excitement simmered, Dad quietly walked through the mounds of wrapping paper and disappeared. I watched him slip through the basement door.

In a moment he reappeared. He carried a lovely, spindled doll cradle in his arms. A shiny red bow was tied in soft loops and a tiny blanket rested inside.

My eyes fell to my niece. She sat pretzel-legged on the floor and her long blond hair fell forward as she embraced a brand new doll.

My dad knelt and placed the cradle in front of her. Her eyes widened in disbelief and love and she fell into his arms.

I glanced at my other niece. Her eyes were filled with hope. My dad caught this, too. And once again, he disappeared. There was also a cradle for her new baby.

My husband's arm slipped around me, and he lifted his hand to brush away my tears. The scenes had been beautiful. I'd been blessed to witness such loving exchanges. My little boys clambered to my lap and I pulled them close. I snuggled into the weight of them and closed my eyes.

I didn't notice that Dad had disappeared again.

When I opened my eyes, Dad was walking toward me. He held a beautiful cradle in his arms. His eyes held mine.

I didn't understand. I scanned the room for my nieces. They were in the corner, playing with their dolls. Two cradles. I glanced at my boys — several crouched over action figures and dinosaurs. They wouldn't want to play with a cradle. It didn't make sense. But when I looked back at Dad, he didn't release my gaze.

"For me?" I questioned.

Dad nodded. He set the cradle down in front of me.

Tears blurred my vision. I moved my finger along the straight lines, along the curve of the spindles. I touched the soft blanket inside. Then I saw the slip of paper—hidden under the soft folds.

I held it with trembling hands. It was written in my dad's small, neat print:

To Shawnelle's Baby Girl,
The gentle rock of a cradle,
With its precious cargo inside,
Must be what it's like in heaven,
When Jesus is by your side.
I'll always love you, Papa

Emotion swelled my heart and captured any words that tried to form. I silently fell into Dad's arms. "Thank you," was all I could whisper into his neck.

"I don't know when she'll come—maybe it will be your grand-daughter. The cradle's for her—and for you." I could feel the tears from his eyes warm on my cheek.

I held on to my dad until my sweet boys lifted their arms to be included in the embrace. We pulled them in.

The cradle is wrapped in a soft, old quilt, in the back of our deep closet. I don't know who the recipient will be.

I only know that when she arrives, I'll have so much to tell her about my dad.

I'll tell her about how, always, he cradled my heart.

~Shawnelle Eliasen

Fathers, Sons and the Angel in the Stadium

I see great things in baseball. It's our game — the American game.
~Walt Whitman

I remember when I got the call that American Eagle Outfitters would be flying my ten-year-old son to New York for their fall campaign. Immediately, I was excited. Actually, I was over the moon about it, but then I stopped in my tracks. My son, Dalton, is a triplet and we have a daughter as well who was seven. Dalton would miss the whole week of school, but the bigger question was: Who would take him?

I was the obvious choice, but my husband is not the best at juggling things at home. Still, the one time he'd taken a child on a trip to a chess tournament, he missed the flight and had to be rerouted at five the next morning. It had been a total disaster. So, imagine, now my son was about to go to New York with his father for six days. I freaked. New York, to me, is scary, and the trip would involve more airports and planes with his dad.

"You have to hold on to him for dear life everywhere you go," I ordered. We live in Boca Raton, Florida and everything here is usually pretty quiet. New York is tough, or so I thought.

But to my delight, my husband was amazing. He took my son places I would have never dared to go. He took him to Madison Square Park, on a ferry to see the Statue of Liberty, to the New York Stock Exchange, photographed him in front of Trump Tower, Chinatown for dinner, everywhere. He was also taken to many locations around New York for his photo shoot and they had a blast. My husband even had him on the subways!

A few nights into his trip, he wanted to take him to a Mets game—Michael and Dalton—just father and son. They walked around the arena looking for tickets from anyone who had any to sell. They came across a guy who had two over-priced tickets, but my husband did not have enough cash, and so the person selling them said, "Hey, you can leave your son with me while you go find an ATM."

"Uh, no thanks," my husband said. "I'll take him and we'll be right back."

Well, as the two of them continued to walk around the stadium to get some more money, an elderly man tapped my son on the shoulder and kindly asked, "Are you two looking for tickets to the game?" To which, my husband snapped around and said, "Yes, sir, we definitely are." With that, the man—who was with his wife—said, "Great, you can be our guests."

The gentleman informed my husband that he had two extra tickets for their friends that couldn't make it. He then said, "Here you go."

My husband said, "Wow, that's awesome. Thank you. How much are they?"

The man softly said, "Nothing. They're on me. Go get your seats and we'll see you inside."

Michael took Dalton to get a Mets sweatshirt and a hot dog.

"This is sooo cool," my son said. "And the other guy wanted so much money. I like New York!"

The two of them went to find their seats and meet their new friends. They walked into the stands, lower and lower and lower until they ended up three rows back from the first base line. Not a soul was sitting in front of them to block the view! It could not have gotten any better.

A short while later, the gentleman and his wife came and sat down next to them.

"I got to tell you," my husband said, "this is really kind of you. It's not every day that people do this kind of thing. My wife would never believe me."

My son was ecstatic. Not only was he doing a national campaign for an amazing clothing company, but he was three rows back at a Mets game for free! The four of them sat together, talked a bit and watched. About a half an hour into the game the concession guy came around selling beers, at which time my husband said, "No, no, I got it. It's a thank you."

The concession guy insisted that since there are cameras, he must ID everyone, and he meant, "Everyone." The gentleman took out his ID and handed it over, but when he went to put it back inside his wallet, something caught my husband's eye. It was a badge of some sort. My husband dared to ask his wife.

"Um, I noticed a badge in his wallet. Is he in some official department? Is he a police officer?"

The woman quietly whispered, "No, he's not a police officer. He is retired from the New York City Fire Department. He was a captain."

My husband then dared again. "Did 9/11 have an impact on him directly? Was he involved in any way at that time?"

The woman replied, "No, he was retired then, but his son is also in the FDNY and he never came home. He died that day."

My husband was speechless. Then the woman said something that made my husband's heart go heavy. After such a wonderful day, a beautiful sky, a perfect evening game, she said, "He used to come to these games with his son. Now, when our friends can't make it, he waits outside the arena looking for another father and son to share our seats with."

When my husband came home and told me this story, he was right; I could hardly believe it. Those short few moments of conversation spoke volumes. My son had shared—with two total strangers—an appreciation for the relationship of a father and son that will last a lifetime.

This is a huge "thank you" from me, the mom of that cute little boy and amazing father and husband. I hope that gentleman knows what he did for us that day.

~Marni Chris Tice

Seven Minutes

Forgiveness does not change the past, but it does enlarge the future.
~Paul Boese

I inhaled the cool autumn air, heady with the aroma of ocean brine off Long Island Sound. I was on my annual "Girls Fall Weekend Away," a few days of indulgence after my non-stop schedule of teaching and caring for a demanding family. My plans included wine tasting along the coast, fine dining and most importantly, sleeping in until I felt like getting up. *Ahhhh*, I breathed a long sigh of contented pleasure as I slipped into my friend's car, feeling the pleasant buzz of a pre-dinner martini at the hotel. This weekend would be a carefree getaway from the worries, big and small, of my everyday life.

As the car pulled up in front of the restaurant, my cell phone vibrated. "Who could be calling me?" I wondered out loud, fumbling for my bag. I only used my cell phone when traveling, much to my teenage daughter's chagrin, to check in at home or have phone access in an emergency. I had spoken with my husband before leaving the hotel and he reassured me everything was under control. So who could be calling me on a Saturday night at 7:00 PM?

"Hello," I answered, relieved to have caught the call before it went to voicemail, but also slightly miffed to be disturbed.

"Lura, hi, it's Dad. " His voice was rushed and gruff, as if reading from a prepared script. "I just called your home and Peter gave me this number to call you. Do you have a moment? Everything's fine here, everything's fine with your mom, but I'd like to talk to you about something important."

With these words, my pre-dinner buzz dissipated instantly and I was fifteen years old again, caught in irresponsible pleasure seeking, instead of being a good, selfless Catholic daughter.

"Dad, just a second." My hand cupped over the phone, I discreetly waved my girlfriends on into the restaurant. While my initial reaction was sheepishness, I knew the call was serious and wondered if it had to do with his ongoing health problems. Along with the daily struggle of living with an amputated leg due to diabetes, a recent checkup had shown he had major blockage of the arteries and was a "heart attack waiting to happen."

An uneasy apprehension clouded my carefree mood. Despite his health concerns, my first reaction was, "What have I done wrong?" I'd never had a real conversation with my dad before. The only times during my childhood he had sat and talked with me one-on-one involved discipline. Most of the time he avoided his children, staying long hours at work or hiding in his workshop at home. My mom and the maid dealt directly with the demands of eight kids.

I do not have one childhood memory of playing with my dad, reading a book with him or curling up next to him to watch a TV show. Once, in a rare moment of camaraderie, my father took my hand to walk along the beach on a Pacific Coast camping trip, just the two of us for no more than a few minutes. We both shared a profound love of nature and must have instinctively joined together in our awe of this stunning wild coastline. My level of discomfort at being alone with my dad would have erased this memory but for my sister, Mary, mentioning it many times as an example of how I was the "extra special" daughter. It was unthinkable to go to him for solace and guidance when I was hurt or sad. The few times I tried, he'd make short, dry, cutting comments on how I needed to be tougher, put hair on my chest, do things better. His irritation at being forced to interact directly with me was palpable and scorching.

Long ago I had accepted this status quo. He sat at the head of the dinner table every night, led the family to church on Sunday, but was not personally close to any of us except our mother. I hid my disappointment behind the stock phrases for men of his generation. That's how he'd been raised. Dads from that generation weren't expected to play with their kids. He was a good provider.

Now here I was on the phone, forced to talk with him. "Lura," my father continued, as if reading a script, "I'm calling all the kids tonight to ask for their forgiveness. I've finally decided to go ahead with the heart surgery. They'll operate tomorrow. I don't know if I'm going to be alive soon and I want to make amends with each one of you."

"Dad, you don't have to apologize for anything," I hurriedly interrupted, a little disingenuously as I was already feeling an urgent need to end this awkward conversation.

As if he didn't hear me, Dad plowed on. "I'm asking every child's forgiveness for not being the kind of father you needed when you were growing up. I loved all of you very much but it was difficult for me to be close. I know I left that role to your mother. I'm sorry I didn't spend more time with each of you, talking with you and getting to know you. I was a good provider. I gave each of you what I consider to be the foundations of a successful life—faith, moral values, education. But I didn't provide you with the warmth and love a father should give. I want to ask you for your forgiveness."

There was a pregnant pause, and then he added, "Lura, do you forgive me?"

Without hesitating, more in an attempt to end this painful conversation than out of any deep reflection, I answered, "Dad, of course I forgive you."

For the first time, I acknowledged to my dad a lifetime of disappointment and emotional neglect from him. And inexplicably, with that simple direct phrase of forgiveness, much of my bitter disillusionment at having an emotionally absent father began to vanish.

Our conversation was fairly brief. I reassured him he didn't have to go through with the surgery if he didn't want to and he reassured me he felt it was necessary. We ended with an exchange of I love you's. I thanked him for the call. Afterwards, I glanced at my cell phone — the call had lasted a little over seven minutes.

My father did not survive the recovery from his heart surgery. Within a few short weeks, he gradually slipped into a coma from which he never resurfaced. I flew home to stand by his bed in the ICU, amid the maze of wires and tubes that kept him going one labored breath at a time. As I held his hand, his eyes opened and rolled about the room, before fixing themselves with great effort on me. I felt the faint squeeze of his hand and then his lips moved, "I love you." Thanks to his last attempt, so long overdue, to forge a loving bond with me by asking directly for my forgiveness and letting me grant it, I was able to accept those parting words and return them with sincerity.

~Lura J. Taylor

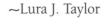

94

Caught on Tape

It's surprising how much memory is built around
things unnoticed at the time.
~Barbara Kingsolver, Animal Dreams

"**A**n early birthday present?" I asked myself as I snatched the square package from my mailbox. The return address told me the box was from my mother in Texas. I hurriedly unwrapped the layers of fiber tape that guarded the prize inside. Finally pulling off the last piece of brown paper, I discovered it wasn't the present I was hoping for after all. "Oh," I said out loud, a bit disappointed when I saw the contents. It was old recording tape, two unlabelled seven-inch reels. I read the note inside. "Found these in the attic," my mother had written. "Thought you might want to have them."

I was curious, of course. Fortunately my workplace had a vintage, mostly unused reel-to-reel tape recorder. I took the mystery bundle to work and during a break, I powered up the machine, threaded up a tape, turned up the volume and hit "play."

Memories suddenly flooded my mind. Events of my childhood rushed at me in fast-rewind. A voice I had not heard in twenty-five years came from the wall-mounted speaker. Amid the scratchy and distorted hisses on the aged tape, I knew the voice in an instant. The unmistakable Texas drawl of my late father, speaking from another time and another place, leaped from the tape. He died when I was only twelve, but now I could almost see him smiling as he spoke to me.

Suddenly, another voice interrupted. It was the voice of a child belting out a song. "Da-vy, Da-vy Crockett, king of the wild frontier!" It was my voice! The mental picture of me as a four-year-old boy, wearing a simulated raccoon-skin cap, half-shouting into the microphone made me laugh. As I listened further, my dad invited me to sing another song. With his help, I struggled through a chorus of "Jesus Loves Me." Soon other voices joined in. My two younger sisters sang along with me. Then, one by one, my father interviewed all three of us about what we were learning in school, our friends, our likes and dislikes. Now and then he added his own thoughtful comments, demonstrating his humor, his unabashed pride in his children, his respect for us, and his surprisingly profound wisdom in even the simplest everyday conversation.

Gradually coming out of my audio-induced trance, an overpowering realization struck me—these old tapes represented a priceless treasure. As the childhood memorabilia continued to play on, I considered all the things my father never achieved in his short thirty-five years on earth. I reflected on all his dreams that went unfulfilled. No doubt he had lofty goals for his life. What a tragic waste, some had said. And I had believed it.

But no longer. Though I didn't recognize it as a youngster, my father had obviously made a conscious effort to leave his children a valuable legacy. I'm not referring to the scratchy audiotapes; those only served to remind me of his real gift. His most valuable offering was himself—his presence, his words, his laughter, his insight, his devotion to pass on to his kids what he knew was genuine and good. My father was not perfect, but he actively and consciously taught us. Even after my father's death, his spoken legacy imperceptibly continued through my teenage years and later into my adulthood. Though his life was short, my father had been a success in what really mattered.

On my drive home that day, I pondered my own responsibility as a father of three young children. What were they receiving from me daily? What were they learning, not in the frequent lectures I gave about keeping their rooms clean or getting to bed on time, but in my everyday conversations with them? Was I leaving a legacy of understanding and patience, of wisdom and truth and love? When the time came for me to be taken from them, would I leave them with something that couldn't be taken away?

That evening as I maneuvered my car into the garage, I had a pretty good idea of what I would find when I walked through the front door. The living room would be littered with toys and books and clothes. The kids would be demanding attention as my wife tried to make dinner. There would possibly be an argument going on. I could react as usual with stern threats or disciplinary measures, then settle in front of the television in an attempt to wind down. Or, I could do something else....

Bursting through the front door, I bellowed out a hearty greeting, and called out, "Hey kids, let's have some fun! Have you ever talked into a microphone?"

~Nick Walker

95

When Daddy Held My Hand

Unable are the loved to die. For love is immortality.
~Emily Dickinson

I vividly remember my father reaching for my hand as we crossed the street. He definitely reached for my hand. I'm certain it wasn't the other way around, for I was far too independent at the tender age of six to need any assistance crossing the street. We lived on a wide city street, and the bus stop located right in front of our house prevented Daddy from ever enjoying the luxury of a convenient parking space. We always had to park across the street and up the block a bit. When you live in the city, someone grabbing for your hand at every intersection becomes second nature to you.

The difference this time, when I was six, is that I remember Daddy's massive calloused hand wrapped around my delicate little fingers and never had I felt so safe. In an instant I learned how much I loved this feeling of total protection. No car, no pickup truck, no bus, not even an eighteen-wheeler could bring harm to me—not while holding Daddy's hand.

Years later I remember Daddy reaching for my hand once again. This time we were headed into the local library where election posters bearing the names of Jimmy Carter and Gerald Ford occupied every inch of available wall space. The voting booths lined one side of the auditorium, while several tables on the other side accommodated registration verification. We stood in line and inched along while Daddy held my hand and explained that he would show me exactly how to cast my vote. Daddy was determined, to say the least, and the poll attendant was none too amused when Daddy followed me into the booth, still holding my hand.

"I'm sorry, Sir, it is against the law to enter a voting booth with a registered voter preparing to cast a ballot," the guard said. His timid tone was no match for Daddy's drill sergeant style.

"She's my daughter and I already know whom she wants to vote for. I just want to show her how to do it," he bellowed. Oh, how my face turned red as I looked pleadingly at the attendant to have mercy and just allow my father to go in the booth with me.

"I'm sorry, Sir," he pressed on. "It's against the law. If she needs assistance I am here to help her."

With a disgusted grunt, Daddy stepped aside.

The calendar pages turned and the next time I recall holding Daddy's hand was several years later. I sat next to Daddy that day in the back seat of a black limousine. I felt like a princess dressed in white, with Daddy looking so handsome in his tuxedo. Just as the driver pulled into traffic, Daddy, reached over and held my hand. Once again his enormous work-worn hand wrapped around mine, instantly calming all my wedding day jitters. He never said a word to me from the time we left our house until we reached the church. But then again, he didn't have to. The strength in his hand said it all. No matter how this giant step in my life turned out, the steadfast strength in Daddy's grip would always be there to comfort me.

The years flew by and Daddy eventually retired. My husband and I visited frequently and often found Daddy at his workbench, working on one project or another while my mother busied herself with household chores or baking. Daddy's health deteriorated at such a slow pace it was easy to ignore, but the last year of his life was an endless string of hospital visits with no promise of any relief or return to good health.

The last time Daddy reached for my hand was about five days before he died. He was taken to the hospital by ambulance and I met him there in the emergency room. Frail and bent over in the wheelchair, with his oxygen canister resting in his lap, he looked up at me and managed a faint smile. God forbid I should detect that he was uncomfortable in any way.

I sat down in the chair beside him as we waited for the doctor. Daddy reached over and held my hand once again. Then he looked at me and said, "Whatever happens, it's going to be okay." For the first time in my life I didn't believe him. I knew then that he was never going to come home from the hospital. I nodded yes and looked down so that he would not see the tears in my eyes. Soon he fell asleep in the wheelchair. He drifted in and out for a few more days and then eventually went to sleep and never woke up.

Through all the stages of my life, Daddy managed to hold my hand in one way or another. I didn't believe him when he told me that last time that everything would be okay. But I know now that he was right. Even from heaven, he reaches out and remains an ever-present positive force in my life. Thanks, Dad, for never letting go.

~Annmarie B. Tait

96

Tuesdays with Daddy

When you look at your life,
the greatest happinesses are family happinesses.
~Joyce Brothers

Many Tuesday mornings, I have coffee with my father. While my mom is at her exercise class, I often stop by my parents' house on my way to work and have a shot of caffeine while my dad relaxes at the kitchen table with his breakfast and his Sudoku puzzle of the day.

Although my father is a man of few words, I really enjoy this time alone with him. Typically, I talk and he listens. Nonetheless, it's quality bonding.

One recent Tuesday, I called my dad to see if I could stop by for a brief schmooze. While I found it a bit unusual when he didn't answer the phone, I assumed he was probably in the shower. Figuring that he would still have time for me, I pulled into his driveway. Yet when I rang the doorbell, no one seemed to be home. I peeked in through the window, noticing the lights that shone from the kitchen, and decided that my dad must be there. He never left lights on when he went out. My dad was, after all, a creature of habit.

I let myself in and called out to my dad.

Silence.

I hurried through his home, checking every room, my pulse quickening as I did so. What if he was hurt? What if I found him lying unconscious on the floor? I tried not to panic. Yet, something just didn't seem right to me.

Upstairs. Downstairs. Still, no Dad anywhere.

I called his cell phone, and heard it ring from the office down the hall.

I ran to the garage, only to discover that his car was still parked in its usual spot. However, the garage door was up and the door from the garage to the laundry room was unlocked. Where would my dad go without his car and why would he leave the house so vulnerable to intruders? Suddenly, I was slightly more than worried. After all, my father was seventy-one years old. Anything could have happened to him. I closed and locked the garage door.

Then, I got in my car and drove to my mother's aerobics class.

On the short drive, I thought a lot about my father and our history together. Suddenly, I was three years old and he was holding me up to the living room window to see the Christmas lights that I loved so much. In his arms, I was safe and secure.

Before long, I was six or seven, and we were at Target, buying cinnamon rolls from the bakery. Cinnamon rolls were always a favorite of my dad's. At age ten, I used to make them from scratch and wake him up with warm breakfast in bed. Those were the days when I felt happy and loved.

Then I was twelve and my dad was amazing all the kids at my birthday party with his magic tricks. Little did we know that his magic was simply basic chemical reactions that my father had learned while getting his Ph.D. in Chemistry. I was so proud of my father for being so special and talented. He'd made my party an incredible success.

When my father taught me to drive, we grew closer despite his frequent stern words. Even when I had my first accident backing into a fire hydrant, I loved my father for being there to make me feel protected.

It was my dad who sat patiently by my side for hours on end helping me with Geometry, and Calculus, and eventually Organic Chemistry. I often thought that my A's in those classes actually belonged to him. He was always willing to help me and made sure I understood what I was supposed to be learning. I could only hope to have half the brains and teaching ability that my father possessed.

When I applied to medical school, my father drove me to my interview in Kansas City. For four hours in the car, he talked to me about the questions he thought I would be asked. He prepped me and quizzed me and helped me formulate my answers. When the interviewers asked me almost every question my father had prepared me for, I was beaming with pride at both my answers and the foresight of the man who had raised me.

As my father walked me down the aisle at my wedding, I tried to look away so as not to show him my tears and not to see his. And when he held my firstborn daughter when she was only minutes old, I thanked God that my dad would be there for her as he had been for me. I was so thankful to my dad for everything he'd taught me and for all the times he'd been there for me. I just couldn't imagine life without him by my side.

And so, as I entered my mother's class, I was anxious and nervous, and a bit overwhelmed from all of my memories. My mom looked at me with happy surprise as she saw me enter the room.

"Mom, where's Dad?" I began hesitantly. "I think he's missing."

"He's working in the yard on the side of the house!" she answered between sit-ups.

"Oops!" I giggled. "I'd better go back. I think I've locked him out!" And I hurried to my car and raced back to my parents' house.

When I arrived there a few minutes later, my dad was obliviously trimming bushes.

"Hey, Dad!" I yelled out and promptly told him about my fears of the last half hour.

My dad began laughing his typical laugh that was always familiar and comforting and promised that he wasn't planning on dying any time soon.

I was so thankful that I still had my daddy. He would still be there for me as he always had been.

And so, as I unlocked the door to my father's house, we went inside for our usual cup of coffee and a huge sigh of relief.

Thanks, Daddy, for all the memories and more importantly, for all your love.

~Sharon Dunski Vermont

97

One Last Reminder

Feeling gratitude and not expressing it is like
wrapping a present and not giving it.
~William Arthur Ward

"See ya later, alligator."

"After 'while, crocodile."

With twinkly, crinkly eyes, my father would always chuckle at his own wit as he invented each new spin on the old familiar farewell. Knowing his forgetful older daughter so well, he sometimes sent me on my way with a fond "see ya later, procrastinator." I had no comeback for that one.

Daddy was a great "reminder." He was always and forever reminding my sister and me of things we needed to do—boring, practical things like getting the oil changed in the car. Most of the time, his reminders were viewed as unnecessary and intrusive. Until he would have to meet me halfway with my forgotten purse or some other necessity left behind in my eagerness to get away from my parents' house and into my own life.

This life evolved into becoming a teacher with a professor husband and two children. We eventually moved far away from our roots, but we always made the trip back home during our Christmas vacation. During the 1997 visit, I noticed (again) that Daddy was not as young as he used to be. However, he still enjoyed his daily trip to get the mail. It was his opportunity to see people and hear all of the local news. When he had a package to mail, he would arrive at the window with a parcel enclosed in whatever had been handy, such as a shoebox sealed with masking tape. I was happy to see that this daily sojourn was still intact even though his gait had become unsteady and the tremor in his hand had become more severe.

One day I was sitting in the living room across from the stairs when my father came through and began climbing up the steps. His shoulders were slumped, he was moving slowly, and he looked at me with weary eyes. He surprised me by saying in a flat tone, "It's just time for me to go on."

Uncomfortable at hearing those words, I responded lamely with, "Daddy, don't talk like that." He continued with his upstairs errand.

As that year's visit drew to a close, we were packing to go home, trying to carve out enough seating space for the four of us amidst all of our luggage and gifts. My mother had cleaned out some closets and had gathered some remnants of lace and trim for me to take back for use in my future craft projects, and this bundle was to be stuffed in along with all the rest.

We said our fond farewells, crammed ourselves into the van and readied ourselves to head back to our own home, our own routine, our own activities, as we had done scores of times before.

"Love you."

"Love you, too."

"Do you have everything? Your glasses? Did you check one last time?"

"I checked. I think we have everything."

"Call when you get there." (Daddy knew I would forget. He would give us time to drive the 450 miles, and then he would call to make sure we had arrived safely.)

"See ya later, alligator."

"After 'while, crocodile."

Upon returning home, of course we became engrossed in our own schedule, and we were excited because our favorite football team was playing in the National Championship. I was in fun mode when Daddy called. He phoned because in typical fashion I had forgotten the lace that Mother had saved for me. Distracted, as usual, by my own doings, I said off-handedly, "Oh, that's okay. I won't use it right away. I'll just get it the next time."

"I can mail it to you," he offered.

"No, don't go to that trouble."

He had the last word with, "I don't mind. It's no trouble."

We finished our conversation. I hung up and returned to whatever I had been doing before the call, not giving it another thought.

Less than a week passed before I got a 10:00 PM call from my sister on January sixth. Daddy was gone. His heart had failed and he had, as he had said he was ready to do, gone on. In shock, I heard my husband making a reservation for an airplane ticket. Numbness protected me as I took a very turbulent flight back to my home state much sooner than I had anticipated.

My husband and children drove up for the funeral, so we all returned home together. Still in shock, I spent the nine hours in the car trying to sort things out. It was so sudden. He had some health problems, yes, but why now? What had happened? He had experienced some bronchial congestion that day and had seen the doctor. What else had he done? How had he spent the rest of this sixth day of January?

As we pulled into our driveway after the long trip, drained and exhausted, my eye caught sight of something leaning against the front door, the one we never used. I climbed wearily out of the car and trudged up the sidewalk to see what had been deposited there in our absence. It was probably a neighbor's package, left by mistake.

My heart ached when I saw the flimsy brown shirt box, crushed and bent, with masking tape crisscrossed in every direction, turning up at the edges and coming loose at the corners. On the front was my name and address penned in the wobbly cursive handwriting of my father. I checked the postmark: January 6, 1998.

One of Daddy's last acts on this earth had been the mailing of that old lace to his absent-minded daughter. I tried with all my mental might to recall every precious word of that last phone conversation, the one I could not have known would be our final one. Did I say thank you? Did I appreciate his wanting to send the box? Or was

I a bit annoyed at his insistence on taking time and effort to do something so trivial? Did I say I love you? Or was I too eager to get back to my own life, my own schedule? Did I say it? I could not remember. I could only hope that I had.

I saved that tattered box with the shaky handwriting and the ragged tape. I kept it under the bed until we moved from that house ten years later. Even then, I cut out the front where my father had written my name one last time, and I carefully packed it among my treasures.

The old bent box top refreshes my memory about my priorities. It is one last reminder from my father to me: "You are likely to forget many things in your life—your purse, your keys, your glasses, even your dental appointment; but don't forget the most important things. Don't forget to express gratitude to those who love you. Don't forget to pay attention to conversations with your nearest and dearest, for you may need to remember them later. Above all, don't ever forget to say 'I love you' whenever you have the chance. It may be the last."

"Thanks, Daddy. I love you. Oh, just one more thing—I almost forgot—see ya later, alligator."

~Jan Hamlett

Heart Strings

To a father growing old nothing is dearer than a daughter.
~Euripides

Every year of my childhood, our family of six would take a summer vacation. Over the Sacramento River and through the Idaho woods to our grandmother's house we'd go.

Trips were simpler then. No itinerary, no restaurants, no motel reservations, no travel kits or GPS units dictating the miles. Just a few old maps, historical landmarks, rest sites and Burma-Shave signs marked our route along the highway.

We were a large family on an educator's budget so we packed our own food, slept in the car while our parents drove through the night, or stayed at the welcoming homes of our relatives for reunion family fun from the West Coast to the Midwest prairies of North Dakota.

Travel may have been simpler then, but the packing ritual of the family station wagon was not. My father planned the placing and stuffing of camping gear, coolers and suitcases, cramming the luggage rack, every cubby and space beneath the seats. There was a method to the madness, but only my father understood the logistics.

The car sat ready overnight as we all tried to sleep until the 4:00 AM start time. The loading of our family into the car was no less strategic than the astronauts strapping into their seats before they are blasted off into space.

The back seat was loaded first. My sister, Dawn, sat in the center with her feet on the hump of the floor that could get uncomfortably warm. My brother was on the passenger side, his scouting experience earning him the official map-reading position of authority. I was on the driver's side with my feet on everyone's flip-flops, activity books, comics and magazines. My youngest sister, Tammy, was in front between Dad and Mom, in a seat with her own play steering wheel, horn, blinkers and all. My mother sat with her feet on a cooler filled with the chicken she had fried, boiled eggs, rolls, fruit, celery, chips, and salami and cheese sandwiches.

Before my father got in the car, he checked us all for safety and comfort and then did something my fourteen-year-old heart will never forget. In a gesture of respect, love, and appreciation for my self-taught ability, my father handed me my guitar in its stiff cardboard case, and helped slide it behind me on top of everything else, into the perfect pocket he had created for it. It was a safe spot, protected from roughhousing and direct sunshine, and it was easily accessible for me to play.

How understandable it would have been for him to say that there was no room for that big awkward thing or that it was a bother, or that he didn't want to hear that "noise" through the whole trip. But that wasn't my dad's way. He packed it, guarded it at gas stops, encouraged my song writing and sang along as I struggled to strum the right strings.

Now, I'm the one packing the car to drive my dad and mom to vacation at our lake cabin. My husband and I built the cabin with my parents' comfort and my mother's wheelchair in mind. Every year, I load the car to its last inch. When I can't find room for another thing, I slam the trunk, always relieved when I hear the soft thud of a job well done and not the clanging sound of overloaded resistance.

Ready to go, my father helps my mother into the car. Even though it's painful for him to bend his knees, my father insists she sit in the front.

One time, my father stopped before getting in the car.

"No room for this?" he asked, pointing to my guitar case left in the entryway.

"Not this trip, Dad," I said, trying not to show my disappointment.

I locked up the house while my father struggled to wedge himself into the crowded space allotted him. I backed out of the driveway and we headed the three hours north.

When we pulled into the dirt road of the cabin, I parked and hurried to help my mother out of the car and into her wheelchair.

After making sure she was comfortable inside the cabin, I went to unload the car. It was only then that I realized that my father wasn't on the deck taking in the blue beauty of the lake. He was still sitting in the back seat.

"Cindy, can I have a little help here?" he laughed. "I'm kinda stuck."

Puzzled, I went around to his side of the car and saw what the problem was. There, on his lap, for three hours, without a word of complaint, he had held my guitar, wedged between his knees and the back of my seat. He was in obvious discomfort.

I hurried to move the front seat forward so I could pull the guitar case out.

"Dad, you didn't have to do that!"

"Sure I did, Cindy. I always make room for what's important to me, and what's important to me is you." He winced as I helped him up and out.

Stretching his knees before he could walk, my father looked out at the lake and breathed in the piney air. He smiled, despite his pain. "I'm grateful that you make a place for us here."

"Dad, I always make room for what's important to me," I repeated his words to him, "and what's important to me is you."

~Cynthia M. Hamond

Just a Little Phone Call

*A man cannot free himself from the past more easily
than he can from his own body.*
~André Maurois

The backs of my thighs were beginning to feel cold from the linoleum. I had been sitting there for twenty minutes trying to make a phone call, but had only managed to push three of the numbers. This wasn't the first time I had attempted to call him. But something deep inside said this was the day.

I inhaled deeply, dialed the phone number and exhaled. Through the pictures that had been torn and tossed, the memories that had been forgotten and the stories that had been left untold, that phone number was etched in my mind. It stayed there despite my attempts to forget. It was as if my mind knew I might want it someday.

"Hello." It was him, I was certain. The voice was so familiar—a combination of Yonkers and a rough life of sixty-five years. Although I was calling from my kitchen thirteen states away, his voice overwhelmed the space as if he were in the same room. For a moment I couldn't breathe. I thought about hanging up.

"Hello," he repeated.

"Hey, Dad, it's me, Kierstan."

Without missing a beat he responded. "Well hello stranger, what's new?"

Did he really just ask me "what's new?" What an absolutely complicated question, yet so expected. Where could I start? I could share how the weather had turned really cold and my herbs are starting to die. I've never been able to keep anything alive. Perhaps I could brag for a few minutes about installing a light dimmer. Maybe he would like to hear about my successful Thanksgiving dinner that I cooked entirely by myself for my boyfriend and me. I'd even admit the turkey was slightly dry. This sounded like typical father/daughter subject matter. The only problem was, we weren't typical. It had been fourteen years since we'd last spoken. Yet the comfort in his voice bid me on and I was desperate to keep that connection.

How do you sum up half of your life? In fourteen years I went through middle school, high school, college, a year of law school and eventually earned a master's degree. I had lived with my grandma and grandpa. I had lived with my aunt and uncle. I had lived with a roommate. I had lived alone. I was with my mother, his wife, before she died. I had been to four continents. I had lived in five different states. I had been married. I was divorced. All of this would be news to him.

The last time I had seen my dad I was in sixth grade. I thought about starting there. I ended up winning that science fair, thanks for the help. I broke up with Tom a few days later. I wore braces most of middle school, although the gap between my two front teeth was never corrected. I joined the middle school cross country team. I loved running though I've never been very good. When I looked back I realized the moments that make up everyday life are experienced with wholeness from using all your senses. Despite the desire to share my past, pieces would be missed in its retelling.

Part of me thought I'd really like to take this slowly, just tell him a little at a time, bite-size pieces. He would understand that, he's a chef. But another part of me had this impulse to tell him everything as fast as I could. I couldn't be sure if he would answer again should I call another day. I needed to tell him who I was, just so he would know. But how do you tell someone who you are when you aren't absolutely certain yourself?

For years I would say to myself, "If I ever talk to my dad again, I'm going to tell him...." I wished now I had written some of those things down. I wished now I hadn't waited so long to call. But I felt fragile beneath the strength of his words, or rather, his silence. I had woken up this morning with the realization that if my dad chose to hang up the phone or talk to me, either way I would manage. I would heal. I was prepared for that. From the initial hello, I felt complete in spaces I had not realized were empty. I am so glad he did not hang up.

"What's new, Dad?" I said. "Well, everything's new and so much is exactly as you'd remember. I made it; or rather I'm making it every day. I'm not perfect but I just recently decided that I am pretty proud of the woman I'm becoming, and I think, should you choose to get to know me, you might be proud of me, too. I miss mom. I became a social worker and I'm certain she influenced that decision. By God's sense of humor I look just like you, Dad. I'm creative like you, though in different ways. I'm not particularly religious, though I think God's been looking out for me. Most importantly, I'm not angry anymore. I guess what I am trying to say is, if you call me I'll answer."

He gave me the score of the Cub's game, recited to me a lamb recipe I will never make and told me he had a box of pictures. Would I like it if he sent them? He wasn't overly sentimental but he was exactly as I remembered, and that seemed enough. The conversation flowed easily. We laughed a lot. So much of my sense of humor comes from him. After about an hour, we decided to hang up, but before we did he surprised me.

"I love you," he said.

And just like that, I felt like someone's daughter.

~Kierstan Gilmore

The Shrubbery Massacre

Weed 'em and reap.
~Author Unknown

Fathers may have all kinds of virtues, but usually there is one great virtue that defines who they are. For some fathers it might be a love of the outdoors that they pass on, or just plain toughness. My father possesses more virtues than this story can contain, but he has one virtue that is truly great—forgiveness.

I was not an easy boy to raise. I was born in the lying down position, and as far as I was concerned, that was my natural state—lying down, and certainly not doing physical labor. In this way I was the opposite of my father.

My father has worked physically demanding jobs his whole life. Not only that, but while working these physically demanding jobs, he'd been running a landscaping business on the side. As his only son, I was conscripted into landscaping against my will.

I may have set a world record for whining as a child. I didn't complain all the time. In fact, I was a very happy kid. Except for when labor was thrown into the mix. My dad would take me with him to rake someone's lawn, or haul away a brush pile, and I would complain nearly the whole time. But did he ever give up on getting me to work? No.

When I went off to college, only forty-five minutes from my parents' house, I would work for my dad on the weekends. It was during one such weekend in the spring that the calamity happened.

As a part of my general disdain for physical labor, I've never liked gardening. Especially weeding. Unfortunately, this was often what was asked of me, since the more skilled gardening tasks such as planting bushes, trees, and flowers, required my father's extraordinary green thumb. Now, if there is a job I do not want to do, I tend to rush through it as quickly as possible in order to get it over with. This proved to be a big mistake.

My father had asked me to weed a horribly overgrown flowerbed in front of a client's house. I sighed when I got to the job site, because I could see a few nice looking lilies surrounded by a wreck of tangled undergrowth, and strangely well-rooted weeds.

I went to work with fervor, using an axe and a shovel when I had to. I hacked and dug all around the lilies. I was saturated with sweat, and coated in dirt and woodchips, but I was exultant. I had conquered the tenacious weeds, hacked them to pieces and dug them out of the earth. But I had a funny feeling. Should I have stopped and questioned why the roots were so tough? I called my dad.

After a brief question and answer session, my error became apparent: I had just axe-murdered about twenty-five shrubs. Shrubs my father had planted the previous year. Once he told me what I'd done, I winced and awaited a tongue-lashing. I'd just weeded the entirely wrong area, and undone hours of his painstaking labor. But do you know what he did? He just laughed, long and hard. Let me tell you, that made the painful process of replanting them, which I did immediately to the best of my ability, easier.

My father is sixty-four now, and is still in better shape than I, at half his age, thanks to his non-stop physical activity. I certainly did not inherit his tolerance for physical labor. But what I hope I inherited is one of his greatest gifts, the ability to forgive, and maybe even laugh a little.

~Ron Kaiser, Jr.

Is Mom There?

A son is a son till he takes him a wife,
a daughter is a daughter all of her life.
~Irish Saying

In the depth of my despair, only one voice would do — my mother's. I called home to connect with her soothing tones, but jarringly, my dad answered the phone. My mom was out. Playing mah-jongg, my father said from the phone's other end.

"Oh," I said, disappointment evident in my voice. "Tell her to call me when she comes in."

"What's wrong?" Dad asked.

"Nothing," I said, though it was the kind of answer meant to deflect rather than inform. I really didn't want to tell my father what was wrong. At the time, I was a twenty-three-year-old woman with a college degree and a full-time job. But at that moment, I was a girl whose heart had been broken by her boyfriend. And I needed my mother.

Mom was the one a girl talked to about such things. My mom had always been my confidante. Besides, she was an enthusiastic supporter of my decision to move from New Jersey to Massachusetts, a move I undertook ostensibly for my career, but which was made easier by the fact that this boyfriend just happened to live in Massachusetts, too.

My father, on the other hand, was less exuberant. "He doesn't love you," he had told me one Sunday just after the boyfriend left following a weekend visit.

"What do you know?" I snapped, anger rising in me like mercury in a July thermometer.

"I can just tell. He's not committed to you," my dad answered with a flat tone that infuriated me even more.

"That's just not true," I countered, turning on my heel and storming away, wondering how he dared to have the audacity to judge my relationships. Indignant, I was stung by his insensitivity and callous treatment of the man who was the love of my life. We never talked again about my relationship with the boy in question.

When I packed up the U-Haul and moved to Massachusetts a few months later, my mom quietly tucked $50 in my pocket as a "good luck" gift. She gave me a hug and told me how excited she was for me. My father, on the other hand, gave me a hug and said little—uncharacteristic of the opinionated guy he was.

It was all so exciting. I lived in a cute little apartment, with a fun (but totally consuming) job, and a boyfriend whom I saw on weekends. It seemed perfect. Over time, though, my boyfriend started offering reasons why this or that weekend would not be good for us to get together. By the time I'd been there for six months it became clear that the boy did not love me. He was half-heartedly trying to make it work (out of guilt, perhaps, for allowing me to move to his home state). But I suddenly realized that if I was to have any self-respect, I had to end the relationship. I called him and told him so, and he didn't try to talk me out of it. "I guess you're right," he said into the phone. "Can't we be friends?" he asked. "No," I said. "I don't want to be your friend." And so the phone call and the romance ended with a receiver click.

It was poignant and sad and so terribly hard. That's when I called my mom. How awful that she wasn't there.

"What's wrong, honey?" my father asked into the phone.

"I don't want to tell you," I said, my voice cracking.

"But why?" he asked.

"Because you'll say 'I told you so,'" I croaked.

"What happened?" he asked again. And it spilled out. I told him of the phone call with the boyfriend—what I'd said, what he'd said, what I'd said, and ultimately, how it all had ended.

"Aw, honey," my dad said, "that must have been very hard for you."

"It was."

"I would never say, 'I told you so.'"

And then I sobbed in earnest as I slid down the stark white kitchen wall on which I'd been leaning and melted like a puddle on the floor. Dad stayed on the phone with me for close to an hour. We talked like we'd never talked before. Those things I thought I could say only to my female parent turned out to be okay to say to my dad. He listened, and by doing so acknowledged that the relationship I was mourning had been significant and real. He was thoughtful and comforting, and most of all, he made me feel loved.

By the time we were finished, I was exhausted.

"Should I have mom call you when she gets home?" he asked.

"No," I answered. "I'm tired and I want to go to bed. Tell her I'll talk to her tomorrow."

That evening was a turning point in my relationship with my father. We'd always shared an unstinting love for one another, but for affairs of the heart, it just always seemed more logical to speak with my mother. My dad proved that even though he had an instinct to protect his one and only daughter from that which might hurt her, he also had the capacity to listen and counsel with genuine care and compassion. It didn't lessen the communication I shared with my mom, but it gave me another ear, and another viewpoint.

Three years later, when I brought home a different guy, my father had a totally different reaction: "I like this boy," he told me. "He cares about you. I can just tell." I married that one. And my father danced happily at our wedding.

~Andrea Atkins

Thanks Dad

Truly Grand Dads

The Pinch Hitter

They say genes skip generations.
Maybe that's why grandparents find their grandchildren so likeable.
~Joan McIntosh

With a tray full of refills of popcorn, I rushed back into the living room just as Jason squealed, "Mom!" His voice raised an octave. "Hurry! You gotta see this!" Popcorn flew across the floor as his arm connected with the tray, oblivious to anything but the game on TV. "Look! Look! It's a pinch hitter! Larkin's a pinch hitter, just like me." It was easy to ignore the popcorn scattered all across the room as I joined my son on the couch. His enthusiasm was contagious. The couch shifted as he plopped down, then shot right back up again. "This is it! He's gonna do it! I know he is." We were about to witness what some would tout as the greatest World Series game ever played.

I've never been a huge fan of the game, but when I hear the bat connect with the ball, the cheering crowd and the sports announcer racing to keep up with the runner as he tears for home plate, I can't help but love the memories it evokes. The sound of baseball always takes me home.

Dad was a sportswriter and a diehard fan. He could rattle off stats, quote game scores and give an illustrated rendition of a pivotal moment in the most colorful language. He rubbed elbows with the likes of Nolan Ryan and shoulder pads with football great, Frank Gifford.

In those days, before the invention of split screens, it wasn't unusual to hear one ballgame blaring on the radio while Dad sat entranced, watching another on TV. My siblings and I assumed all kids in America went to bed on Monday nights with Howard Cosell's staccato delivery as backdrop to their mom's bedtime story. Whistles, referee showdowns and the roar of fevered crowds played soundtrack while visions of popcorn and peanuts danced in our heads.

Somehow, that sports-fanatic gene skipped my generation, and to my dad's disappointment, neither of my brothers shared his love for baseball. It wasn't until the summer of 1991 that Dad found his pinch hitter.

By then, Dad had moved on to other playing fields. He no longer covered the sports scene, but wrote for a public relations firm that took him to bigger fields around the globe. The pencil that was once tucked behind his ear disappeared and a briefcase, suit and tie, took its place.

We visited Mom and Dad that July. And though Disney World scored a run, it was the bond that developed between my dad and oldest son, Jason, that knocked the ball clear out of the park. At eleven years of age, Jason embodied everything my father had longed for in a son. He was a baseball fan. He also believed my dad was the epitome of a true hero. And there, on my parents' couch, one aging used-to-be sportswriter and one stars-in-his-eyes eleven-year-old boy became the best of friends.

Dad and Jason spent every waking moment together. They discussed the sports page over coffee and cold cereal, scoured the shops for baseball cards and then watched a recap of all the day's baseball scores before going to bed—just to get up and do it all over again.

As each great game eventually comes to an end, so too did our vacation. But Jason's newfound love for baseball didn't die once we hit home, and neither did his love for his grandpa. Somehow, my son had managed to break through the tough exterior and got to know the real man—something I had not been able to do until I saw him through the eyes of my child.

About two weeks after our return from Florida, I found Jason studying the flipside of his baseball cards and carefully taking notes.

"What are you working on?" I asked, curious as to why he'd taken an old picture of himself out of the family album.

"I'm making á surprise for Grandpa," he said, without looking up.

"So what's a pinch hitter?"

"Grandpa said it's someone who stands in for someone else and takes their place at bat." He chewed his lip as he thought a moment, then showed it to me. "Do you think Grandpa will like it?"

"He'll treasure it," I choked out.

September 1st dawned like any other Sunday morning back then. Frantic chaos ensued as we scrambled to eat, dress and make it to church on time. The ringing phone was just one more interruption in an already harried morning. But shocking news that my father had died the night before while away on a writing assignment shook me fully awake. I was stunned. Images of the extraordinary bond between my father and my son flashed over and over, then stuck on replay. Sadness weighed heavy on my heart. I knew the worst was yet to come. I had to tell Jason that his grandpa, his new best friend was gone.

My father was buried with his glasses and one other item. Tucked inside Dad's coat pocket was the picture of a pint-sized, blond-headed, swinger-to-be, up at bat. Jason had transformed the photo of himself at nearly two years of age into a rookie card. On the backside he'd listed fictitious statistics in perfect baseball lingo, the envy of any major league hero. Included was the title: Pinch Hitter. It was obvious the card hit a grand slam when Dad received it. Dad considered it priceless.

It was the bottom of the 10th inning and bases were loaded. Popcorn littered our family room floor as tension filled the air. We watched, with bated breath, as Minnesota's Gene Larkin stepped up to the plate. Peña, of the Atlanta Braves, stood on the pitcher's mound. You could have heard a pin drop. Peña wound up, then let the ball fly. Larkin swung. And connected. The pinch hitter drove in the winning run, making the Twins the 1991 World Series champs.

"Grandpa would have loved it," Jason said, his face flushed with excitement. And I had to agree. He would have loved the game, but not as much as sharing it with his stand-in.

~Dawn Lilly

103

Everlasting Lessons

A grandfather is someone with silver in his hair and gold in his heart.
~Author Unknown

While the women of our family slept in pre-dawn darkness, Granddad and I grabbed buckets and rods and slipped into his brown Zephyr station wagon. Rumbling up and down the hills of our Pittsburgh neighborhood, we were off on an adventure just for the guys. We sat side by side on the front seat as the music of Granddad's oldies filled the car. When we pulled up to a creek behind a gas station, soft light spread across the sky. We were there. I stepped out and waited for the magic to start.

Wearing a trucker hat and overalls, Granddad transformed into a master fisherman. His face glowed as he dipped his worn bucket into the green water and slowly pulled it up. Like a kid in awe of a magician, I gazed wide-eyed at the hundreds of minnows that swam inside.

Back then I was just a nine-year-old boy happy to be spending time with Grandpa. But years later, memories like that one would mean much more. They were lessons in living and manhood. They were touchstones that anchored me in values and faith. And one day, those moments with Granddad would save me from myself.

Some boys look to their fathers for direction. I had my mom's dad. Where my father's presence was scarce, my Granddad was my rock. He imparted wisdom like he sowed seeds in his garden. He planted the knowledge and waited for it to sprout.

Any time we spent together was an opportunity to teach. He

schooled me in the importance of learning new things. "You can play anytime," he would say in the accent that revealed traces of his West Virginia childhood. "Crack open a book and learn something." As I watched him work on car engines in the yard, he would tell me how important it was to learn a trade: "That's something no one can take away." When I would trail him around our backyard garden and help him tend to the tomatoes and green beans, he would tell me about enjoying God's blessings.

Then Granddad got sick. His pecan-colored skin turned pale. His hair, always dyed jet black, showed its true silver. I watched his body weaken and his fight for living slip away. Ten days before my fourteenth birthday, my Granddad died of prostate cancer. Losing him was like losing my compass. Everywhere I turned, I was lost. Not only did I no longer have a father figure in my life, I felt abandoned and alone. Suddenly, I was left to be a man on my own. Or at least that's what I thought.

I turned my back on the lessons Granddad taught me and started making bad choices. I stopped going to church. My birthdays, because they fell right after yearly anniversaries of Granddad's death, were painful reminders he was gone. So I stopped celebrating them.

One day, I looked at myself in the mirror and saw someone I didn't know. My eyes looked cold and hard. My heart was ice. I knew I was at a turning point. I could keep following the path I was on and end up defeated or dead. Or I could choose the road to hope. Right then, my grandma said something that shook me to the bone: "Your Granddad would be heartsick to see you like this." Softly at first and then louder, I could hear his voice in my ears: "Learn a trade. Crack open a book. Be a man who makes his family proud." The lessons Granddad taught me as a child returned to lead me when I needed them most.

Turning things around was a process. I stopped hanging out. I started learning an automotive trade. Slowly, purposefully, I started to find my way.

Today, I'm a husband and father. I own my home and work hard six days a week as a detailer at a car dealership. I dream of one day owning my own business. I know Granddad would be proud.

I go to his grave sometimes and thank him for filling me with lessons that live on like his memory in my heart. At my house, I have a picture of Granddad. His eyes crinkle with joy as he smiles. It's my reminder to be the kind of man he was.

~Kevin Price as told to Kelly Starling Lyons

104

Chicken Soup
for the Soul

Doting Dad

Great fathers get promoted to grandfathers.
~Author Unknown

"**I**t's time," I told my mother over the phone. Well, really, did I actually say those words? I've no idea, but I do know that Mom and Dad dropped everything and were there at the hospital all day while I was in labor wishing for it to be over already.

My father still had his own medical practice and my mother managed his office. Whatever their plans had been, whatever patients were scheduled, I don't know. They must have cancelled them all in order to be there with me.

Dad bonded with my daughter the moment he set eyes on her.

Still exhausted from forty-six hours of labor and a C-section, I was scheduled to go home to our multi-level townhouse.

"No." Dad wouldn't hear of it. He and Mom not only offered us a place in their house, but also gave us their bed. "We have those electric beds. You can raise up the top to sit without using your stomach muscles," Dad explained.

"And you don't even have to get out of bed to nurse," Mom added.

So while I bonded with my firstborn, my parents' love for her continued to grow as well. Unexpectedly, I developed a new understanding of my father. Of course I don't remember my own infancy. I grew up attached to my mom. My brothers had Dad and I had her. We cooked together while Dad, when he was home, played chess with my brothers. During my childhood, Dad had to be gone long hours. It was his job. The phone rang anytime day or night with people who needed him.

As my daughter grew, so did Dad's devotion. "How high's the fever?" he asked when I called to say my baby was ill. "Get your coat, we're going," I heard him say to Mom as I looked at the thermometer.

"It's 102, Dad. I can handle it." They lived sixty miles away. "You don't need to come all this way for nothing." Part of me felt hurt. Didn't they trust my ability as a mother? By the time they arrived, her fever had broken. "I'm sorry you wasted all that time."

When Dad walked in, face contorted with worry, he was not my dad, the doctor. He was Grandpa. And he had to see his grandbaby. "Seeing you is never a waste of time."

"You really need to get out more," Mom insisted. "Take a break." She knew that I always needed alone time.

"And go on a date," Dad added, meaning that he wanted time with my daughter without my husband or me around.

Long-distance babysitters. I'm sure there were plenty of capable teenagers in the neighborhood who would have loved the babysitting job. But, no. My parents drove an ever-longer trip as traffic increased over the years. There were many times when it made more sense for Mom to come by herself. After all, when Dad wasn't seeing patients, he wasn't making any money. Didn't matter. The weight of raising his own children now lighter on his shoulders, he would make the time. He had missed out on many of the small things in his own children's lives, not by choice but by circumstance. And now he could make up for it by being an active grandpa.

My parents took my daughter to the park, to the theater, to museums. They treated her to wonderful meals from different types of restaurants and never passed up an opportunity to let her find a favorite something in a gift store. Mom might have said no—she often did when I was a kid. But Dad couldn't deny my daughter anything.

When baby number two came along, Dad stepped up in a big

way, keeping my four-year-old daughter happy, stimulated and occupied, while Mom helped me recover and take care of my newborn daughter. "Come on, Grandpa, let's go to the park."

"Just what I was going to say." He'd take her hand and off they would go.

And then I had a son, Dad's first grandson. We spent the summer after he was born at my parents' house. My son developed colic within days of our arrival. Every evening just as we sat down for dinner, the screaming would begin. Such a content, easy baby the other twenty-three hours, for an hour every day he was inconsolable. Hearing him cry contracted every muscle in my body.

"He senses your stress," Mom said.

I sighed. "He's the one making me stressed."

Dad was somehow unaffected. Once again sacrificing his time with the family and a hot dinner, he'd take my son outside and hold him gently. Humming, singing, talking, all in a soothing voice, Dad walked around and around the yard. The wobble that occurred as he walked on uneven legs helped rock the baby to sleep.

I never thought much about what kind of father my dad had been, what he was like when I was a baby, what he went through to provide for us and still try to spend as much time with us as possible. It took me being a mom, watching him as a doting, self-sacrificing grandfather, to really appreciate all he did for me as a child. His giving never ends.

"Come on, Grandpa," my daughter said to him once again. "Let's go play."

I looked at him as he got up to leave the company of adults. "Thanks, Dad."

~D. B. Zane

105

Running the Gauntlet

Watching your daughter being collected by her date feels like handing over a million dollar Stradivarius to a gorilla.

~Jim Bishop

About the time I was beginning to get serious about a boyfriend, a major holiday would come around and I would start sweating. Christmas, Thanksgiving and Easter were big in our family and required a large meal with all the relatives. These dinners were the bane of my existence because if I was dating, the boyfriend had to come. No excuses.

I knew why we had this rule. It was so my father and grandfather could run my dates through what I called "the gauntlet." No matter how closely I tried to stay attached to my date's arm and protect him from the pair, they always managed to remove him from the crowd and put their questions to him.

With an uncanny sixth sense, I always knew when they had him, and I would try in vain to rescue him before my grandfather asked the big question: "Are you going to marry my granddaughter?" Typically, he inserted this question out of the blue with little warning.

It didn't matter if I had been dating for a week, a month, or a year. If my grandfather got hold of him, the question would be asked.

I tried to prepare my dates, but they never seemed to understand how bad it would be. They never took me seriously. My grandfather knew I would warn them, so he would change his questions. If Grandpa couldn't get a good read on a fellow from the marriage questions, he went on to other ones: "How soon are you planning to have children?" Anything that was highly embarrassing to me would do. My dad always went for the financial questions: "How do you plan on putting a roof over her head and food on the table?" "What do you think of your boss?" To my grandfather, it didn't matter about the little things. He'd grown up in the Depression and fought in World War II. Performance under pressure was the best measure of a man.

As a decade went by and no boyfriend made it to a second family function, I decided enough was enough, and for two years I didn't bring anyone, telling my family I had sworn off men. I thought that would fix things, that they would be so glad when I dated someone, that they would stop chasing them all away. Thanksgiving was approaching and I had been dating a guy all summer. It wasn't serious. We just had a lot of fun together. I hadn't said much to my family about him and didn't plan to. I wasn't inviting him to Thanksgiving. I had learned my lesson and there was no way this one was going through the gauntlet.

As the holiday approached, my date asked about my Thanksgiving plans. I told him about dinner with my family, thinking he would realize I was busy. Instead I found myself telling him what time dinner was and calling my mother to set another place at the table.

This one, I didn't even warn about the gauntlet. I wasn't in love.

Sure enough, I had dish duty and left my date alone with both my father and grandfather in the other room. I was being pumped by the women in the kitchen for details on the man. I wasn't providing much. All of a sudden it got quiet. Not a dish clinked and the football game was muted. I was putting something away in the dining room china cabinet and had a clear view of the living room. There was my date, my grandfather standing on his one side and my father on the other.

"So, do you plan on marrying my granddaughter?" I wanted to drop through the floor. I wasn't going to marry this guy. We were just friends.

"Yes, sir I do," he replied, looking right at my grandfather.

Then my father stepped in. "How do you plan on supporting her?"

He told them about his job and then they moved on to other less controversial subjects.

The football game came back on, dessert was served and everything went on as before, with quite a few more smiles from the women and advice on how to cook a turkey when it was my turn to host Thanksgiving. I, on the other hand, was a bit shell-shocked.

Somebody had passed the gauntlet. I had to rethink my whole take on this man. I watched my date for the rest of the afternoon, realizing he was something special as he played with my nieces, helped my grandmother carry dessert dishes, and argued about football with my brothers and uncles. Needless to say, he did go on to marry me and has fit into my family ever since.

It wasn't until years later that I learned my grandfather was more concerned with how my dates answered his questions than with what their answers were. If they broke eye contact, the deal was sealed; this man could not be trusted and was not for me.

My grandfather is looking down from heaven, but my dad will be ready. I am looking forward to watching the gauntlet in action. You see, I have a fifteen-year-old daughter who will be dating in a couple of years. I want her dates to pass the same test. I can still see the twinkle in my grandfather's eye when my husband answered his questions and received a nod of approval. Fathers and grandfathers do know best, no matter how embarrassing the process of running the gauntlet may be.

~W.S. Gager

106

I Call Him Papa Jim

Remember, we all stumble, every one of us.
That's why it's a comfort to go hand in hand.
~Emily Kimbrough

I was thirty when he became my father. He was tall, a strikingly handsome retired Army Major, with military bearing and manner intact. But I didn't feel intimidated. Mostly, I just felt grateful. You see, he'd been my friend before he met my mother, and I knew the kind of character he had. I knew firsthand the kind of man he was, and I was thrilled that, by marrying my mother, he was about to become a part of our family forever. So, though I'd previously called him "Jim," on that chilly November day, as he took his vows with Mama by his side, I called him by a new name. I called him Papa Jim. He was my new dad.

I have a birth father and I have no ill will toward him. I just don't know him, and he does not know me. He left us when I was fifteen years old. He has a new family, with a wife and children I've never met. Since he left, I have graduated from high school and college with honors, married, divorced, remarried. I have overcome battles with anorexia, infertility and a brain tumor. I've birthed three daughters, fulfilled a childhood dream of becoming a writer, and won first place in the women's division of a skeet-shooting contest! If my biological father spent a day with me now, he'd have to start from scratch. He would not know the woman I've become. Papa Jim, however, does.

Papa Jim has done one thing that sets real dads apart.

He's been there. With me, for me, beside me, every step of

the way. Through the proverbial thick or thin. For the last eighteen years.

I remember the day I gave birth to my first daughter, Zoe, after twelve long years of infertility. Papa Jim stood alone in the waiting room, pacing nervously, pushing his hands deep into his pockets, and waiting while my mother and my daughter's father stayed with me in the delivery room. Papa Jim was there, standing by my bed with tears in his dark eyes when I handed my brand-new daughter up to him. "Meet your granddaughter," I said, and he reached down to take her in his arms. In that moment, I remembered the countless sacrifices he'd made for the previous nine months—the dinners he ate alone so my mother could be with me when I thought I was going to miscarry, the patience he'd shown during my many late-night calls to her, when I was afraid because my baby hadn't moved much during the day, or when I felt an unexpected pain.

When, two years later, my marriage ended, Papa Jim drove from Georgia to Indiana to move my baby girl and me back home. He'd had a heart attack by then, but you'd never have known it by the way he walked briskly up and down the flight of stairs to my apartment. He carried Zoe's baby bed, the sofa, our table and the 101 boxes of her toys, our clothes, my dishes... my LIFE... out to the truck. He worked tirelessly and efficiently, and I had to force him to stop now and then. "Let's do this," he would say. "Let's keep going, honey."

I didn't know then, nor did he, that this would only be the first of many moves he would help me, and my three younger sisters, with over the years.

On the day of my brain surgery, Papa Jim and my mother were the last people I saw before the surgery. Watching him there, standing strong beside my weeping mother, I felt safe, like I always have since he entered our lives. A few weeks after the surgery, I ended up living with my girls at my parents' home to recuperate. Papa Jim quietly moved his beloved train collection and military library into storage to make room for us.

It wasn't easy. Papa Jim likes peace and order and quiet. Life with three young granddaughters is antithetical to his military-trained sense of order and restraint. There were times I could see frustration growing in his eyes, and there were times he was unable to keep it in. A sharp word, an edgy response to a question, would pop out. But nearly as the words were spoken, Papa Jim would come to me, or the girls, and apologize.

"Honey, I'm so sorry. I don't know what gets into me," he would say, regret obvious in his voice and eyes.

That is how he is—quick to apologize, accept blame, and honest as the day is long.

He also adores our mother. They are inseparable. They get up at the same time and go to bed together at the same time. They grocery shop together. And he sacrifices for her. For years he has had a dream of returning to Hawaii. He was stationed there years ago and has never lost his love of the islands. But he puts that dream off, year after year, because other things keep coming up. Like the times my sisters and I have moved back in with them. Like the moves he has helped each of us with. Like raising grandchildren.

Four years ago, my parents took in my sister and her new twin baby boy and girl. My sister and her other five children moved out after a few months, but the twins stayed with Mama and Papa Jim, who agreed to raise them. Papa Jim spent months changing diapers, warming baby bottles, searching for missing pacifiers. He has logged countless miles walking crying babies back and forth in the hallways of their home, patting small backs, trying to soothe restless babies back to sleep. The twins are four now and he plays ball with them in the yard, sits patiently by the kiddie pool in the backyard, stands by with paper sacks while they run around picking up pecans, and holds glass jars for their firefly collections on summer evenings.

I honestly can't remember my life before he came into it, and I cannot imagine my life without him in it. I love him so much, my amazing, my fabulous Papa Jim.

~Donna Reames Rich

My Father—My Son

Every generation needs regeneration.
~Charles H. Spurgeon

Dad and I stood outside the window, looking in.

"In the back," I said as I pointed through the reinforced glass.

Dad just looked and smiled, and didn't say much as he saw his new grandson for the first time. He didn't usually express himself when it came to matters of the heart, at least to me, and this time he saved it for my wife, Linda.

"He's the first Xavier grandson," Linda said he told her gently, his soft smile shining, as he stood beside her hospital bed.

Dad was already being called Grandpa by a half-dozen little ones, but this was his first son-of-a-son.

"The next generation…" he said.

He had become a grandfather more than a dozen years before, and I remember well that day when my oldest sister had her first son. I heard the news as soon as I walked in the door from school, and as most annoying nine-year-olds would do, I asked if we were supposed to call him Grandpa now. He just looked at me, so I never called him Grandpa again.

Dad worked pretty much non-stop in those days, one of the sacrifices of self-employment. We didn't see him much, though he was always there for the really important times, things like birthdays and graduations and weddings and births—and every night for dinner. Dinner was never once put on the table until Dad walked in the door.

Mom would have it ready, ready and waiting, and when Dad came in the door he washed his hands and we all sat down. It was the rule, but we knew it simply as dinner.

Although he sometimes made mistakes, he was a great father. He never told me how to raise my sons, not in words. But everything I know about being a father, I learned from him.

Thirty-four years have passed fairly quickly, it seems, for without too much effort I can still look at Brent and see him as a newborn, with light blond hair covering the top of his head.

And as we raised him, Linda and I made mistakes. Some of them were inherited—things like sometimes putting work ahead of my kids. Some were mine and mine alone, like making their childhood stricter than mine had been because I didn't want them to make the same blunders I had made. I doubt they ever noticed.

But as my sons grew, I wondered if I had done enough, worked with them enough, taught them enough, to be better fathers when the time came, than I had been. I sincerely hoped so.

I stood in the hospital waiting room. It wasn't as we thought it would be that night, my son and I. I felt his fear, though it was truly more his than mine, and I tried to offer a few words of encouragement. He resisted my efforts, as he often does when dealing with matters of the heart. He is so much like his grandfather the similarities sometimes scare me.

And so I watched him, hoping I could help, to be there if he needed me, though he rarely does. I followed him as he walked toward the recovery room while the doctor explained that everyone was okay, mother and baby. Everything had worked out just fine despite the last-minute scare.

I saw him, his hands freshly scrubbed. I saw him follow the nurse, and I watched him as he saw her—his daughter, my granddaughter—for the very first time.

And I saw him smile, a smile I had not seen on him but once before, on his wedding day some years ago.

"The next generation," I thought, as I looked at her perfect little face and thanked Colleen for bringing us this breathtaking little girl. And then somebody called me Grandpa.

When my father became a grandfather all those years ago, I don't know if he immediately felt, as I did just a few weeks ago, a change. For me, it signaled an added responsibility, for now there's another generation to worry about. And I can only hope that the guidance I gave my son as he was growing up was enough—enough for him to draw upon as he teaches this precious little girl—for it's his turn now.

My father—my son. The wisdom of the older generation, the energy of the younger. Life is truly amazing.

~Gary B. Xavier

Meet Our Contributors

Linda Apple is the author of *Inspire! Writing from the Soul*. Her stories have appeared in eleven *Chicken Soup for the Soul* books. Linda is also a motivational speaker and currently serves as the Arkansas Regional Speaker Trainer for Stonecroft Ministries. Please visit her website at www.lindacapple.com or e-mail her at lindacapple@gmail.com.

Teresa Armas has her Bachelor of Arts and Master of Education from California State University, Los Angeles. She is in the field of education. Her children's book, *Remembering Grandma*, was a finalist for the Tomas Rivera Children's Book Award. She enjoys traveling, writing and spending time with her children and family, who are her inspiration.

Ronda Armstrong and her husband enjoy ballroom dancing. They chase after two beloved cats and connect with family and friends. Ronda's essays and stories have appeared in *Chicken Soup for the Soul* books, *The Des Moines Register* and *Knee High by the Fourth of July* — a Midwest anthology. E-mail her at ronda.armstrong@gmail.com.

Andrea Atkins is a writer whose work has appeared in many national magazines including *Woman's Day*, *Good Housekeeping*, *Better Homes & Gardens* and others. She is the mom of two daughters and is married to David Hessekiel.

Caitlin Quinn Bailey is the communications coordinator for a nonprofit and has always been a writer, thanks to the incredible support of her family. On April 24, 2010, her dad will give her another priceless gift—walking her down the aisle on her wedding day. Thanks, Dad. E-mail her at caitlinqbailey@gmail.com.

Kathleene S. Baker and husband Jerry reside in Plano, Texas with two pooches, Hank and Samantha. A precious Schnauzer named Josey inspired her first writing experience. As a freelancer, she has contributed to newspapers, anthologies, magazines, online e-zines, and writes a weekly column entitled "Heart of Texas." Visit her website at www.txyellowrose.com.

Kerrie R. Barney still lives with her parents, still loves to knit and crochet—and still takes advantage of her dad's unraveling skills when a project goes awry. She lives and writes in the beautiful high desert of central Oregon.

Jill Barville is a professional wordsmith who writes everything from newspaper and magazine articles to PR copy and computer manuals. She lives in Spokane, Washington with her husband and three kids and within walking distance of her parents. They have dinner together most Sundays. Contact her via e-mail at jbarville@msn.com.

Tina Bausinger has previously published poetry and short stories and is a humor columnist for the University of Texas at Tyler. Tina enjoys reading and spending time with her husband Lee and their three children. Please e-mail her at tinaboss71@yahoo.com.

Donna Buie Beall is a freelance writer and adjunct English professor at Brewton-Parker College in South Georgia. This is Donna's second publication in *Chicken Soup for the Soul* and she is working on her first novel.

Cindy Beck lives in Utah with her husband, two cats, and a short, fat dog. As a published author of numerous stories and co-author of a book of humorous anecdotes, Cindy spends her time writing for books, magazines, and doing a humor column for the newspaper. Visit her at www.bythebecks.com.

June Harman Betts is the author of The Echoes in My Mind series: *Father Was a Caveman*, *We Were Vagabonds* and the upcoming release, *Executive*. She enjoys writing, spending time with her family, volunteering and traveling. Learn more at www.authorsden.com/junehbetts.

Robin Pepper Biasotti received her Economics degree from the University of Notre Dame and her J.D. from the University of Dayton. She resides in Connecticut with her husband and four children. Prior to working as a stay-at-home mom, Robin was a family law attorney.

Cynthia Blatchford works as a full-time dental assistant and enjoys writing during her spare time. She hopes that she can help others heal through the written word based on her own life's experiences. She can be reached via e-mail at cindy_700@hotmail.com.

Sharon Beth Brani is a single mother of two precious daughters, a licensed professional counselor and adoption coach. She has had more than 400 stories and articles published in a variety of publications including *Chicken Soup for the Soul*. Visit her website at www. heartprintsadoption.com.

Tim Brewster is an accountant and outdoor enthusiast living in Alberta, Canada with his wife and two daughters. Together they enjoy skiing, fishing, cycling, skating, camping, telling stories, and looking at the stars.

Elaine Bridge worked in the woods on the West Coast as a forester before becoming a stay-at-home mom to her three boys. Now living in Ohio she works part-time in a grocery store and is devoted to developing her relationship with God, caring for her family and writing inspirational material.

Christine Brooks is a freelance writer, ocean activist, and surfer who believes in taking care of the ocean, an enormous inspiration in so many aspects of her life. Her second book, *A Voice To Be Heard*, is due out in 2010. For more information please visit www.fourleafclover.us.

Barbara Canale is a freelance writer and columnist for the *Catholic Sun* in Syracuse, NY. She has been published in *Chicken Soup for the Veteran's Soul, Chicken Soup for the Adopted Soul* and *Chicken Soup for the Soul: Count Your Blessings*. She is the author of *Our Labor of Love: A Romanian Adoption Chronicle*. She enjoys biking, skiing, and gardening.

Tracy Cavlovic recently returned to the workforce after being a stay-at-home mom for ten years. She has two amazing boys who keep her busy and entertained with their hockey dreams. Her dream is to continue to write and have it enjoyed by others. Please e-mail her at tracycavlovic@sympatico.ca.

Karen Gray Childress lives in the Midwest. She enjoys writing, traveling, working with soft pastels, and spending time with her family. Additional information is available at www.karenchildress.net.

Jane Choate is a graduate of Brigham Young University and has been weaving stories in her head for as long as she can remember. In recent years, she has made her dream of becoming a published writer come true.

Sheila Curran is the author of *Everyone She Loved*, about a woman's efforts to protect her own family even after her own expiration date has come and gone. Her first book, *Diana Lively Is Falling Down*, is a romantic comedy Jodi Picoult called warm, funny, inventive and original and Booklist called a gem. Visit www.sheilacurran.com for more information.

Danielle is finishing her last year of high school and plans to attend college next year, studying in the field of psychology. She is a member of her school cheerleading team and also enjoys skiing. Please e-mail her at Danielle0971@aim.com.

Lola Di Giulio De Maci is a contributor to several *Chicken Soup for the Soul* books. She gathers inspiration for her children's stories from her now-grown children and the children she's taught over the years. Lola has a Master of Arts in education and English and continues writing from her sunny loft overlooking the San Bernardino mountains. E-mail her at LDeMaci@aol.com.

Although blind, **Janet Perez Eckles** thrives as a Spanish interpreter, international speaker, writer and author of *Trials of Today, Treasures for Tomorrow — Overcoming Adversities in Life*. From her home in Florida, she enjoys working on church ministries and taking Caribbean cruises with her husband Gene. She imparts inspiration at: www.janetperezeckles.com.

Barbara Edwards is a wife and the mother of two young men. She works as a newspaper reporter and at an elementary school in Northern California. Barbara enjoys traveling, shopping, watching college football, and writing for teens and preteens. Please e-mail her at bandked@yahoo.com.

Shawnelle Eliasen and her husband Lonny raise their five boys in an old Victorian on the Mississippi River. She home-teaches her youngest sons. Her work has been published in a number of magazines. She writes about life, family, friendship, and God's grace.

Melissa Face lives in Virginia. She teaches Special Education and writes as often as possible. Her work has appeared in newspapers, magazines, and several anthologies. Visit her blog at www.melissaface29.blogspot.com or e-mail her at writermsface@yahoo.com.

James S. Fell, MBA, CSCS, is a husband, father, runner, weightlifter and fitness author. In addition to writing for a variety of respected fitness magazines he is the author of *Body for Wife: The Family Guy's Guide to Getting in Shape*. Visit: www.bodyforwife.com or e-mail him at james@bodyforwife.com.

A graduate of the University of Pennsylvania, **Sally Friedman** has been writing personal commentaries for four decades. Her work appears in *The New York Times*, *The Philadelphia Inquirer*, *AARP The Magazine*, and various other national, regional and local publications. She is a frequent contributor to the *Chicken Soup for the Soul* series. E-mail her at pinegander@aol.com.

Originally from upstate New York, **Rachel Furey** is a current Ph.D. student at Texas Tech. She is a previous winner of Sycamore Review's Wabash Prize for fiction. Her work has also appeared in *Women's Basketball Magazine*, *Chicken Soup for the Soul: Twins and More*, *Freight Stories*, *Squid Quarterly*, and *Waccamaw*.

W.S. Gager writes the *Mitch Malone Mystery* series and teaches English at Baker College in West Michigan. Her first book, *A Case of Infatuation*, was the winner of the 2008 Dark Oak Mystery Contest. Check out her mysteries at www.wsgager.com or e-mail her for more information at wsgager@yahoo.com.

Bryan Gill received his B.A. in Communication from Auburn University and his Master of Divinity from Beeson Divinity School. He is the Baptist Collegiate Ministry director for Metro Memphis, Tenn. Bryan authored *31 Verses Every Teenager Should Know*, a devotional book (Student Life; Birmingham, 2009). He enjoys photography and kayaking.

Kierstan Gilmore received her Bachelor of Arts from The Catholic University of America and her Master of Social Work from Saint Louis University. She is a psychiatric social worker for the time being, but hopes to one day call herself a real writer. Please e-mail her at kierstan.gilmore@gmail.com.

Jenna Glatzer (www.jennaglatzer.com) is the author or ghostwriter of eighteen books including *The Marilyn Monroe Treasures* and the authorized biography, *Celine Dion: For Keeps*. Her latest collaboration is *Unthinkable* by Scott Rigsby, the first double-amputee to finish the Hawaiian Ironman triathlon. She and her daughter live in New York.

Ashlan Gorse is a correspondent and fill-in anchor for *E! News*. She received her BA from the School of Journalism at the University of North Carolina, Chapel Hill. When Ashlan isn't following movies, fashion and celebrities you can find her traveling around in search of the perfect glass of pinot.

Amanda Green was born and raised in Texas and now lives in New York City. Her writing has appeared in *New York Press*, *The Guardian*, *Mr. Beller's Neighborhood*, and The New York Times' City Room blog. She writes about her misadventures in the city (and beyond!) at www. noisiestpassenger.com.

Tina Haapala doesn't play guitar like her dad, so she hopes to strike a chord with her writing. This is her fourth contribution to *Chicken Soup for the Soul*. Tina's website, www.excuseeditor.com, strives to help aspiring writers. If you would like to hear "Tina Marie '73," e-mail her at tinamarie73@gmail.com.

Cathy C. Hall is a freelance writer and humor columnist from Georgia. Her byline has appeared in newspapers, magazines, and anthologies. She often writes about family and friends. So, if you've ever met Cathy, she's probably written about you. Find out more at www.cathy-c-hall.com.

Jan Hamlett is a freelance writer who resides in Little Rock, Arkansas. She is a retired English teacher who enjoys reading, gardening, following SEC football, and traveling. Jan's stories have appeared in *Women Alive* magazine, *The Wittenburg Door*, and the online publication *Bewildering Stories*. You may e-mail her at jt1950@yahoo.com.

Cynthia M. Hamond has numerous stories in over twenty-five *Chicken Soup for the Soul* books as well as other major publications, including *Woman's World* magazine and King Features Syndication. Cynthia has received two awards and two of her stories have been made for television. Cynthia is available for school visits and group talks. Learn more at www.Cynthiahamond.com.

Charles E. Harrel served as a pastor for thirty years before stepping aside to pursue writing. He has over 280 published works. His stories and devotionals have appeared in twenty books, including *Chicken Soup for the Father & Son Soul*. Charles enjoys photography, playing guitar, and family camping trips.

Heidi Durig Heiby has worked as a German and English teacher and tutor and lives in Ohio with her husband Fritz and their daughter Anna. Heidi enjoys reading, writing, her wonderful writers group, travelling, cooking, the outdoors, and the company of close friends and family. Please e-mail her at hheiby@yahoo.com.

Patti Callahan Henry is a *NY Times* bestselling novelist. She has six novels with Penguin/NAL. Patti has been hailed as a fresh new voice in southern fiction. She has been short-listed for the Townsend Prize for Fiction and has been nominated for the Southern Independent Booksellers Alliance Fiction Novel of the Year. She lives outside Atlanta with her husband and three children. Website: www.patticallahanhenry.com.

Elizabeth Herrera received her Master's Degree in Educational Leadership in August, 2004. She is a career counselor and has always enjoyed working in social service environments and working with underserved populations. She enjoys traveling, running and spending time with her husband.

Fracia Heter resides in Wellington, Kansas, where she was born and raised. She received her Associate of Arts degree in 2009. Fracia enjoys reading, creative writing, shopping, and spoiling her Shih Tzu, Emma. She can be reached via e-mail at fmarie1211@aol.com.

Kathy Irey is a social worker and freelance writer in Pittsburgh. (Go Steelers!) Her work has appeared in numerous publications including *The Secret Place*, *Devo'Zine*, and *Affaire de Coeur*. Among her passions are waterslides, wave pools, her alma mater, Penn State, and women's history.

Ron Kaiser, Jr. teaches English and college writing classes in vibrant and beautiful New Hampshire with his absolutely radiant wife. After his aforementioned lovely wife and wonderful family, his second love is writing fiction. He is currently seeking a publisher for two novels and a short story collection. Please e-mail him at kilgore.trout1922@ gmail.com.

J. Aday Kennedy is an award-winning multi-published author of inspirational/Christian pieces and of children's literature. Three picture books are under contract eagerly awaiting publication. She is a ventilator-dependent quadriplegic making her dreams come true a story at a time. As a speaker, Aday entertains, instructs, motivates and inspires audiences of all ages. www.jadaykennedy.com & http:// jadaykennedy.blogspot.com.

Jess Knox was published in 2009's *Chicken Soup for the Soul: The Cancer Book*. She graduated from the University of Southern California in 2007 with a degree in Screenwriting and currently works for Omnipop Talent Group in Los Angeles. Please e-mail her at knox.jess@gmail.com.

Robyn Kurth is a freelance writer whose work has appeared in various publications and websites. She is a regular contributor to Examiner. com as the Orlando Parenting Examiner. Robyn has been published in several anthologies, including *Chicken Soup for the Chocolate Lover's Soul* and *The Ultimate Christmas*. She can be reached at rwordworks@ earthlink.net.

Nine years ago, **Victoria LaFave** surrendered her marketing career to pursue her dream as a writer and mom. She had a story published in the book, *My Teacher Is My Hero*, and also had her work published in *Parents*, *FamilyFun* and *Woman's Day* magazines. She can be reached at vrlafave@sbcglobal.net.

John Lavitt would like to say that he was right and his father was wrong when it came to prognostications about his future, but he would be lying. Despite his father's protestations, John still works in Hollywood, still writes poetry, and still believes he will hit that home run.

Dawn Lilly calls the Pacific Northwest the perfect place to live, write and garden. A wife, mother and grandmother, Dawn inherited her passion for writing from Doug Miles, her father, her first editor, and the inspiration behind "The Pinch Hitter." You can contact Dawn at 22dlilly@gmail.com.

Amy Lyons is a Los Angeles-based writer and editor, who has worked for *The Boston Globe* and countless publications in Los Angeles. She loves putting words on paper, seeing live theatre, listening to music and spending time with family and friends. E-mail her at amykly@yahoo.com.

Kelly Starling Lyons is Kevin Price's sister and a North Carolina children's book author. Find out more about Kelly at www.kellystarlinglyons.com. This story is dedicated to Kelly and Kevin's grandfather, Thurman Starling.

Timothy Martin is the author of four books and seven screenplays. He has three children's novels scheduled for release in 2010. Tim's work has appeared in numerous *Chicken Soup for the Soul* books. His TV reality show *Repossessed* is in development at Indigo Films. He can be reached at tmartin@northcoast.com.

Bonita Y. McCoy resides in Alabama with her three wonderful sons and her husband of twenty years. She received her Bachelor of Arts in Journalism with a minor in English from Mississippi State University and is currently teaching high school English. The McCoy family loves to go RVing and have had many adventures in their RV, properly named Seymore.

Abby McNutt received her Bachelor of Science degree at St. Gregory's University in 2002. She teaches transitional first grade in Oklahoma. She enjoys working with children, especially those of divorce and plans to write a book about her experience as a child of divorce. Please e-mail her at ramcnutt2000@yahoo.com.

Kimberlee Murray is a wife and proud mother of two boys, Nicholas and Christopher. She keeps very busy with her active family and in her downtime writes about how to keep life simple in her blog, "Life Isn't Rocket Science," (http://kimberleemurray.blogspot.com). You can e-mail her at kbernard53@hotmail.com.

Sheila Myers writes for an international non-profit by day, and for herself the rest of the time. She is working on a science-fiction book for young adults. E-mail her at sjblomyers@sbcglobal.net.

As the former Kansas City Fox TV 4 parenting expert, **Brenda Nixon** (www.BrendaNixon.com) is the author of the award-winning *The Birth to Five Book*, host of *The Parent's Plate* radio show, and a popular speaker to parents and childcare professionals. She lives in Ohio with her husband and near her three grown children.

Kirsten Ogden grew up in Hawaii, but now makes her home in Los Angeles where she teaches writing at Pasadena City College. She is a poet laureate of Gambier, Ohio, and also teaches poetry in the public schools with the California Poets in the Schools program. Visit Kirsten's blog at www.eatthepaper.com.

Jill Olson graduated from the University of North Carolina at Chapel Hill in 1993 with a degree in economics. She then moved to New York

City, where she worked for a hedge fund, analyzing global currency and bond instruments. Since 1999, Jill has been involved with several non-profit organizations, all focused on breaking the cycle of poverty.

Dr. Debra D. Peppers, a retired English teacher, university instructor, radio and television host, author, and Emmy award-winning playwright, was inducted into the prestigious National Teachers Hall of Fame. A member of the National Speakers Association, Dr. Peppers is available for bookings at 314-842-7425 or www.pepperseed.org.

Mark Damon Puckett has written for *Saveur* and *Greenwich Magazine*. He received his M.F.A. in Creative Writing from the University of Houston; his M.A. in English and his M.Litt. in African-American Studies from Middlebury. His stories have appeared in *Gulf Coast*, *The Crescent Review* and *The Tusculum Review*. Please check out: www.markdamonpuckett.com.

Jennifer Quasha is a freelance writer and editor, who, despite baboon attacks, still loves to travel to exotic locales. Check out her website at www.jenniferquasha.com.

D.R. Ransdell teaches writing at the University of Arizona. Her CD of mariachi music is titled *Diana canta la venganza*, or *Diane Sings Revenge*. She also has a collection of cat poems: *The Secret Lives of the Pink House Cats*. She recently completed a six-concert tour in China with the Southern Arizona Symphony Orchestra. Please visit her website at www.dr-ransdell.com.

Natalie June Reilly is a single mother of two extraordinary teenage boys, a full-time football mom and the author of the children's book, *My Stick Family: Helping Children Cope with Divorce*. Natalie lives and loves in gratitude every day and she welcomes you to reach out to her at natalie@themeanmom.com.

Eric T. Reuscher received his Bachelor of Arts from the University of

Pittsburgh in 1987. He works in development at the Eastman School of Music. Eric enjoys golf, gardening, sports and spending time with family and friends. He continues to write stories for children and teens. Please e-mail him at pitt8787@yahoo.com.

Donna Reames Rich is an avid writer, and has written on a freelance basis for the past twenty years. She is also a psychiatric registered nurse. She loves her three dogs and one cat, but the absolute most fun she has is being a mother to her three lovely, lively daughters—Zoe, Chloe and Caroline. Please e-mail her at donnachloe@yahoo.com.

Sallie A. Rodman is an award-winning author with numerous stories appearing in *Chicken Soup for the Soul* anthologies, various other anthologies and magazines. She lives in Los Alamitos, CA with her hubby Paul, Mollie the Beagle and Inky the cat. Sallie attributes her successes in life to her father and his values. Reach her at sa.rodman@verizon.net.

Stephen Rusiniak is a husband and father of two and a former police detective who specialized in and lectured on juvenile and family matters. He now shares his thoughts through his writings and has appeared in various publications, including the anthology *Chicken Soup for the Father & Son Soul*. E-mail him at stephenrusiniak@yahoo.com.

Heather Simms Schichtel is a writer, special needs advocate and mom to three-year-old Samantha. This is her second *Chicken Soup for the Soul* publication. She would like to thank her dad for providing the inspiration behind Morey. You can reach Heather at www.samsmom-heathers.blogspot.com.

Joel Schwartzberg is an award-wining writer and author of *The 40-Year-Old Version: Humoirs of a Divorced Dad* (www.40yearoldversion.com), which was released with reviews in 2009. His personal essays have appeared in *The New York Times Magazine*, *Newsweek*, the *New York Daily News*, *New Jersey Monthly*, and elsewhere.

Michelle Sedas is the author of *Welcome The Rain* and *Live Inspired*, coauthor of *The Power of 10%*, host of the *Inspired Living Café*, and cofounder of Running Moms Rock. Michelle graduated from Texas A&M University and lives in Texas with her husband and two children. Visit her at www.michellesedas.com.

Michael Jordan Segal, who defied all odds after being shot in the head, is a husband, father, social worker, freelance author (including a CD/Download of twelve stories, read with light background music, entitled *Possible*), and inspirational speaker. He's had many stories published in *Chicken Soup for the Soul* books. For more information visit www.InspirationByMike.com.

A native of Los Angeles, CA, **Al Serradell** now resides in Oklahoma City where he works as a Workforce Center Manager for the State of Oklahoma between his real hobbies of rescuing Chihuahuas and writing stories.

Sara F. Shacter is a children's writer. Her articles have appeared in such publications as *Highlights for Children* and *World Book's Childcraft Annuals*. She made her fiction debut with the picture book *Heading to the Wedding*. A former teacher, she loves speaking at schools. Please visit her at www.sarafshacter.com.

Kathleen Shoop earned her Ph.D. at the University of Pittsburgh in 1999. She writes novels, has articles regularly published in magazines and newspapers, and works part-time at a K-8 school in the city of Pittsburgh. She also has a wonderful husband and two children who never fail to make her laugh out loud. Please e-mail her at jakenmax2002@aol.com.

Curtis Silver is a freelance writer residing in a three-bedroom house in Sarasota, FL with his wife and three kids. When he's not writing, he suffers the daily grind of commuting to work and pretending to be smart. He can be contacted via e-mail at cebsilver@gmail.com, via Twitter at cebsilver or at http://cashorcheckonly.wordpress.com.

Adrian R. Soriano resides in San Antonio, Texas. He is happily married with a wonderful wife, Jennifer, and three children named Jasmine, Abigail, and Adrian Jr. This is his first article and he is honored to have it published. With God all things are possible—Matthew 19:26.

Diane Stark is a former teacher turned stay-at-home mom and freelance writer. Her first book, *Teachers' Devotions to Go*, was released in the fall of 2009. Diane lives in southern Indiana with her husband Eric and their five children. She can be reached at DianeStark19@yahoo.com.

Elissa Stein's latest book is *FLOW: the Cultural Story of Menstruation*. Previously she published *City Walks with Kids: New York*, interactive thank you notes, and visual iconic pop culture histories. She runs her own graphic design business and also practices yoga, knits, and collects vintage coats. She lives in the NYC area with her family.

Annmarie B. Tait lives in Conshohocken, PA with her husband Joe and Sammy the "Wonder Yorkie." She has contributed to the *Chicken Soup for the Soul* series, *Reminisce* magazine and *Patchwork Path*. When not writing, Annmarie enjoys cooking along with singing and recording American and Irish folk songs which reflect her heritage. E-mail her at irishbloom@aol.com.

Lura J. Taylor is an early retirement attorney who enjoys teaching French, traveling and taking care of her family and pets. She is currently working on a graphic novel about her early adult years in Wichita and Lawrence, Kansas. Please e-mail her at ltaylor94@gmail.com.

Marsha D. Teeling is a grandmother to two wonderful children, Madison, 5, and Logan, 3. She enjoys writing as a hobby, while working full-time as a case manager for critically ill children. Married to her soul mate, Anthony, for thirty years, she enjoys gardening, needlework, reading and friends. Her twin sister lives close by.

Marla H. Thurman lives at home in Signal Mountain, Tennessee, with her two dogs, Oreo and Sleeper. Her dad still rescues her on occasion.

Marni Tice is a stay-at-home mom raising her triplet boys and daughter. She had been a court reporter for many years and now owns her own legal transcription company in South Florida. She loves to write and is currently working on her first novel. Please e-mail her at Ameriscopes@aol.com.

Christine Trollinger is a freelance writer from Kansas City, MO. Her short stories have appeared in several books and magazines. She enjoys travel, gardening and spending time with her family.

Megan Tucker-Hall is a junior at the University of Tennessee at Chattanooga where she is majoring in Psychology. She hopes to attend medical school in 2011. She enjoys reading, volunteering in her community, traveling, and spending time with her sorority sisters. She can be reached at PrimRose8806@aol.com.

Dave Ursillo received his Bachelor of Arts in Political Science from the College of the Holy Cross in 2008. He is a writer, aspiring career author and life coach. He writes self-help and inspirational nonfiction and offers his writings for free online at DaveUrsillo.com. E-mail Dave at Dave@DaveUrsillo.com.

Sharon Dunski Vermont is a full-time wife and mother and part-time freelance writer and pediatrician with an MD degree from the University of Missouri-Kansas City. Her husband Laird, daughters Hannah and Jordyn, and parents Neil and Harriet Dunski are the inspiration for everything she writes. You may e-mail her at svermont1987@yahoo.com.

Sydney Wain is a high school freshman. She has been on the honor roll all her life, and is on her school volleyball team. She loves to go to the mall with her friends. Sydney is eager to do well in school and attend college somewhere in Europe to study international relations.

Nick Walker is an on-camera meteorologist for The Weather Channel, and songwriter/author of *Sing Along with the Weather Dude*, a CD/Book teaching children weather basics, and *Don't Get Scared, Just Get Prepared*, teaching severe weather preparedness. Contact Nick at his "Weather Dude" website at www.wxdude.com.

Terrilynne Walker is the mother of five children and six grandchildren, and an educator in the Florida school system. She wishes that her dad had lived long enough to know her family, not only for its accomplishments, but for the kind, gentle spirit it inherited from him.

Stefanie Wass lives in Ohio with her husband and two girls. Her essays have been published in numerous newspapers and anthologies, including five *Chicken Soup for the Soul* anthologies. Stefanie is currently seeking representation for her first children's novel. Visit her website at www.stefaniewass.com.

Gail Wilkinson lives in rural Illinois in a lively household of husband, kids and pets. She works as a human resource director for a software company. Gail is particularly interested in stories that preserve and honor family histories. Her middle grade novel about her grandparents' lives, *Alice and Frosty: An American Journey*, is to be published in 2010 by Iowan Books.

Karyn Williams is the eldest daughter of Orlando Magic Executive Pat Williams, and "big sister" in a family of nineteen children adopted from all over the world. She is a staff songwriter with Universal Music, an author and recording artist. Her first full-length studio album will release in early 2010. You can visit her at www.karynwilliams.com.

Paul Winick, M.D., lives in Florida with his wife Dorothy. He practiced pediatrics for thirty years. He has two children and five grandchildren. Paul is a Professor of Clinical Pediatrics at the University of Miami, School of Medicine. This is his fifth *Chicken Soup for the Soul* contribution. He has published a memoir, *Finding Ruth*, and many prize-winning stories. E-mail him at paulwinick@pol.net.

Ray M. Wong is a devoted husband and father. He's also a freelance writer and contributes the column "Family Matters" to newspapers in the United States. He has completed a memoir called *Chinese-American: The Journey Home*. Visit his website at www.raywong.info. Or e-mail him at Ray@raywong.info.

Mary Jo Marcellus Wyse is a 2006 graduate of Vermont College of Fine Arts' MFA in Writing Program and is currently finishing a novel about a father-daughter relationship. She loves being a stay-at-home mom to two wonderful kids. Mary Jo and her family live outside of Boston.

Gary B. Xavier, an author and lecturer throughout the U.S. and Canada, has published numerous mechanical trade textbooks. He writes a Sunday newspaper column, magazine articles, and was published in *Chicken Soup for the Father & Son Soul*. Married to Linda for thirty-nine years, he has two grown sons and a granddaughter. He can be contacted at gary_xavier@yahoo.com.

D. B. Zane is a writer, teacher and mother of three. In her free time, she enjoys reading, walking the dog, and taking her kids to visit their grandparents. Please e-mail her at dbzanewriter@gmail.com.

Heidi L.R. Zúñiga has lived her whole life in Gilbert, Arizona. She is the third youngest child of eleven in her family. Heidi has five brothers and five sisters and loves having a big family. She keeps herself busy, growing up with sports and small jobs on the side. Heidi along with a sister and two friends created their own little businesses to earn money.

Meet Our Authors

Jack Canfield is the co-creator of the *Chicken Soup for the Soul* series, which *Time* magazine has called "the publishing phenomenon of the decade." Jack is also the co-author of many other bestselling books.

Jack is the CEO of the Canfield Training Group in Santa Barbara, California, and founder of the Foundation for Self-Esteem in Culver City, California. He has conducted intensive personal and professional development seminars on the principles of success for more than a million people in twenty-three countries, has spoken to hundreds of thousands of people at more than 1,000 corporations, universities, professional conferences and conventions, and has been seen by millions more on national television shows.

Jack has received many awards and honors, including three honorary doctorates and a Guinness World Records Certificate for having seven books from the *Chicken Soup for the Soul* series appearing on the New York Times bestseller list on May 24, 1998.

You can reach Jack at www.jackcanfield.com.

Mark Victor Hansen is the co-founder of Chicken Soup for the Soul, along with Jack Canfield. He is a sought-after keynote speaker, best-selling author, and marketing maven. Mark's powerful messages of possibility, opportunity, and action have created powerful change in thousands of organizations and millions of individuals worldwide.

Mark is a prolific writer with many bestselling books in addition to the *Chicken Soup for the Soul* series. Mark has had a profound influence in the field of human potential through his library of audios, videos, and articles in the areas of big thinking, sales achievement, wealth building, publishing success, and personal and professional development. He is also the founder of the MEGA Seminar Series.

Mark has received numerous awards that honor his entrepreneurial spirit, philanthropic heart, and business acumen. He is a lifetime member of the Horatio Alger Association of Distinguished Americans.

You can reach Mark at www.markvictorhansen.com.

Wendy Walker began writing and editing several years ago while staying home to raise her children, and is now the author of two novels, *Four Wives* and *Social Lives*, both published by St. Martin's Press. She recently edited *Chicken Soup for the Soul: Power Moms* (2008) and *Chicken Soup for the Soul: Thanks Mom* (2010).

Before becoming a mother, Wendy worked as an attorney in private practice both in New York and Connecticut, and served as a *pro bono* lawyer at the ACLU. While attending law school at Georgetown University, she spent a summer in the Special Prosecutions Division of the U.S. Attorney's Office for the Eastern District of New York.

Wendy obtained her undergraduate degree from Brown University with a double major in economics and political science. Her junior year was spent at the London School of Economics. Upon graduating, she worked as a financial analyst in the Mergers and Acquisitions department of Goldman, Sachs & Co. in New York.

As a young girl, Wendy trained for competitive figure skating at facilities in Colorado and New York. She now serves on the board of Figure Skating in Harlem, an organization committed to the development of underprivileged girls, which she has supported since 1997.

Wendy lives in suburban Connecticut and is busy raising her three sons and writing her third novel.

About Scott Hamilton

1984 Olympic gold medalist **Scott Hamilton**, the popular and beloved figure skater, is also a network TV skating commentator, actor, performer, producer, Emmy Award nominee, bestselling author, philanthropist and cancer and brain tumor survivor.

Scott's life work includes advocating his message that anything is possible with fortitude and determination. He is a motivational speaker for a wide variety of groups and organizations. Scott speaks to audiences, from 500 to 1,500, about his life, his road to Olympic Gold, and his battle to overcome cancer.

As an author, Scott received notable critical praise for his *New York Times* bestselling autobiography *Landing It* (Kensington Books, October 1999), an intimate look at his professional and personal life both on and off the ice.

Scott appears regularly on television and is a popular guest on national news shows, such as *The Today Show*, entertainment news programs, and in various national news publications, such as *People* magazine. He made his motion picture debut in *On Edge*, a 2001 mockumentary of figure skating, and starred in the motion picture *Blades of Glory*, with Will Ferrell and Jon Heder.

Audiences have watched Scott perform with numerous U.S. symphony orchestras in his own *Scott Hamilton's American Tour*, and in fifteen national touring seasons with *Stars on Ice*, which he also co-created. Scott served as co-producer of *Stars on Ice* until his retirement from the tour in April 2001. For two seasons since then, he returned to *Stars on Ice* as a special guest star in select cities, and he continues to be the creative producing force behind each annual production.

During a fourteen-year tenure with the CBS Television Network, Scott covered multiple Olympic Games. He recently signed a three-year exclusive agreement with NBC Sports to cover all of the network's skating broadcasts, including the Winter Olympics in 2010.

Scott was inducted into the United States Olympic Hall of Fame in 1990. In that same year, he also became a privileged member of the World Figure Skating Hall of Fame.

Scott participates in numerous charitable organizations. He is the official spokesperson for Target House at St. Jude Children's Hospital in Memphis, Tennessee, as well as for his own Scott Hamilton CARES Initiative (Cancer Alliance for Research, Education, and Survivorship) at the Cleveland Clinic Taussig Center in Cleveland, Ohio. Scott also maintains the website www.Chemocare.com, and serves on the Board of Directors for Special Olympics.

Scott married former nutritionist Tracie Robinson in 2002 and the couple now has two sons, Aidan and Maxx. When Scott is not working, performing or promoting his charitable causes, he can be found on the golf course or spending time with his wife and children at home in Nashville, Tennessee.

Thank You!

The strength of family ties has been brought to life by the emotional depth and honesty embedded within the stories from our contributors. Not every story could be used, but every story added to the richness with which we were able to explore the relationships of fathers, step-fathers and grandfathers in this book. I offer my deepest gratitude to the thousands of people who submitted their personal, heartfelt stories. By sharing your experiences and insights, you help create the special bond that exists among the vast Chicken Soup for the Soul readership.

Chicken Soup for the Soul: Thanks Dad was truly a collaborative effort! Assistant Publisher D'ette Corona read thousands of submissions and worked with every contributor during the editing process. Publisher Amy Newmark guided the crafting of the manuscript from start to finish with a clear vision for what this book should be. Editors Kristiana Glavin and Barbara LoMonaco perfected every line with meticulous editing. And a big thanks to Brian Taylor at Pneuma Books for the handsome cover design and layout.

Under the leadership of CEO Bill Rouhana and President Bob Jacobs, Chicken Soup for the Soul continues to connect millions of people every year through the most human, relevant topics. It is truly a privilege to be a part of this team.

~Wendy Walker